Encyclopedia of MATLAB: Science and Engineering

Volume VII

Encyclopedia of MATLAB: Science and Engineering Volume VII

Edited by **Louis Young**

LANRYE
INTERNATIONAL

New Jersey

Published by Clanrye International,
55 Van Reypen Street,
Jersey City, NJ 07306, USA
www.clanryeinternational.com

Encyclopedia of MATLAB: Science and Engineering
Volume VII
Edited by Louis Young

International Standard Book Number: 978-1-63240-195-3 (Hardback)

Contents

Preface

Over the recent decade, advancements and applications have progressed exponentially. This has led to the increased interest in this field and projects are being conducted to enhance knowledge. The main objective of this book is to present some of the critical challenges and provide insights into possible solutions. This book will answer the varied questions that arise in the field and also provide an increased scope for furthering studies.

Proportional-integral-derivative (PID) controllers are widely regarded as the most important tool for a control engineer. However, in today's era of computer science, MATLAB has acquired the position of an essential tool for the modern system engineering. This book has been written in a manner to serve as a practical guide for both practicing engineers and engineering students. Numerous applications use MATLAB as the working framework which shows that it is an effective, comprehensive and handy technique for performing technical computations. This book discusses various prominent applications in which MATLAB is used: in image processing algorithms, and from Graphic User Interface (GUI) design for educational purposes to Simulink embedded systems.

I hope that this book, with its visionary approach, will be a valuable addition and will promote interest among readers. Each of the authors has provided their extraordinary competence in their specific fields by providing different perspectives as they come from diverse nations and regions. I thank them for their contributions.

Editor

Part 1

Modelling, Identification and Simulation

MATLAB in Biomodeling

Cristina-Maria Dabu
CRIFST – Romanian Academy
Romania

1. Introduction

Mathematical modeling and computer simulations are widespread instruments used for biological systems study.

Matlab and Simulink are powerful, high-level programming language which offer the opportunity to apply the principles of linear systems theory in the analysis of biological systems; the opportunity to develop adequate computer simulation techniques and algorithms in order to model dynamic responses of physiological systems, and to collect and analyze data and to visualize the results information for the simulation processes

2. Systemic modeling in biosciences

Models are extremely useful in understanding how the neuronal cell stores, computes, integrates and transmit the information necessary for the survival of the organism. Computer assisted models permit also to create a variety of test scenarios that would be too difficult, expensive or dangerous to allow to happen in reality.

The main goal in modeling and simulation in the area of Biosciences is to develop integrative models and simulation which allow the dynamic representation of signaling and metabolic networks in the neuronal cell as open systems with distinct input and output ports and specific response mechanisms. The systemic approach in the actual researches in the field of biomodeling aim to fit together the different level at which complex biological systems are working, from genes through cells, organs to the whole organism (Noble, 2002). The majority of biological and physiological control systems are nonlinear and the control is often accomplished parametrically.

Biological systems are hierarchical systems, characterized by:

1. Each level has unique language, concepts or principles;
2. Each level is an integration of items from a lower level; discoveries or descriptions at i-th tlevel aid understanding of phenomena at i+1 level;
3. Relationship between levels is not symmetrical;

In fig.1. is presented the algorithm used for developing biological systemic and mathematical models. Control systems theory, applied in the neuronal modeling, is used to analyze the dynamic properties of the neuronal metabolic and signaling pathways and to understand the role of feedback loops in the reaction networks. The essence of this approach lies in the dynamics of the system and cannot be described merely by enumerating the components of the system. In the systemic approach, the neuronal cell is considered an open system with distinct input and output ports and specific response mechanisms.

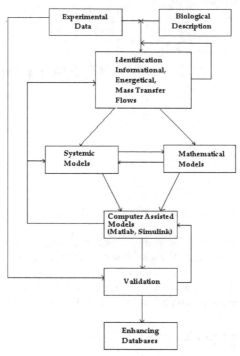

Fig. 1. The algorithm for developing systemic and mathematical models in neurobiology

Biological systems are adaptive systems, stable, equipped with control mechanisms (feedback) extremely fine (Heinrich, 1996). In fig.2 we have considered a model rule to regulate processes within the neuron, a model that, in various forms, otherwise we will find all subprocesses in regulating cell.

In the neuronal cell, extracellular and intracellular stimuli are captured and measured by specialized receptor structures located in the cytoplasm and in the cell membrane. Stimuli are represented by various substances that circulate in the body (hormones, oxygen ions, different protein structures), environmental factors (radiation, temperature variations, etc.) and electrical impulses from adjacent cells. Based on these stimuli, and coded programs to DNA, control mechanisms (feedback) provides nerve cell adaptation to environmental conditions. They aim to develop cell responses to stimuli coming from the external environment and internal, depending on the deviation e(t) measured between the model output (encoded at the genetic level) $y_M(t)$ and output biosystem (neuronal cell) y(t).

$$\varepsilon(t) = y_M(t) - y(t) \tag{1.1}$$

Under ideal operating conditions for the neuronal cell $\varepsilon(t) \to 0$

Where:
u(t) = input size
r(t) = size reference
y(t) = output size
p(t) = disturbance

Models about the mechanisms of neuron refers to adaptive changes in cell metabolism, compared with the extracellular environment. In the presence of enzymes, synthesized as a result of chemical reactions, substances taken from the cell improper turns feeding their cell substance. Exchange with the outside is permanent and will work antientropic cell, because it will prevent their growth through disruption of entropy.

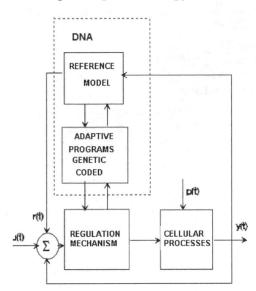

Fig. 2. The systemic model for the regulation processes in the neuronal cell

3. Neuronal cell processes modeling

3.1 The systemic and mathematical models of protein synthesis in the neuronal cell

From the systems theory viewpoint, the neuronal cell is an open system with distinct input and output ports and specific response mechanisms. Signaling action through the pathways result in different categories of cellular responses like ionic channel opening or closing, neuronal differentiation or neuronal cell death. The dynamical models of signaling pathways are nonlinear and the analysis of their behavior in challenging request specific algorithms.

In a first approximation, the protein synthesis process at neuronal level may be modeled like a open three-compartmental system (fig.3.)

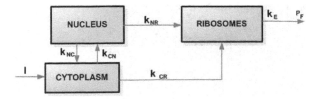

Fig. 3. The three-compartmental model for the protein synthesis process

The equilibrium equations which are describing the system are:

$$\frac{d}{dt}q_N(t) = (-k_{NC} + k_{CN})q_C - k_{NR}q_R \tag{2.1.1}$$

$$\frac{d}{dt}q_C(t) = (k_{NC} - k_{CN})q_N - k_{CR}q_R + i(t) \tag{2.1.2}$$

$$\frac{d}{dt}q_R(t) = k_{NR}q_N - k_{CR}q_C - k_e P_f(t) \tag{2.1.3}$$

Passing in the matrix form, we have:

$$\frac{d\overline{q}}{dt} = A\overline{q} \tag{2.1.8}$$

$$\begin{pmatrix} q_N(t) \\ q_C(t) \\ q_R(t) \end{pmatrix} = \overline{q} \qquad \frac{d}{dt}\begin{pmatrix} q_N(t) \\ q_C(t) \\ q_R(t) \end{pmatrix} = \frac{d\overline{q}}{dt} \qquad \begin{pmatrix} 0 \\ I(t) \\ -k_e P_f(t) \end{pmatrix} = \overline{b} \tag{2.1.5}$$

$$\begin{pmatrix} 0 & (-k_{NC} + k_{CN}) & -k_{NR} \\ -(-k_{NC} + k_{CN}) & 0 & -k_{CR} \\ k_{NR} & k_{CR} & 0 \end{pmatrix} = A \tag{2.1.6}$$

Using the substitutions (2.5) and (2.6) we get the next afine equation:

$$\frac{d\overline{q}}{dt} = A\overline{q} + \overline{b} \tag{2.1.7}$$

With the initial condition: $\overline{q}(t_0) = \overline{q}_0$

In order to solving this equation, we have firste to determinate the solution of the homogenous equation:

$$\frac{d\overline{q}}{dt} = A\overline{q} \tag{2.1.8}$$

The General solution of such an equation is:

$$\overline{q}(t) = Ce^{A(t-t_0)}, A \in M_{3,3}(R) \tag{2.1.9}$$

where:

$$e^{A(t-t_0)} = \sum_{n \geq 0} \frac{A^n(t - t_0)}{n!} \tag{2.1.10}$$

The proper values of matrix A, used in the study of the protein synthesis process stability are:

$$\lambda_1 = 0$$

$$\lambda_2 = i\sqrt{k_{CR}^2 + k_{CN}^2 + k_{NR}^2}$$

$$\lambda_3 = i\sqrt{k_{CR}^2 + k_{CN}^2 + k_{NR}^2}$$

(2.1.11)

The main biochemical process in the protein synthesis is the formation of the peptide bound. The necessary information for the synthesis of a protein is stored at the specific structural gene level coded as purines and pyrimidine bases of DNA molecule structure. To each amino acid is corresponding a characteristic group of three bases, called codon, the total number of specific combinations being 64. Through a process of transcription, the code is transferred in the form of an m_{RNA} molecule, synthesized in the nucleus and then transferred into the cytoplasm. The RNA molecule acts on the ribosomes, in the initiation stage of synthesis process. During the transcription process, each sequence of DNA is copied into a corresponding sequence on the m_{RNA}.

The RNA synthesized in the neuronal cell nucleus is transferred through the nuclear pores in the cytoplasm in two forms: m_{RNA} and t_{RNA}, each of the two macromolecular structures fulfilling specific roles in the synthesis the proteins. Also, in the cytoplasm of amino acid activation occurs in the presence of ATP, under the influence of specific amino-synthase, resulting in an amino-AMP synthetase complex. In this specific t_{RNA}, also synthesized by the DNA transcription synthase is released, forming amino acid-activated t_{RNA} complex.

Amino acids activated and coupled with t_{RNA}, reach the ribosomes structures where protein synthesis takes place in three phases:

- initiation phase
- elongation phase
- termination phase

In the protein synthesis process are implied:

- DNA
- Amino acids
- Ribosomal RNA (r_{RNA})
- Messenger RNA, formed the nucleus (m_{RNA})
- Cytoplasmic transfer RNA (t_{RNA})
- Enzyme activation of amino acids (amino t_{RNA}-synthase)
- Initiation Factors
- Transfer Factors
- Termination factors

The initiation phase

The protein synthesis process is triggered under the influence of initiation factors existing in the cytoplasm, and, especially, the m_{RNA}, which contains an initiation codon Uracil-Guanine-Adenine (UGA), which is fixed on the 40S ribosomal subunit. On the initiation codon is fixing the initiation t_{RNA}, which is containing the initiation anticodons (sequence complementary codon UGA) and carries the emtionina. The t_{RNA} initiation is carried at the P-site P-peptidyl from the 60S subunit (Haulica, 1997).

The elongation phase

On the codone that follows the initaiting one, is fixing itself the corresponding t_{RNA} which is bringing the first aminoacid from the proteic sequence, and positioning itself on an second site (A) from the 60S subunit. When two t_{RNA} molecules are fixed on the ribosome, is acting a ribosomal transpeptidase which is transferring the formilmetioninic residue from the P site t_{RNA} on the A site t_{RNA}, forming a dipeptidil-t_{RNA} is. Then, through a phenomenon of translocation, during which the ribosome dipeptidil-t_{RNA} is and moving in opposite directions on the distance of a codon, dipeptidil reach the site of P-t_{RNA}, and the site of, remained open, it's loaded with fixed t_{RNA} the second amino acid sequence. By repeating the process, to add new amino acids, in accordance with the code sent. The process described is carried out based on energy supplied by ATP and GTP, and elongation of existing factors in the cytoplasm (Haulica, 1997).

The terminal phase

Is triggered by m_{RNA} termination codon (UGA or UAA), reached the site of the codon A. t_{RNA} is not fixed, but protein termination. At this point, unlink transpeptidase peptide chain composed of the last t_{RNA}. Peptide passes into the cytoplasm, being separated into ribosomal subunits (Haulica, 1997).

Based on bio-physiological processes described above, we have developed the following model for the systemic process of protein synthesis in the neuronal cell (fig.4), where:

DNA = deoxyribonucleic acid

m_{RNA} = messenger ribonucleic acid

t_{RNA} = transfer ribonucleic acid

r_{RNA} = ribosomal ribonucleic acid

In the cytoplasm, the conservation equations for t_{RNA} and m_{RNA} mass will be:

$$\frac{dM_{RNA_t}}{dt} = Q_{RNA_{t_P}} + Q_{RNA_{t_L}} - Q_{RNA_{t_D}} - Q_{RNA_{tAMP}} \tag{2.1.12}$$

$$\frac{dM_{RNA_m}}{dt} = Q_{RNA_{m_P}} + Q_{RNA_{m_L}} - Q_{RNA_{m_D}} - Q_{RNA_{m_R}} \tag{2.1.13}$$

Where:

M_{RNAm}, M_{RNAt} = mass of m_{RNA}, respectively mass of t_{RNA};

Q_{RNAmP}, Q_{RNAtP} = m_{RNA} flows, respectively t_{RNA} flows, coming from the nucleus into the cytoplasm through nuclear pores;

Q_{RNAmL}, Q_{RNAtL} = m_{RNA} flows, and that t_{RNA}, which are in free state in the cytoplasm;

Q_{RNAmD}, Q_{RNAtD} = m_{RNA} flows, and that t_{RNA}, degraded citosolic nuclease;

Q_{RNAmR} = flow mRNA, ribosomal binding sites linked in t_{RNA};

$Q_{RNAtAMP}$ = = flow, which combined with amino-AMP-synthetase complex, forming a complex amino acid-activated tRNA (Dabu, 2001)

When the cell is in rest, we have:

$$\frac{dM_{RNA_m}}{dt} = 0 \tag{2.1.14}$$

$$0 = Q_{RNA_{m_P}} + Q_{RNA_{m_L}} - Q_{RNA_{m_D}} - Q_{RNA_{m_R}} \qquad (2.1.15)$$

$$\frac{dM_{RNA_t}}{dt} = 0 \qquad (2.1.16)$$

$$0 = Q_{RNA_{t_P}} + Q_{RNA_{t_L}} - Q_{RNA_{t_D}} - Q_{ARN_{tAMP}} \qquad (2.1.17)$$

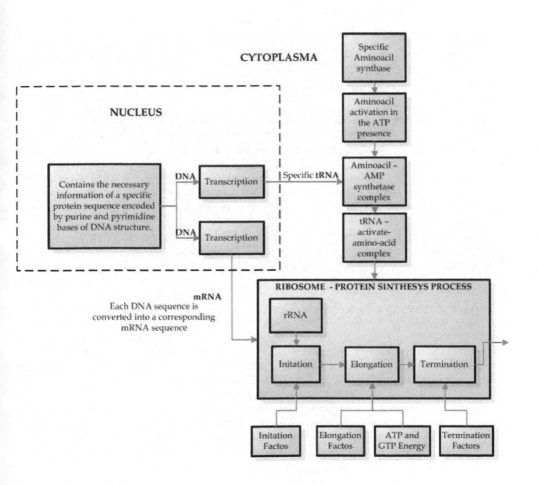

Fig. 4. The multi-compartmental model of protein synthesis process in the neuronal cell

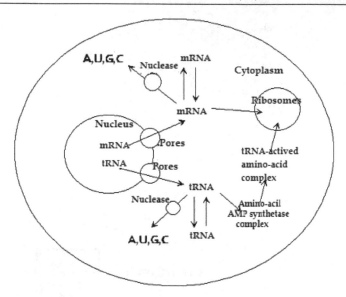

Fig. 5. Chart status for tRNA and mRNA in the neuronal cell

3.2 Modeling the behavior of Ca^{2+} ions as second messengers

The dynamical model for the Ca^{2+} regulation is nonlinear and the analysis of this process behavior request specific algorithms and tools. MatLab and Simulink offer adequate tools and algorithms for modeling these kind of processes.

In a neuronal cell in resting state, Ca^{2+} concentration is maintained at values below 10^{-7} mol/l, because the existing balance between influx and efflux of Ca^{2+}. Ca^{2+} influxes that may come from outside the cell by IL-type channels, the ISA, the messengers I, or G protein receptor complex or other messengers (cAMP, cGMP, IP4). Another source is the influx of Ca^{2+} stores in cell Ca^{2+} bound in the mitochondria or reticulum endo (sarco) plasma. Increasing concentrations of free cytoplasmic Ca^{2+} is compensated (in the idle state of the cell) by effluxes equivalent achievement either to exter (pump ATPase Ca^{2+} receptor-operated and how other messengers II system and antiport third Na$^+$/Ca^{2+}) or to deposits (by the Ca^{2+} ATPase) (Haulica 1997).

Cell activation through the occurrence of an action potential (AP) or through the coupling action of a messenger I with specific receptors, stimulates the Ca^{2+} influx and mobilization of deposits. When the concentration of cytoplasmic free Ca^{2+} exceeds the threshold value of 10^{-5} mol/l, cell response is triggered by Ca^{2+} as second messenger. Depending on the receptors involved in the process and the path followed, cell responses may get different aspects: the degradation of cAMP and cGMP, the formation of cGMP and cAMP, glycogenolysis, the release of synaptic neuromediators, protein synthesis, etc.

The effects of activation of other second messengers, Ca^{2+}-CaM complex, modulatory activated creates the possibility of two or more lines of receptor-activated intracellular signaling a significant effect on the final pool of the cell response (Rousset et al. 2003)

3.2.1 Modeling the behavior of neuronal Ca^{2+} when cell is in rest

When the cell is at rest, free cytoplasmic Ca^{2+} concentration is maintained at values below 10^{-7} mol/l, and the system is described by the following equation (Dabu, 2001):

$$\begin{cases} \dfrac{d[Ca_L^{2+}]}{dt} = Q_{Ca^{2+}_{I_L}} + Q_{Ca^{2+}_{I_{SA}}} + Q_{Ca^{2+}Msg_I} + Q_{Ca^{2+}G} + Q_{Ca^{2+}Mit} + Q_{Ca^{2+}RE} - \\ \qquad\qquad\qquad\qquad\qquad\qquad -Q_{Ca^{2+}EATP} - Q_{Ca^{2+}LATP} \end{cases} \qquad (2.2.1)$$

Where:

$[Ca^{2+}_L]$ = concentration of free Ca^{2+} in nerve cell cytoplasm in a state of rest;

$Q_{Ca^{2+}_{IL}}$ = influx of extracellular Ca^{2+} ion channels IL;

$Q_{Ca^{2+}_{ISA}}$ = influx of extracellular free Ca^{2+} ion channels ISA;

$Q_{Ca^{2+}\ MsgI}$ = free extracellular Ca^{2+} influx through messengers I.

$Q_{Ca^{2+}G}$ = free extracellular Ca^{2+} influx through G protein;

$Q_{Ca^{2+}Mit}$ = flow freely from the mitochondrial Ca^{2+} deposits

$Q_{Ca^{2+}RE}$ = free flow of Ca^{2+} from the endoplasmic reticulum;

$Q_{Ca^{2+}EATP}$ = efflux by intracellular free Ca^{2+} ATPase pump;

$Q_{Ca^{2+}LATP}$ = intracellular free Ca^{2+} flux through the ATPase of caught and stored Ca^{2+} in mitochondria

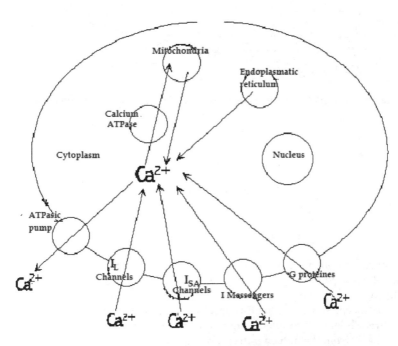

Fig. 6. The states chart for Ca^{2+} inside the neuronal cell in rest state

3.2.2 The cellular response modeling

Ca^{2+} acts as a messenger II in activating the cellular response when the neuronal cell is activated either by the occurrence of an action potentialor after coupling a messenger I with a specific receptor and the concentration of Ca^{2+} free in the cytoplasm exceeds the threshold value of about 10^{-5} mol/l. At the occurrence of an action potential in the neuronal cell as result of releasing the synaptic mediator in the synaptic space, the membrane depolarization at terminal button level stopes the penetration of Na^+ from outside the cell and generate the increasing of Ca^{2+} influx inside the cell.

The ions penetrate from the extracellular environment through two kinds of channels:
1. voltage-dependent Na^+ channels opened by action potential
2. voltage-dependent ionic channels, which are opened with a certain delay.

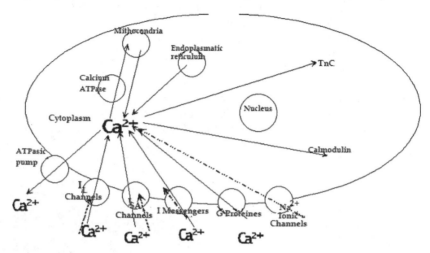

Fig. 7. States diagram for the free Ca^{2+} as cell reponse initiator in the activated neuronal cell cytoplasm

$$\begin{cases} \dfrac{d[Ca_L^{2+}]}{dt} = Q_{Ca^{2+}I_L} + Q_{Ca^{2+}I_{SA}} + Q_{Ca^{2+}Msg_I} + Q_{Ca^{2+}G} + Q_{Ca^{2+}Mit} + Q_{Ca^{2+}RE} + \\ \qquad\qquad + Q_{Ca^{2+}Na^+} - Q_{Ca^{2+}EATP} - Q_{Ca^{2+}LATP} - Q_{Ca^{2+}Cmd} - Q_{Ca^{2+}TnC} \\ \qquad\qquad\qquad\qquad\qquad\qquad\qquad\qquad \dfrac{d[Ca_L^{2+}]}{dt} \geq 0{,}99 * 10^{-5} \end{cases} \qquad (2.2.2)$$

Where:
$[Ca^{2+}_L]$ = free concentration of the nerve cell cytoplasm in rest state;
$Q_{Ca^{2+}IL}$ = influx of extracellular Ca^{2+} ion channels IL;
$Q_{Ca^{2+}ISA}$ = influx of extracellular free Ca^{2+} ion channels ISA;
$Q_{Ca^{2+}MsgI}$ = free extracellular Ca^{2+} influx through Messengers I channels.
$Q_{Ca^{2+}G}$ = free extracellular Ca^{2+} influx through G protein channels;
$Q_{Ca^{2+}Mit}$ = flow freely from the mitochondrial Ca^{2+} deposits
$Q_{Ca^{2+}RE}$ = free flow of Ca^{2+} from the endoplasmic reticulum;
$Q_{Ca^{2+}EATP}$ = efflux by intracellular free Ca^{2+} ATPase pump;
$Q_{Ca^{2+}LATP}$ = intracellular free Ca^{2+} flux through the Ca^{2+} ATPase of captured
and stored in mitochondria Ca^{2+};
$Q_{Ca^{2+}Na^+}$ = Ca^{2+} influx through voltage-dependent Na^+ channels opened by action potential
$Q_{Ca^{2+}Cmd}$ = free flow of cytoplasmic Ca^{2+} which combines with Calmodulin

$Q_{Ca^{2+}TnC}$ = free flow of cytoplasmic Ca^{2+}, which combine with TnC

In order to developing the model in SIMULINK, in order to describe the behavior of intracellular Ca^{2+} as messenger II, the following things were considered:
- description of the biological process
- analysis of a great number of lab tests regarding the behavior of Ca^{2+} , including:

The models that were built are characterized by the fact that, for input data that is similar (from the point of view of equivalence with the real world) to measurable input data for the real system in laboratory conditions, the output data, from point of view of values and evolution in time, was very close to the experimental data obtained from the lab tests.

Also, the obtained models have been verified, to establish their validity and adjustments were made where it was required, for a higher fidelity of the models.

The models were developed with MATLAB 4.2 for Windows and SIMULINK 1.3. In their development, the following were considered:

1. Intracellular Ca^{2+} is one of the most important messengers II, having a decisive role in secretion, motility, intermediary metabolism, cellular division, and cell death;

2. Intracellular Ca^{2+} concentration is very important in information processing at neuronal level;

3. The mechanisms for regulation of Ca^{2+} distribution within a neuronal cell include mainly non-linear processes, whose kinetics depends both on time and space

4. Not all the sub-systems that contribute to the regulation of intracellular Ca^{2+} concentration operate at the same rate. Some are rapid systems, while others are slow systems, with delays and idle periods;

5. Research demonstrated the existence of more Ca^{2+} transport sub-systems at neuronal level: mitochondrial sub-system, endo(sarco)plasmatic reticulum sub-system, ionic channels transportation, Ca^{2+} ATPases transportation and transport through Na^+/Ca^{2+} ion exchangers

6. Laboratory tests carried out on mouse hippocampus cells demonstrated that, following and action potential, intracellular Ca^{2+} concentration could reach the value of 1mM, while, at rest, intracellular Ca^{2+} concentration is about 0.1 mM. Laboratory tests analysis, performed with the FURA-2 system have shown that the induction of an intracellular depolarization, following 10-20 action potentials, increases the level of intracellular Ca^{2+} concentration within soma and proximal apical dendrites from 0.02-0.05 mM to 0.1-0.2 mM. The time required for the concentration level to come back to the initial value was about 100 ns. Other similar Laboratory tests analyzes have shown that the level of intracellular Ca^{2+} concentration could increase by 400-500% as a response to an electric pulse applied for 500 ms, with a comeback to the initial value period of 5 s.

7. Fluctuation of the Ca^{2+} concentration at cell level depends on:
   - the volume of the substance where the process takes place;
   - local diffusion coefficient
   - geometry of the elements and structures analyzed (Dabu,2008)

In figures 8 and 11 are presented the Simulink models for the regulation of the Ca^{2+} in the neuronal cell in rest state and activated state of the cell. The input ports are the input ionic channels and receptor sites from the neuronal membrane where signaling molecules initiate coupled sets of chemical reactions within the cellular space The output ports are the output ionic channels and the specific binding sites from the neuronal membrane where the signaling molecules are binding and initiate bio-chemical reactions outside the cell.

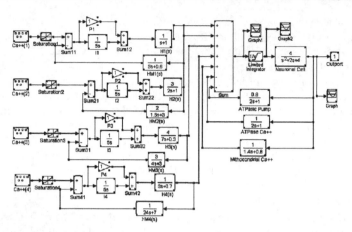

Fig. 8. The Simulink model for the regulation of the Ca²⁺ in the rest state of the neuronal cell
The results of the simulations are Presented in figures 9 and 10

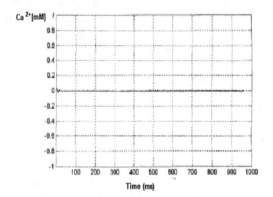

Fig. 9. Simulation results with low variation of Ca²⁺ concentration

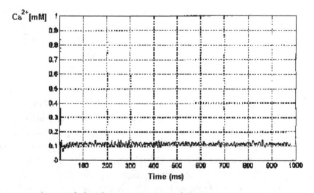

Fig. 10. Simulation results with higher variation of Ca²⁺ concentration

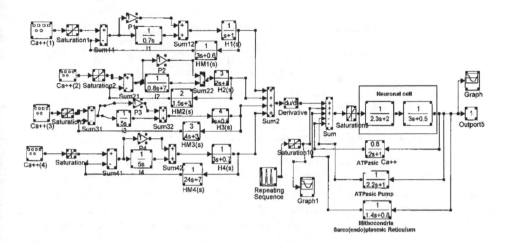

Fig. 11.The Simulink model for the regulation of the Ca²⁺ in the activate state of the cell

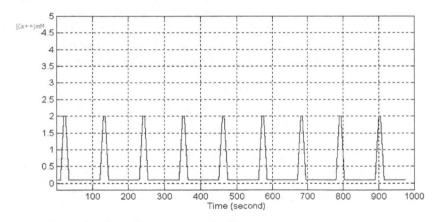

Fig. 12. Simulation for the activate neuronal cell

4. Matlab and simulink in computer assisted modeling and systemic approach for aerobic bioremediation

The aerobic bioremediation treatment process technology use special bacteria blends engineered in order to biodegrade the organic contamination (fig. 13) into harmless carbon dioxide and water, to derive energy, with no potential environmental impacts, as compared to conventional burning methods. Some of the carbon is used by bacteria as "food" to derive new carbohydrates, proteins and nucleic acids for growth. One bacteria category is initializing the process, and other bacteria families are continuing the process (figure 2). The absence of one bacteria species from the bacteria blend is diminishing the purifying capacity of the whole system .

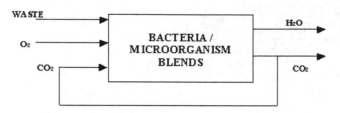

Fig. 13. The systemic model for aerobic bioremediation

For bioremediation to be effective, microorganisms must enzymatically attack the pollutants and convert them to harmless products. As bioremediation can be effective only where environmental conditions permit microbial growth and activity, its application often involves the manipulation of environmental parameters to allow microbial growth and degradation to proceed at a faster rate. The most used procedures for environmental parameters manipulation are: biosparging, bioventing, the use of oxygen releasing compounds; pure oxygen injection, hydrogen peroxide infiltration, ozone injection. All these procedure add in the contaminated area supplemental supply of oxygen which becomes available to aerobic, hydrocarbon-degrading bacteria. Like other technologies, bioremediation has its limitations. Some contaminants, such as chlorinated organic or high aromatic hydrocarbons, are resistant to microbial attack. They are degraded either slowly or not at all, hence it is not easy to predict the rates of clean-up for a bioremediation exercise. There are no rules to predict if a contaminant can be degraded (Rockne et al., 2000).

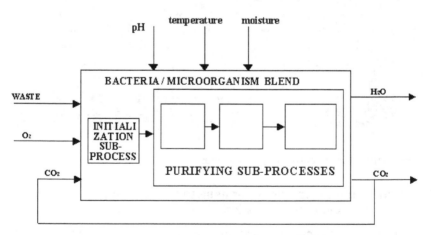

Fig. 14. The compartmental systemic model for aerobic bioremediation

Microbial growth and activity are readily affected by pH, temperature, and moisture. Temperature affects biochemical reactions rates, and the rates of many of them double for each 10°C rise in temperature. Above a certain temperature, however, the cells die. Available water is essential for all the living organisms, and irrigation is needed to achieve the optimal moisture level. The amount of available oxygen will determine whether the system is aerobic or anaerobic (fig.14)

Biomodeling using Simulink and Matlab can provide important answers regarding the mechanisms of biodegradation reactions and the evolution of degenerative capabilities in bacteria/microorganisms. They are usefully to predict the outcome of the bioprocesses and to evaluate the time and the costs of the intervention, it is necessary to create and use systemic and computer assisted mathematical models to describe the bioremediation processes (Dabu 2004).

For developing such models, it is necessary to look down the following steps:

1. Establishing the scope of the required treatment;
2. Identifying the inputs and outputs of the system;
3. Identifying the environmental parameters which affect the process and the corresponding sub-processes (bioavailability, penetration or uptake of the compounds trough the cell envelope, flow and transport, biochemical reactions, release of products);
4. Identifying the inhibitory and activator effects of different compounds or microorganism classes;
5. Identifying the compartmental systemic model of the process.
6. Identifying the transfer functions which are describing every compartment of the model and the transfer function for the entire model (Dabu & Nicu 1998, Dabu 2004).

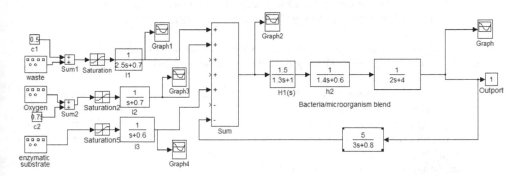

Fig. 15. The Simulink model for an anaerobic bioremediation process

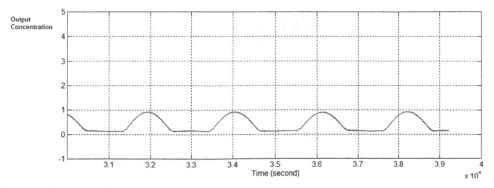

Fig. 16. The simulation output

5. References

B. N. Anderson & R. D. B. N. Anderson & R. D. Henkler. (2000). Monitoring and Control of Field Bioremediation. Biotechnology 2000:Proceedings of the 11th International Biotechnology Symposium & 18th DECHEMA Annual Meeting on Biotechnology, Berlin. Section VI, Environmental Biotechnology, pp. 403-407

Cristina – Maria Dabu, M. D. Nicu, "Environmental Biotechnologies and their Implications in Ecological Problems", Modern Biotechnologies and the Environment Protection, 1998, 130-135;

Dabu C.M. Contributions about mathematical and computer aided modeling of neuronal structures applied in radiobiology, "Politehnica" University of Bucharest, 2001, pp 5-15

Dr. Cristina –Maria Dabu,. Environmental Biotechnologies and the environment quality A.G.I.R. Bulletin, no. 4, 2004, 85-88;

Dabu C.M. Computational Models end e-Science, Dr. Eng. Cristina – Maria Dabu, E_COMM_LINE 2005 Volume, 2005, pp351-355

Jiri Dambrosky, Computer modelling of microbial hydrolytic dehalogenation, Pure &Appl. Chem., vol.70, No.7, 1998, 1375-1383;

Gonzalez Perez P.P, Modelling intracellular signalling networks using behaviour-based systems and the blackboard architecture, Universidad Nacional Autónoma de México, pp.1

Haulica, I., Fiziologie umama, Editia a II -a, Ed. Medicala , Bucuresti, 1997, pp 45-99

Heinrich, R. & Schuster, S. 1996 The regulation of cellular systems. New York: Chapman & Hall

Rockne, K. J., J. C. Chee-Sanford, R. A. Sanford, B. Hedlund, J. T. Staley, S. E. Strand (2000) Anaerobic naphthalene degradation by microbial pure cultures under nitrate-reducing conditions. Applied Environmental Microbiology. 66 (4), 1595-1601.

Matthieu Rousset, Thierry Cens, Sophie Gavarini, Andreas Jeromin, Pierre Charnet, Down-regulation of Voltage-gated Ca2_ Channels by Neuronal Calcium Sensor-1 Is _ Subunit-specific, The Journal of Biological Chemistry, Vol. 278, No. 9, Issue of February 28, pp. 7019–7026, 2003

Noble, D. 2002 Modeling the heart—from genes to cells to the whole organ. Science 295, 1678–1682. (doi:10.1126/science.1069881)

Shreedhar Maskey, Andreja Jonoski, Dimitri P. Solomatine, Groundwater Remediation Strategy Using Global Optimization Algorithms, Journal of Water Resources Planning and Management, 2002, 431-440;

M. Vidali, Bioremediation. An overview, IUPAC, Pure and Applied Chemistry 73, 2001, 1163–1172

2

Automotive Sketch Processing in C++ with MATLAB Graphic Library

Qiang Li
Jilin University
P. R. China

1. Introduction

The purpose of automotive sketch processing is to separate the sketch into patches and extract the useful information and apply it to assist 2D to 3D transformation. How to extract the useful information depends on what the resources are, what kinds of information are needed, and what methods are applied. In sketches, the information may be extracted from features such as the geometry features, shading, colours and lighting. Geometry features are the most important because they contain the information to identify and distinguish between forms. For example, edges can be used to determine the shapes, and areas can be used to match the size.

This chapter introduces a way to make the automotive sketches ready for 2D to 3D transformation. Three aspects of problems are discussed including the pre-processing of sketches outside computer, the processing of pre-processed sketches inside computer, and the extraction of features. Some of sketch processing algorithms are implemented in C++ using the MATLAB image processing toolbox, Graphic Library and Math Library. Some have been developed from scratch. The work describe in this chapter is concerned with the production of a feasible routine, from the point of view of application, which is capable of dealing with the real world characteristics of automotive sketches. There is no established method which provides a suitable starting point for the transformation of real automotive sketches. The combined algorithms, which are discussed in this chapter, have been found to be useful.

2. A glimpse of the 23D system

A brief set of requirements, from a usability point of view, for 2D to 3D tool can be summaried as follow:

- Can deal with 2D sketches and 3D models.
- Intuitive, simplified and robust.
- Flexible and expandable.
- Compatible with other CAD and CAM systems.

Following the above requirements, a prototype of 2D to 3D system, called "23D", has been implemented to support the novel method of transforming 2D automotive sketches quickly into 3D surface models.

2.1 The development environment

The main development language is Microsoft Visual C++® (Ladd, 1996; Seed, 1996; Smith, 1997; Schildt, 1998) with OpenGL® (Kilgard, 1996; Wright & Sweet, 1996; Fosner, 1997; Silverio et al., 1997; Chin et al., 1998; Segal & Akeley, 2001), MATLAB® C/C++ Math and Graphics Libraries (MathWorks, 2001). The basic functions and some algorithms are implemented based on the Open Geometry (Glaeser & Stachel, 1999), MATLAB optimisation toolbox (MathWorks, 2000), spline toolbox, and image processing toolbox (MathWorks, 2001), Image Analysis Pro (IaePro) (Matthews, 2002) and Microsoft VisSDK (The Vision Technology Group, 2000).

2.2 Multiple working modes

The system needs to deal with 2D sketches and 3D surface models, and transformationfrom 2D to 3D as well. Therefore, the working modes should be easily exchanged between 2D and 3D. In the system, the multiple working modes have been implemented for 2D and 3D manipulations. It is easy to switch the modes, see Fig. 1. 2D sketch is considered as the background in 3D space. Therefore, the 2D working mode is that the background plane containing the sketch is displayed without the 3D models, see Fig. 1a; the 3D working mode is that the 3D models are displayed without the background, see Fig. 1b; and the mixed working mode is that both the 3D models and the 2D background are displayed at the same time, see Fig. 1c. The 2D sketch background is not affected by any 3D manipulations.

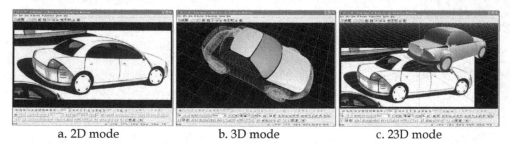

a. 2D mode   b. 3D mode   c. 23D mode

Fig. 1. Three working modes

3. The pre-processing of a sketch

The sketches are not realistic images. The forms and shadings may contain many inconsistencies compared with a true projection of a possible real object. In addition, the reverse transformations from 2D to 3D are rather complicated and contain possible ambiguities, in that a 2D shape may represent many possible shapes in 3D. Therefore, some assumptions have to be made in order to simplify the problem. The fundamental assumptions made here include:

- The scanned sketches will be pre-processed to reduce the inconsistencies in them. The end result of the pre-processing will be that boundaries are complete and are all closed contours or silhouettes. Any key lines will be clear and without ambiguities so as to give enough information for further processing. With these conditions satisfied, the sketch can be separated into patches which can be represented by parametric models.

- Shadings of sketches may be ignored initially, since many techniques of the representations in sketches are not realistic and exact. To derive meaning from them requires psychological interpretation of the intention of the designer, which is beyond the scope of this project.
- Any side, front, rear or top view of automotive model in the sketches is considered to be orthographic projection, others such as front or rear ¾ perspective views are considered to be perspective projection.
- Minor details are ignored and allowing concentration on the major ones which establish the essential 3D geometry. It is possible that these could be restored after the basic form has been determined, perhaps using parts from a parts library.
- There is a limit to the exaggeration of forms in a sketch that can be used. Designers often do use exaggerated geometry to achieve a desired mood. If translated into 3-D, the resultant model will also contain exaggerated geometry.
- No attempt is made to correct ambiguities of the reverse transformation automatically. These functions are best left for user intervention. The user is likely to be the stylist, who is in a good position to judge which of a number of possibilities best represents the intended vehicle.

As known, not all the sketches are suitable for 3D modelling by the 23D system, but many do contain the required characteristics. There are many different styles in automotive sketching, according to the stylist's personal practice. The information contained varies at the different conceptual design stages, and is not exactly correct in geometry shape and projection, because the sketches are not real-world images. Humans can easily interpret the shape through adding additional information, in the form of prior knowledge of automotive forms to the sketches and ignoring the faults according to this knowledge. However, the computer is not as agile as the human. It must have available enough information to create the shape, which can come from various sources. One approach is to establish a powerful knowledge database to support the object recognition; another approach is to add the information before image processing. The former needs larger investment and longer time to train the computer, and the later needs less investment and is easy to realize. Two examples of the use of an original sketch as a basis for two well established edge detection algorithms are shown in Fig. 2c and 2d. The results show that they are difficult to be interpreted, even by a human. If the results are to be interpretable by a computer program, significantly more sophisticated processing will be required. Therefore, it is necessary and feasible to establish some input requirements for the sketches that will be used for 3D modelling by the method proposed in 23D system, and will form the requirements for the pre-processing stage. The requirements are relative. The more powerful the pre-processing method is, the lower the requirements for the interpretive program are. The original sketches are drawn by stylist, as shown in Fig. 2a and 2e. The results after pre-processing are shown in Fig. 2b and 2f.

The aim of the pre-processing of sketches is to allow the requirements for the interpretive program to be met by a greater variety of original sketches. Essentially, the pre-processing emphasises useful features in the sketches and eliminates useless ones. According to the analysis of Tingyong Pan (Pan, 2002), the form-lines and form-shadings should be enhanced and kept, and the non-form-lines and non-form-shadings should be ignored. The vehicle components should be simplified in details and ambiguities removed. One of the important requirements is that the input sketches should have completed and closed contours or silhouettes. Any key form-lines should be clear to give enough information to the further processing. For example, the original sketches (Fig. 2a and 2e) leave some missing and unclear contours or silhouettes to give an imaginary space. These should be redrawn by stylists, see the sketches in Fig. 2b and 2f. All the silhouettes are closed and clear. Some details are ignored such as small lights, highlights, and shadings. The shading information can be separated from the contour or silhouette information. If the shading information is important and near realistic, and is within the closed contours, it can be kept. Otherwise, it should be ignored or further processed to a suitable form. The shadows of the vehicles are deleted, and the completed silhouettes of wheels are added, which are very important for the determination of the 3D coordinates. Side elevations, front and rear ¾ perspective views are the best starting point for system processing.

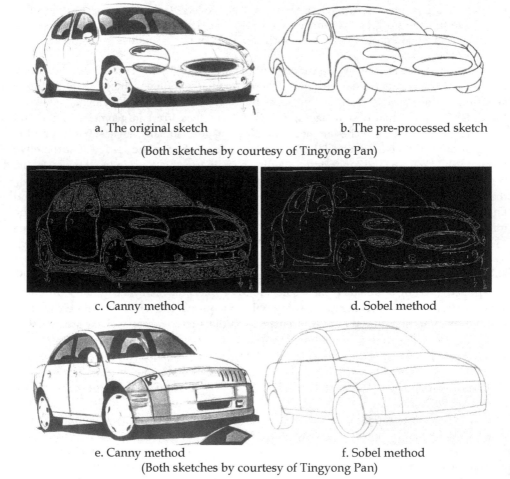

a. The original sketch   b. The pre-processed sketch
(Both sketches by courtesy of Tingyong Pan)

c. Canny method   d. Sobel method

e. Canny method   f. Sobel method
(Both sketches by courtesy of Tingyong Pan)

Fig. 2. The pre-processing of the sketch

It is also important to produce pre-processed sketches with simple patches, which can be represented using existing parametric models.

Because the features extracted from sketches are currently pixel-based in order to keep the balance between the speed of processing and the precision of calculation, the suitable size of input sketches should be carefully considered.

4. Sketch processing

Even though the sketches have been pre-processed before scanning, they also need to be subject to further image processing before transforming them into 3D. Some basic functions - such as the adjustment of lightness, hue, and saturation, the exchange from colour to grey scale and B&W, the erasure of unnecessary areas in the sketch, the separation of form from non-form line and shading - are used before edge detection and segmentation. To decrease the size of the dataset and smooth the boundaries, B-spline or NURBS curve fitting to the outlines are applied. These form-lines are disassembled into spline segments and are used to build up the patches, which represent the whole surface model.

The original sketches (if applicable) or pre-processed sketches still need to be processed further in order to obtain a sketch with single pixel edges and closed boundaries, and this sketch is separated into patches for the downstream processes. Therefore, it is necessary to investigate a set of efficient image processing algorithms for this application.

4.1 Image mode selection

There are many modes for the different purposes of raster image processing including colour and non-colour ones. Some typical colour modes such as RGB (red, green and blue), HSV (hue, saturation and value), HLS (hue, lightness and saturation), and CYMK (cyan, yellow, magenta and black) have been described in the books (Foley et al., 1996; Salomon, 1999). The Adobe Photoshop 6.0 supports colour modes such as RGB, CYMK, Lab (lightness, green-red axis and blue-yellow axis), Indexed Colour, and HSB (hue, saturation and brightness), and non-colour modes such as Greyscale, Multi-channel, Bitmap and Duotone.

There are four modes for image displaying and processing supported by the 23D system: RGB colour, 256 greyscale, 16 greyscale, and black and white (B&W). The internal format is RGBA colour; therefore the modes can be changed reversibly. The algorithms of greyscale are different. For example, the Image Analysis Explorer Pro (IaePro) supports three methods to obtain a greyscale as follows.

$$A_{ij} = \begin{cases} 0.2125R_{ij} + 0.7154G_{ij} + 0.0721B_{ij} & \text{Greyscale BT709} \\ 0.299R_{ij} + 0.587G_{ij} + 0.114B_{ij} & \text{Greyscale Y} \\ 0.5R_{ij} + 0.419G_{ij} + 0.081B_{ij} & \text{Greyscale RMY} \end{cases} \quad (1)$$

However, for simplification, the transformation from RGB to 256 greyscale used here is an average algorithm of the colour RGB values (Jain, 1995, pp. 281).

$$A1_{ij}\Big|_{\substack{i=0,\cdots,BmpBgr\_w-1 \\ j=0,\cdots,BmpBgr\_h-1}} = \frac{1}{3}(R_{ij} + G_{ij} + B_{ij}) \quad (2)$$

Where $A1_{ij}$ is the greyscale value of a point in image including three components R_{ij}, G_{ij} and B_{ij}; $BmpBgr\_w$ and $BmpBgr\_h$ are the width and the height of sketch in pixels, respectively. In B&W mode, the two levels are obtained from a point between 0 and 255 to bisect the whole range. A similar function is used in Adobe Photoshop 6.0 (Adobe, 2000).

$$A2_{ij}\Big|_{\substack{i=0,\cdots,BmpBgr\_w-1 \\ j=0,\cdots,BmpBgr\_h-1}} = \begin{bmatrix} 0 \\ 1 \end{bmatrix} = \begin{bmatrix} 0 \\ 255 \end{bmatrix} \quad \begin{matrix} 0 \le A1_{ij} < D_L \\ D_L \le A1_{ij} \le 255 \end{matrix} \tag{3}$$

Where $A2_{ij}$ is determined by $A1_{ij}$, and D_L is a threshold to determine a dividing level. The default of D_L is 192, and can be adjusted. The change from 256 greyscale to 16 greyscale is obtained according to the average rule. A coding scheme proposed in 23D system is that the values of 16 intervals are increased through adding the value 17 for smoothness and keeping it spanning to the two ends (0 and 255).

An example is shown in Fig. 3 for the four modes of processing allowed by the system.

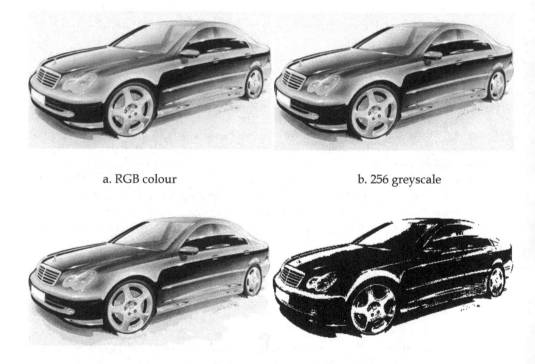

a. RGB colour   b. 256 greyscale

c. 16 greyscale   d. B&W with a threshold of 192

(Colour sketch by courtesy of geocities.com)

Fig. 3. The four display modes of the system

$$A3_{ij}\Big|_{\substack{i=0,\cdots,BmpBgr\_w-1 \\ j=0,\cdots,BmpBgr\_h-1}} = \begin{bmatrix} 0 \\ 1 \\ 2 \\ 3 \\ 4 \\ 5 \\ 6 \\ 7 \\ 8 \\ 9 \\ 10 \\ 11 \\ 12 \\ 13 \\ 14 \\ 15 \end{bmatrix} = \begin{bmatrix} 0 \\ 17 \\ 34 \\ 51 \\ 68 \\ 85 \\ 102 \\ 119 \\ 136 \\ 153 \\ 170 \\ 187 \\ 204 \\ 221 \\ 238 \\ 255 \end{bmatrix} \quad \begin{array}{l} 0 \le A1_{ij} < 16 \\ 16 \le A1_{ij} < 32 \\ 32 \le A1_{ij} < 48 \\ 48 \le A1_{ij} < 64 \\ 64 \le A1_{ij} < 80 \\ 80 \le A1_{ij} < 96 \\ 96 \le A1_{ij} < 112 \\ 112 \le A1_{ij} < 128 \\ 128 \le A1_{ij} < 144 \\ 144 \le A1_{ij} < 160 \\ 160 \le A1_{ij} < 176 \\ 176 \le A1_{ij} < 192 \\ 192 \le A1_{ij} < 208 \\ 208 \le A1_{ij} < 224 \\ 224 \le A1_{ij} < 240 \\ 240 \le A1_{ij} \le 255 \end{array} \tag{4}$$

4.2 Brightness and contrast adjustment

The adjustments of brightness and contrast supply the basic means of image enhancement, which compensate for the losses caused by imperfect scanning methods. The algorithm from MATLAB (MathWorks, 2001) *imadjust* function was used to control the values of RGB components directly. The brightness f_b can be adjusted as follows.

$$f_b = \begin{cases} \left. \begin{array}{ll} f_{b0}(255-b)/100 & t \ge b \\ f_{b0}(255-t)/100 & t < b \end{array} \right\} & f_{b0} \ge 0 \\ \left. \begin{array}{ll} f_{b0}t/100 & t \ge b \\ f_{b0}b/100 & t < b \end{array} \right\} & f_{b0} < 0 \end{cases} \qquad f_b \in [0,255] \tag{5}$$

Where f_{b0} is the original value of brightness; t and b are the top and the bottom values of brightness. They are adjusted by f_b, $t = t + f_b$ and $b = b + f_b$; h and l are the highest and the lowest values among the values of RGB. The differences are defined as $dx = h - l$, $dy = t - b$. They are limited within 0~255.

$$\begin{cases} h = l + (255-b)dx/dy, t = 255 & t > 255 \\ h = l - bdx/dy, t = 0 & t < 0 \\ l = h - tdx/dy, b = 0 & b < 0 \\ l = h - (t-255)dx/dy, b = 255 & b > 255 \end{cases} \tag{6}$$

If the original value $f_{c0} \ge 0$, the contrast f_c can be adjusted as

$$f_c = f_{c0}dx / 200 \qquad f_c \in [0,255] \tag{7}$$

Then h and l should be adjusted as $h = h - f_c$ and $l = l + f_c$. Otherwise, the image is not enhanced. The boundaries should be adjusted again.

$$\begin{cases} h = x_0 + 0.5dy / k & y_1 \geq t \\ h = 255; t = y_1 & y_1 < t \\ l = x_0 - 0.5dy / k & y_2 \leq b \\ l = 0; b = y_2 & y_2 > b \end{cases} \text{ where } \begin{cases} k = tg[arctg(dy / dx)(100 + f_c)] \\ x_0 = 0.5(h + l), y_0 = 0.5(t + b) \\ y_1 = y_0 + k(255 - x_0) \\ y_2 = y_0 - kx_0 \end{cases} \tag{8}$$

The Gamma value f_γ is adjusted according to the original value $f_{\gamma 0}$ as follow.

$$f_\gamma = \left(f_{\gamma 0} / 5\right)^{1.2} \qquad f_\gamma \in [1,10] \tag{9}$$

Therefore, the RGB values of each pixel can be calculated as follow.

$$\begin{bmatrix} R_{ij} \\ G_{ij} \\ B_{ij} \end{bmatrix} = \begin{bmatrix} b + (t - b)\left(C_\gamma\right)^{(R_{ij}-l)/(h-l)} \\ b + (t - b)\left(C_\gamma\right)^{(G_{ij}-l)/(h-l)} \\ b + (t - b)\left(C_\gamma\right)^{(B_{ij}-l)/(h-l)} \end{bmatrix} \qquad \begin{array}{l} i = 0, \cdots, BmpBgr\_w - 1 \\ j = 0, \cdots, BmpBgr\_h - 1 \end{array} \tag{10}$$

The dialog window and examples are shown in Fig. 4. The range of the sliders is ± 100.

4.3 Edge detection

Many algorithms for edge detection have been developed for different image resources. Because the sketches are not the real-world images and can be pre-processed before imported into the system, the edge detection is just a simple routine to quickly find the necessary points for the further processing. Therefore some basic and common algorithms are implemented into the system including *Sobel, Prewitt, Roberts, Canny, Zerocross, Direct* and *Sobel+*. The system was built using the MATLAB C++ Math Library and the Graphics Library (MathWorks, 2000). The dialog window is shown in Fig.5, which is similar to the MATLAB find edges function.

Some examples are shown in Fig. 6 and Fig. 7. In most cases, the algorithms from the MATLAB edge functions can give good results for original sketches, shown in Fig. 6. However, they give poor results on pre-processed sketches, shown in Fig. 7b and Fig. 7d. The pre-processed sketches are composed of sets of dense and thick strokes coming from a quick expression of the edges according to the original sketches. Therefore, a hybrid algorithm, *Direct*, is proposed to deal with such styled sketches.

The idea comes from a demo – *Region Labelling of Steel Grains* – in the MATLAB image processing toolbox. Two binary images are obtained from pre-processed sketches by using low and high thresholds. The edge points from low threshold image are used to delete the same points from high threshold image. The left edge points from the high threshold image are considered as the edges. In this way minor regions caused by strokes are deleted. The result is shown in Fig. 7c produce from a thick edge image.

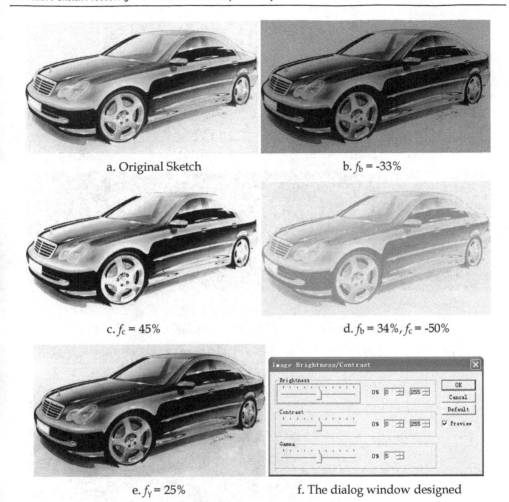

a. Original Sketch   b. $f_b = -33\%$

c. $f_c = 45\%$ d. $f_b = 34\%, f_c = -50\%$

e. $f_Y = 25\%$ f. The dialog window designed

Fig. 4. The samples of the brightness and contrast adjustment

Fig. 5. The dialog window of *Find Edges* function

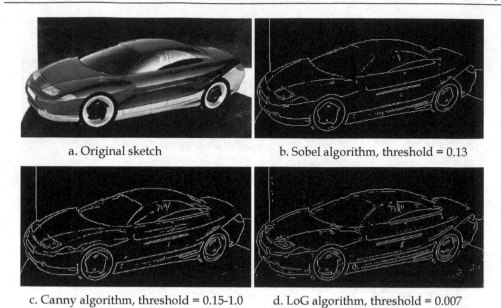

a. Original sketch   b. Sobel algorithm, threshold = 0.13

c. Canny algorithm, threshold = 0.15-1.0   d. LoG algorithm, threshold = 0.007

(Original sketch by courtesy of Cor Steenstra, Foresee Car Design)

Fig. 6. Edge detection of the original colour sketch with the different algorithms

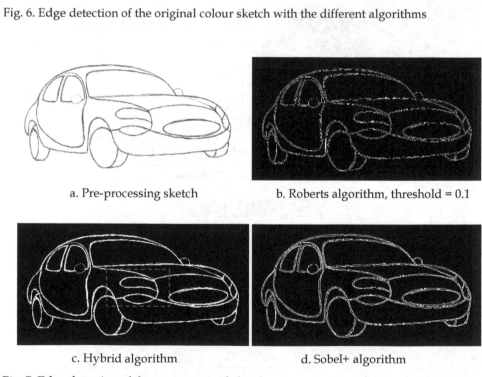

a. Pre-processing sketch   b. Roberts algorithm, threshold = 0.1

c. Hybrid algorithm   d. Sobel+ algorithm

Fig. 7. Edge detection of the pre-processed sketch

To obtain a satisfactory result, it is crucial to select a suitable threshold for edge detection. However, some problems are still left such as thick edges, double edges and broken edges which cause unclosed boundaries, and small 'spurs' or 'prickles'. Therefore, further processing is needed to eliminate these problems.

4.4 Edge morphing

Edge morphing can further refine the image obtained from edge detection. This function is implemented using the MATLAB *bwmorph* function including the method *Bothat*, *Bridge*, *Clean*, *Close*, *Diag*, *Dilate*, *Erode*, *Fill*, *Hbreak*, *Majority*, *Open*, *Remove*, *Shrink*, *Skel*, *Spur*, *Thicken*, *Thin* and *Tophat*, as shown in Fig. 8. It can apply specific morphological operations to the binary image. Repeated application of these operations may be necessary. *Infinite* means that *Times* are determined by the methods automatically.

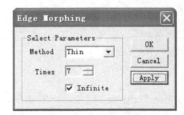

Fig. 8. The dialog window of *Edge Morphing* function

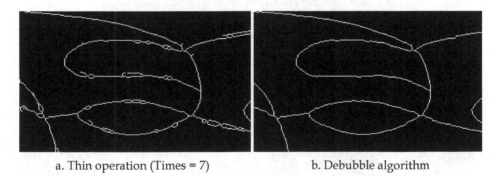

a. Thin operation (Times = 7)   b. Debubble algorithm

Fig. 9. Edge thins and debubbles (Please refer to Fig. 7c)

When the edges are not single pixels such as the ones shown in Fig. 7c, edge morphing should be applied. The result after the seven applications of the thin operation is shown in Fig. 9a. The edges become the single pixels, but with some small holes and spurs. This is still not a satisfactory starting point for the transformation. The bubbles and spurs must be eliminated.

4.5 Debubble – a hybrid algorithm

It has not proved to be possible to obtain the required result using a single method. Different hybrid methods have been applied to achieve a good result. Here is a hybrid algorithm proposed in this research to perform an operation of deleting the small holes and spurs, such as shown in Fig. 9a. The algorithm entitled *Debubble*, shown in Fig. 10, applies firstly the *Bwlabel* algorithm in MATLAB to find the small bubbles (holes), which are determined by the bubble size parameter. Once the small bubbles are found, they are filled into solid areas. Then the *Skel* and *Spur* algorithms are applied to obtain the single pixel edges. The actual bubble size is the percentage of the maximum size in pixels, which is compared with the image size in pixels. For example, to obtain the result in Fig. 9b, the actual bubble size is 165, and the image size is 524288 (1024×512). This is just 0.0315% of the image size – very small bubbles! In this case, all the bubbles those are smaller than 165 are deleted. The result shown in Fig. 9b is quite acceptable. Using the *Direct*, *Thin*, and *Debubble* algorithms for the pre-processed sketches can give a good result.

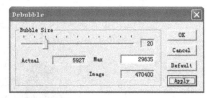

Fig. 10. The dialog window of *Debubble* function

4.6 Edge refinement

Once satisfactory edges are obtained, the image is ready for segmentation. However, there are still anomalies that must be handled. For example, see the case in Fig. 11a, the crossing point of the three patches is not unique. This produces three crossing points. In order to delete this small error, the edge points must be checked and refined.

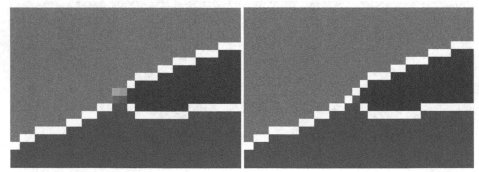

a. Crossing points are not unique   b. Unique crossing point

Fig. 11. Crossing point searching

An algorithm is proposed here to perform this operation. It is described as follow:
- Every point is checked in the whole image.
- If it is an edge point, a counter is set with initial value of zero. The point is the current point.
- The eight neighbours of the current point are checked one by one from 0 to 7, see Fig. 12a.
- Once a neighbour point is edge point, the counter is increased by one.
- The current neighbour point is anomaly point, once the counter reaches three within the eight neighbours.

- The last current neighbour is deleted.

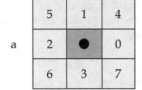

3	2	1
4	●	0
5	6	7

a

5	1	4
2	●	0
6	3	7

b

Fig. 12. Eight-neighbour graph

The result is shown in Fig. 11b. Now the three patches share the same single pixel boundaries and have a unique crossing point.

4.7 Patch segmentation with colours

It is easy to separate an image with closed boundaries into patches by applying the MATLAB *Bwlabel* function, and it can then be displayed with the different colour maps. The *Pseudo Colormap* includes *Autumn, Bone, Colorcube, Cool, Copper, Flag, Gray, Hot, HSV, Jet, Lines, Pink, Prism, Spring, Summer, White* and *Winter*, as shown in Fig. 13. The label 0 is assigned to the boundaries between the patches. Label 1 is assigned to the background and used as the silhouette of the whole vehicle. From label 2 onwards, they are assigned to the patches which form the surfaces of the vehicle. After labelling, a pseudo colour map is added for separating the patches. The labelled image is shown in Fig. 14.

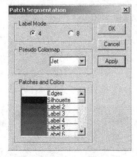

Fig. 13. The dialog window of *Patch Segmentation* function

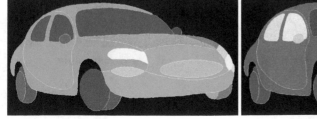

a. Labelled sketch   b. Multiple Selection of patches

Fig. 14. The sketch after segmentation

As well as the labelling and colour mapping, some other tasks are performed at the same time, such as finding out the start points of each patch on the boundary and the maximum rectangles containing each patch, initialising the boundary node data and searching all the sequential nodes and the crossing points on the boundary of each patch, and calculating the areas and centres of patches.

4.8 Curve fitting

After the segmentation, the sketch is separated into small patches with zigzag boundaries. In most cases, the shape does not vary largely compared with the original sketch. However, at some corners which contain crossing points, the shape may look strange. The use of spline curve fitting can smooth the zigzag boundaries and provide modification of the shapes if necessary.

The patches are selected by the user, shown in Fig. 15b, for performing the curve fitting. The basic functions are implemented from the MATLAB *Splinetool* function in the spline toolbox [THEM01c]. The similar dialog window, as shown in Fig. 16, was designed. An example is given to demonstrate the curve fitting process, shown in Fig. 15 (refer to the area in Fig. 7c). Comparing the areas from Fig. 15a and Fig. 15d, the boundary of the light is smooth and its shape has been improved.

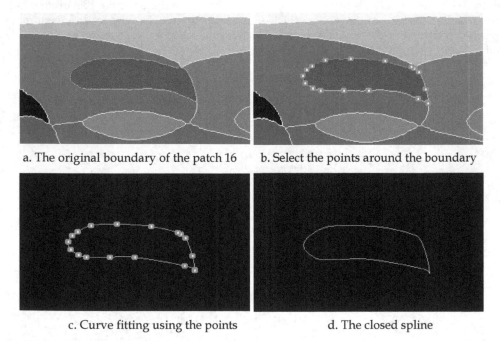

a. The original boundary of the patch 16   b. Select the points around the boundary

c. Curve fitting using the points   d. The closed spline

Fig. 15. The curve-fitting and shape modification

5. Feature extraction

The features include the point, curve and patch features extracted from the sketch, which are put into a data structure.

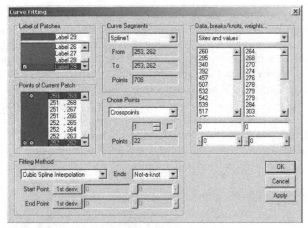

Fig. 16. The dialog window of *Curve Fitting* function

5.1 Data structure for sketch

The points after labelling contain a lot of information for further processing and analysis. Therefore, it is important to establish an efficient data management system. A proposed sketch structure is shown in Fig. 17. The basic unit is a single point, a set of points presents a curve, a close curve or several curves stands for a patch, all the patches make a vehicle.

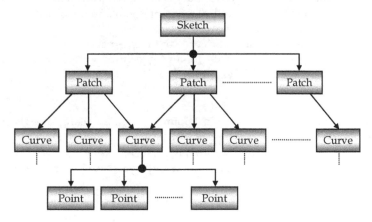

Fig. 17. Sketch data structure

5.2 Point features

After labelling, the sketch becomes a two-dimensional integer array. Zero stands for boundaries as known, but it is necessary to find out which patch it belongs to. They are just the separate edge points with the value of zero at the moment, nothing else. They should be reorganised to useful data.

As the basic unit from data structure, 2D point contains three basic features – the coordinates {x, y}, attributes (crosspoint, selected, breakpoint), and links (previous point, next point).

After labelling, each boundary point has at least two different neighbours. If more than two, the point is a crosspoint. If the point is selected for spline fitting, the selected attribute is true. If the point is used for breaking whole boundary into pieces, the breakpoint attribute is true. The links like a chain join the separated points into a sequential structure. The extraction of point features follows the other feature calculations.

A simple algorithm searching related neighbours is developed as follows

- Assume that the current point is an edge point. The eight neighbours of the current point are checked one by one from 0 to 7, see Fig. 12a.
- Once a neighbour is not an edge point, the first related neighbour is found and saved.
- Carry on searching, any different neighbour will be saved until all neighbours are checked. Return the number of related neighbours and an array containing the different neighbours.
- If the number of related neighbours is greater than two, the current point is a breakpoint.

5.3 Curve features

A set of edge points around a patch make a closed curve. Each closed boundary may have more than one curve segments, i.e., each segment has its own point set. The point sets may be sparse for curve fitting in order to reduce the size of data and obtain a precise representation of the sketch. The following features need to be extracted in a curve:

- Number of points, and the coordinates of each point (values)
- Number of breakpoints if a closed boundary is broken down to several segments.
- The first point and the last point, if the last point is equal to the first point, it is a closed boundary.
- Curve type, either the outer silhouette curve or the internal curve

If using spline fitting to present a curve, the following features need to be extracted.

- Number of selected points for curve fitting
- Fitting method selected.
- End conditions.
- If the point doesn't belong to the original boundary point, a changed tag is given.
- If displaying a spline, a view tag is given.
- If displaying marks on each node, a mark tag is given.

A searching algorithm of boundary curve point setting is based on single pixel has been developed as follows.

- If a point is an edge point and one of its neighbours is the patch, the edge point belongs to the patch.
- The first edge point is the start point of boundary curve, and it becomes the current point, previous point 1 and previous point 2.
- Check the eight neighbours of the current point using the graph in Fig. 12b.
- Once a neighbour point is the edge point and it belongs to the patch, and it is not the previous point 1 and 2, it is a new edge point. Add it to the curve.
- The new edge point becomes the current point. Repeat the same procedure from beginning, until the point is equal to the first point.

In the algorithm, two previous points are used to determine the direction of processing. Using the neighbour graph in Fig. 12b will obtain slightly smoother curves than using the one in Fig. 12a.

5.4 Patch features

Several curve segments are joined together into a closed curve to form a patch. The following features can be extracted.

- The patch serial number, i.e. the label number
- The colour and the title of patch
- If selected for display or processing, a selected tag is given
- The minimum rectangle containing the patch
- The area and centre of the area of patch, the area value is the number of points within the patch. The centre is the sum of coordinates divided by the area.

5.5 Sketch features

When a sketch is separated into patches, the features such as the number of patches and each patch features will be obtained. The neighbourhood will be established. Each patch has the number of neighbours, the shared boundaries with the neighbours. A boundary with one neighbour is the outer silhouette, with two is the inter boundary. The features directly derived from the sketch are shown in Fig. 18.

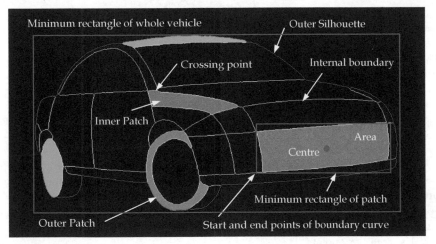

Fig. 18. Features in sketch

Currently, the features directly used for the 2D to 3D transformation are the area and centre of patch. However, more features can be extracted from the points and basic features for further application. It is easy for humans to distinguish where the patch belongs to, what size it is, and where the characteristic points are located. The use of human recognition of patches can help provide a direct and interactive transformation from 2D to 3D, without the need for sophisticated recognition methods. For example, the features such as the position of patch, size and curvature can be used to determine which part of surface it belongs to; the features such as the principal axis of ellipse, size and position can be used for determine the position and tangent points of wheels for coordinate system determination; and features such as symmetric points from breakpoints and the curve between the them, and shading features can be used to determine the curvature of surface, the difference of the areas of 2D patch and its corresponding 3D surface can be used for the adjustment of coordinates. This can all be done in a straightforward manner so long as the patch is correctly identified, which is most readily done by human intervention (although an automated, possibly artificial intelligence based method for this may be feasible, but is outside the scope of this research).

6. Implementation of MATLAB functions

As mentioned above, the 23D system has been implemented the MATLAB functions. Differing from the proposed method of MATLAB implementation, our method was to apply directly the kernel part of their functions. At first, the MATLAB *.m files were converted into *h and *.cpp files of C++. Then, it was to extract the kernel part of the function, and to add them into the 23D system. It was necessary to implement all the related functions. Therefore, no *.dll or *.lib files of MATLAB were used. This method is quite simple and easy to change or enhance the implemented functions.

7. Conclusion

The approach here has been to reduce the problem of pre-processing of the sketch into a number of separate stages, each of which refines or extracts a particular piece of information embodied in the sketch. Some conclusions are summarized below:

- The pre-processing of sketches plays an important role for the input sketches. The more precise the sketches are, the easier the sketch processing is. Pre-processing can be used to translate 'imprecise' sketches to more 'precise' ones, providing a better starting point for the transformation process. This approach allows the system to deal with sketches that have roughly closed boundaries, in turn allowing easier separation into patches.
- For the pre-processed sketches, the related processing algorithms have been investigated in order to obtain the separated patches with single-pixel and closed boundary, which are ready for the 2D to 3D transformation. Facing the specific sketches, some existing or new algorithms and new hybrid algorithms have been proposed.
- Some basic features are extracted from the patches to present points, curves and patches. They are listed below.
  - The boundary points
  - The relationships of the patches
  - The minimum rectangle containing the patches
  - The start and end points for each boundary
  - The areas and geometric centres of the patches
  - The attributes of the points whether they are the selected, break or crossing points

Related searching and calculating algorithms have been also developed. Some features are discussed and may be applied in further research.
- The sketch processing and feature extraction depend on the raster data. Therefore, the method is device dependent. The inherent error is one pixel. Increasing the sketch size can reduce error. But the important issue is the quality of the input sketch. A good sketch will produce significantly better results.
- Curve fitting supplies an additional way to improve the patches. Through the selection and modification of the edge points, the shapes of the patches can be smoothed or even

be changed in some places. This process allows resolution of a further set of imperfections in the original sketch.

- Direct implementation of MATLAB functions is a feasible way to enhance 23D system functions.

8. Acknowledgment

I would like to take this opportunity to express my special thanks to my supervisor, Dr. R. M. Newman, for his invaluable guidance, supports and helps in the research project. Many thanks also go to the other members of the research group, Prof. M. Tovey, C. S. Porter and J. Tabor, for their ideas, supports and helps in the research project, and T. Y. Pan for his exchanging the information, ideas and supports with me.

I am grateful to a number of staffs and students in the MIS, especial in the CTAC, who have discussed with me on my project and have given me lots of support and help, especially to Prof. Keith. J. Burnham, Mrs. A. Todman, and Miss Y. Xie.

9. References

Adobe System Incorporated. (2000). Adobe® Photoshop® 6.0 user guide for Windows® and Macintosh, Adobe System Incorporated, 90024592

Chin, N.; Frazier, C. & Ho, P. (1998). The OpenGL® Graphics System Utility Library. version 1.3, ed. Leech, J.

Foley, J. D.; van Dam, A. & Feiner, S. K. (1996), Computer graphics: principles and practice, 2nd ed. in C, Addison-Wesley Publishing Company, Inc. ISBN 0-201-84840-6

Fosner, R. (1997). OpenGLTM Programming for Windows® 95 and Windows NTTM. Addison-Wesley, ISBN 0-201-40709-4

Glaeser, G. & Stachel, H. (1999). Open Geometry: OpenGL® + Advanced Geometry. Springer-Verlag New York, Inc., ISBN 0-387-98599-9

Kilgard, M. J. (1996). The OpenGL Utility Toolkit (GLUT) Programming Interface. API version 3, Silicon Graphics, Inc.

Ladd, S. R. (1996). C++ Templates and Tools. 2nd ed., M&T Books, ISBN 1-55851-465-1

Matthews, J. (2002). Image Analysis Explorer Pro. version 1.01, http://www.generation5.org/iae.shtml

Pan, T. Y. (2002). Identification of 3D Information from 2D Sketches in Automotive Design, MPhil paper, School of Art and Design, Coventry University

Salomon, D. (1999), Computer graphics and geometric modelling, Springer-Verlag New York, Inc. ISBN 0-387-98682-0

Schildt, H. (1998). C++ from the Ground up. 2nd ed., Osborne/McGraw-Hill, ISBN 0-07-882405-2

Seed, G. H. (1996). An Introduction to Object-oriented Programming in C++: With Applications in Computer Graphics. Springe-Verlag London Ltd., ISBN 3-540-76042-3

Segal, M. & Akeley, K. (2001). The OpenGL® Graphics System: A Specification. version 1.3, ed. Leech, J.

Silverio, C. J.; Fryer, B. & Hartman, J. (1997). OpenGL® Porting Guide. rev. Kempf, R. ed. Cary, C., Silicon Graphics, Inc.

Smith, J. T. (1997). C++ Toolkit for Scientists and Engineers. International Thomson Computer Press, ISBN 1-85032-889-7

The MathWorks, Inc. (2000). MATLAB® C/C++ Graphics Library – The Language of Technical Computing - User's Guide, version 2

The MathWorks, Inc. (2000). MATLAB® C Math Library – The Language of Technical Computing - User's Guide, version 2

The MathWorks, Inc. 2000, "MATLAB® C++ Math Library – The Language of Technical Computing - User's Guide", version 2, The MathWorks, Inc.

The MathWorks, Inc. 2001, "MATLAB® Compiler – The Language of Technical Computing - User's Guide", version 2, The MathWorks, Inc.

The MathWorks Inc. (2001). MATLAB® The Image Processing Toolbox User's Guide, version 3

The MathWorks, Inc. (2001). Spline Toolbox for Use with MATLAB® - User's Guide, version 3.

The Vision Technology Group, Microsoft Research. (2000). The Microsoft Vision SDK. version 1.2, VisSDK@microsoft.com.

Wright, R. S. & Sweet M. (1996). OpenGL Superbible: The Complete Guide to OpenGL Programming for Windows NT and Windows 95. The Waite Group, Inc.

3

Using MATLAB to Compute Heat Transfer in Free Form Extrusion

Sidonie Costa, Fernando Duarte and José A. Covas
University of Minho
Portugal

1. Introduction

Rapid Prototyping (RP) is a group of techniques used to quickly fabricate a scale model of a part or assembly using three-dimensional computer aided design (CAD) data (Marsan, Dutta, 2000). A large number of RP technologies have been developed to manufacture polymer, metal, or ceramic parts, without any mould, namely Stereolithography (SL), Laminated Object Manufacturing (LOM), Selected Laser Sintering (SLS), Ink-jet Printing (3DP) and Fused Deposition Modeling (FDM).

In Fused Deposition Modelling (developed by Stratasys Inc in U.S.A.), a plastic or wax filament is fed through a nozzle and deposited onto the support (Pérez, 2002; Ahn, 2002; Ziemian & Crawn, 2001) as a series of 2D slices of a 3D part. The nozzle moves in the X–Y plane to create one slice of the part. Then, the support moves vertically (Z direction) so that the nozzle deposits a new layer on top of the previous one. Since the filament is extruded as a melt, the newly deposited material fuses with the last deposited material.

Free Form Extrusion (FFE) is a variant of FDM (Figure 1), where the material is melted and deposited by an extruder & die (Agarwala, Jamalabad, Langrana, Safari, Whalen & Danthord, 1996; Bellini, Shor & Guceri, 2005). FFE enables the use of a wide variety of polymer systems (e.g., filled compounds, polymer blends, composites, nanocomposites, foams), thus yielding parts with superior performance. Moreover, the adoption of co-extrusion or sequential extrusion techniques confers the possibility to combine different materials for specific properties, such as soft/hard zones or transparent/opaque effects.

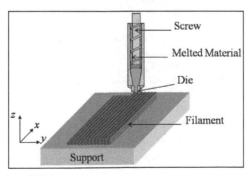

Fig. 1. Free Form Extrusion (FFE).

Due to their characteristics - layer by layer construction using melted materials - FDM and FFE may originate parts with two defects: i) excessive filament deformation upon cooling can jeopardize the final dimensional accuracy, ii) poor bonding between adjacent filaments reduces the mechanical resistance. Deformation and bonding are mainly controlled by the heat transfer, i. e., adequate bonding requires that the filaments remain sufficiently hot during enough time to ensure adhesion and, simultaneously, to cool down fast enough to avoid excessive deformation due to gravity (and weight of the filaments above them). Therefore, it is important to know the evolution in time of the filaments temperature and to understand how it is affected by the major process variables. Rodriguez (Rodriguez, 1999) studied the cooling of five elliptical filaments stacked vertically using via finite element methods and later found a 2D analytical solution for rectangular cross-sections (Thomas & Rodriguez, 2000). Yardimci and Guceri (Yardimci & S.I. Guceri, 1996) developed a more general 2D heat transfer analysis, also using finite element methods. Li and co-workers (Li, Sun, Bellehumeur & Gu, 2003; Sun, Rizvi, Bellehumeur & Gu, 2004) developed an analytical 1D transient heat transfer model for a single filament, using the Lumped Capacity method. Although good agreement with experimental results was reported, the model cannot be used for a sequence of filaments, as thermal contacts are ignored.

The present work expands the above efforts, by proposing a transient heat transfer analysis of filament deposition that includes the physical contacts between any filament and its neighbours or supporting table. The analytical analysis for one filament is first discussed, yielding an expression for the evolution of temperature with deposition time. Then, a MatLab code is developed to compute the temperature evolution for the various filaments required to build one part. The usefulness of the results is illustrated with two case studies.

2. Heat transfer modelling

During the construction of a part by FDM or FFE, all the filaments are subjected to the same heat transfer mechanism but with different boundary conditions, depending on the part geometry and deposition sequence (Figure 2).

Fig. 2. Example of a sequence of filaments deposition.

Consider that N is the total number of deposited filaments and that $T_r(x,t)$ is the temperature at length x of the r-th filament ($r \in \{1,...,N\}$) at instant t. The energy balance for an element dx of the r-th filament writes as:

$$\begin{cases} Energy\ in\ at\ one\ face - Heat\ loss\ by\ convection\ with\ surroundings \\ -Heat\ loss\ by\ conduction\ with\ adjacent\ filaments\ or\ with\ support \end{cases} =$$

$$= Change\ in\ internal\ energy + Energy\ out\ at\ opposite\ face$$

This can be expressed as a differential equation. After some assumptions and simplifications (Costa, Duarte & Covas, 2008):

$$\frac{\partial T_r}{\partial t} = -\frac{P}{\rho\,CA}\left(h_{conv}\left(1 - \sum_{i=1}^{n} a_{r_i}\lambda_i\right)(T_r - T_E) + \sum_{i=1}^{n} h_i a_{r_i}\lambda_i\left(T_r - T_{r_i}\right)\right) \tag{1}$$

where P is filament perimeter, ρ is density, C is heat capacity, A is area of the filament cross-section, h_{conv} is heat transfer coefficient, n is number of contacts with adjacent filaments or with the support, λ_i is fraction of P that in contact with an adjacent filament, T_E is environment temperature, h_i is thermal contact conductance for contact i ($i \in \{1,...,n\}$) and T_{r_i} is temperature of the adjacent filament or support at contact i ($r_i \in \{1,...,N+1\}$, $r_i \neq r$, $T_1,..., T_N$ are temperatures of filaments, T_{N+1} is support temperature). In this expression, variables a_{r_i} are defined as (see Figure 3):

$$a_{r_i} = \begin{cases} 1 & \text{if the } r-\text{th filament has the } i-\text{th contact} \\ 0 & \text{otherwise} \end{cases}, \forall i \in \{1,...,n\}, \forall r \in \{1,...,N\} \tag{2}$$

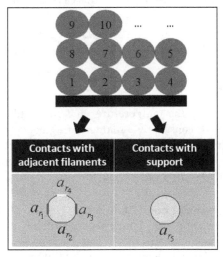

Fig. 3. Contact areas of a filament (n = 5).

Considering that:

$$\begin{cases} b\left(a_{r_1},...,a_{r_n}\right) = h_{conv}\left(1 - \sum_{i=1}^{n} a_{r_i}\lambda_i\right) + \sum_{i=1}^{n} a_{r_i}h_i\lambda_i \\[6mm] Q\left(a_{r_1},...,a_{r_n}\right) = \dfrac{h_{conv}\left(1 - \sum_{i=1}^{n} a_{r_i}\lambda_i\right)T_E + \sum_{i=1}^{n} a_{r_i}h_i\lambda_i T_{r_i}}{b\left(a_{r_1},...,a_{r_n}\right)} \end{cases} \tag{3}$$

equation (1) can be re-written as:

$$\frac{\rho VC}{PL\ b\left(a_{r_1},...,a_{r_n}\right)}\frac{\partial T_r(t)}{\partial t}+T_r(t)=Q\left(a_{r_1},...,a_{r_n}\right) \tag{4}$$

Since the coefficients are constants, the characteristic polynomial method can be used to yield the solution:

$$T_r(t)=\left(T_{r0}-Q\left(a_{r_1},...,a_{r_n}\right)\right)\ e^{\frac{-PL\ b\left(a_{r_1},...,a_{r_n}\right)}{\rho VC}(t-t_r)}+Q\left(a_{r_1},...,a_{r_n}\right) \tag{5}$$

In this expression, t_r is the instant at which the r-th filament starts to cool down or contact with another filament and $T_{r0}=T_r(t_r)$ is the temperature of the filament at instant t_r. Taking k as thermal conductivity, the Biot number can be defined (Bejan, 1993):

$$Bi=\frac{A}{P}\frac{b\left(a_{r_1},...,a_{r_n}\right)}{k} \tag{6}$$

When Bi is lower than 0.1, the filaments are thermally thin, i.e., thermal gradients throughout the cross section can be neglected. In this case, Eq. (5) becomes:

$$Bi\le0.1\Rightarrow T_r(t)=\left(T_{r0}-Q\left(a_{r_1},...,a_{r_n}\right)\right)\ e^{\frac{-PL\ b\left(a_{r_1},...,a_{r_n}\right)}{\rho VC}(t-t_r)}+Q\left(a_{r_1},...,a_{r_n}\right) \tag{7}$$

3. Computer modelling

Equations (5) and (7) quantify the temperature of a single filament fragment along the deposition time. In practice, consecutive filament fragments are deposited during the manufacture of a part. Thus, it is convenient to generalize the computations to obtain the temperature evolution of each filament fragment at any point x of the part, for different deposition techniques and 3D configuration structures.

3.1 Generalizing the heat transfer computations

Up-dating the thermal conditions: The boundary conditions must be up-dated as the deposition develops. The code activates the physical contacts and redefines the boundary conditions for a specific filament position, time and deposition sequence. For all the filaments, three variables need to be up-dated:

- time t_r (TCV-1): instant at which the r-th filament starts cooling down, or enters in contact with another filament;
- temperature T_{r0} (TCV-2): temperature at t_r;
- -vector a_{ri} (TCV-3): in Eq. (3), sets in the contacts for the r-th filament ($i \in \{1,...,n\}$, where n is the number of contacts).

Simultaneous computation of the filaments temperature: During deposition, some filaments are reheated when new contacts with hotter filaments arise; simultaneously, the latter cool down due to the same contacts. This implies the simultaneous computation of the filaments temperature via an iterative procedure. The convergence error was set at $\varepsilon = 10^{-3}$, as a good compromise between accuracy and the computation time.

Deposition sequence: The deposition sequence defines the thermal conditions TCV-1, TCV-2 and TCV-3. Three possibilities were taken in: unidirectional and aligned filaments, unidirectional and skewed filaments, perpendicular filaments (see Figure 4). In all cases, the filaments are deposited continuously under constant speed (no interruptions occur between successive layers).

Some parts with some geometrical features may require the use of a support material, to be removed after manufacture. This possibility is considered in the algorithm for unidirectional and aligned filaments.

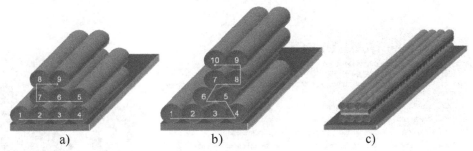

Fig. 4. Deposition sequences: a) unidirectional and aligned filaments; b) unidirectional and skewed filaments; c) perpendicular filaments.

3.2 Computing the temperatures
The computational flowchart is presented in Figure 5 and a MatLab code was generated. In order to visualize the results using another software (Excel, Tecplot...), a document in *txt* format is generated after the computations, that includes all the temperature results along deposition time.

4. MatLab code for one filament layer

In order to illustrate how the MatLab code "*FFE.m*" was implemented, the segment dealing with the temperature along the deposition time for the first layer of filaments, using one or two distinct materials, is presented here. The code has the same logic and structure for the remaining layers.

4.1 Input variables
Two arguments need to be introduced in this MatLab function:
-   A matrix representing the deposition sequence, containing m rows and n columns, for the number of layers and maximum number of filaments in a layer, respectively. Each cell is attributed a value of 0, 1, or 2 for the absence of a filament, the presence of a filament of material A or of a filament of material B, respectively. An example is given in Figure 6.
-   The vertical cross section of the part (along the filament length) where the user wishes to know the temperature evolution with time.

The code includes one initial section where all the variables are defined (Figure 7), namely environment and extrusion temperatures, material properties, process conditions, etc. The dimensions of all matrixes used are also defined.

MATLAB CODE

Definition of the variables

- Deposition mode (number of filaments per layer, total number of filaments and total number of layers): STEP 1
- Computation variables (Step time, convergence error…); STEP 2
- Size of the variables to be used in the code (matrix dimensions); STEP 3
- FFE variables (process variables, filament dimensions and material properties); STEP 4
- Heat Transfer parameters (Heat transfer coefficient, thermal contact conductances); STEP 5
- Computation of the parameters influenced by the contacts; STEP 6
- Computation of the parameters influenced by the material properties; STEP 7
- Definition of the time periods between two successive contacts; STEP 8

MatLab code

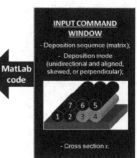

INPUT COMMAND WINDOW
- Deposition sequence (matrix);
- Deposition mode (unidirectional and aligned, skewed, or perpendicular);

- Cross section x.

Computation of the temperature of the first filament (1ˢᵗ layer)

- Activation of the contacts for the first filament (TCV-3); STEP 9
- Computation of b and Q, Eq. (3); STEP 10
- Saving the instants at which the temperatures are computed; STEP 11
- Computation of the temperatures using Eq. (5); STEP 12
- Verification of the value of Bi: if Bi < 0.1, a warning message is shown. STEP 13

Computation of the temperature of the remaining filaments (1ˢᵗ layer)

- Activation of the contacts for the last filament and the previous one in contact with it (TCV-3); STEP 14
- Up-date of b, Eq. (3); STEP 15
- Definition of an additional time period for the last filament deposited STEP 16
- Iterative process to compute the temperatures of the filaments; STEP 17
- Verification of the value of Bi: if Bi < 0.1, a warning message is shown. STEP 18

Computation of the temperature of the remaining filaments (other layers)

- <u>Horizontal contacts</u>: activation of the contacts for the two last filaments (TCV-3).
- <u>Vertical contacts</u>: Depending on filament position and deposition mode, activation of the contacts for the current and adjacent filaments.

- Up-date of b, Eq. (3);

- Definition of an additional time period for the last filament deposited
- Up-date of initial time t, (TCV-1) and initial temperature T, (TCV-2) for filaments with new contacts.

- Iterative process to compute the temperatures of the filaments;
- Verification of the value of Bi: if Bi < 0.1, a warning message is shown.

MatLab code

OUTPUT
- Text Document with evolution of temperature during deposition for all filaments in C:\MATLAB\bin.

Fig. 5. General procedure to compute all the temperatures.

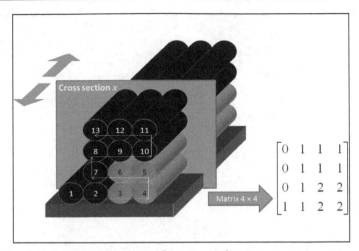

Fig. 6. Example of deposition sequence and corresponding input matrix.

```
function FFE(matrix,x)

%_____ STEP 1 _____
%Definition of the vector that contains the number of total filaments in each layer
matrix_lin = size(matrix,1);
matrix_col = size(matrix,2);
vector = zeros(matrix_lin,2);
contar = 0;
for i = matrix_lin:-1:1
    contar = contar + 1;
    for j = 1:matrix_col
        if matrix(i,j) ~= 0
            vector(contar,1) = vector(contar,1) + 1;
        end
    end
end
%Number of layers
m = length(vector(:,1));
%Number of filaments
n = 0;
for j = 1:m
    if m == 1
        n = vector(1,1);
    else
        if vector(j,2) <= 1
            n = n + vector(j,1);
        end
    end
end

%_____ STEP 2 _____
%Computation variables
passo = 0.05;           %Step time
temp_mais = 15;         %Additional time computation after construction of the part
erro = 0.001;           %Convergence error
```

```
%_____ STEP 3 _____
%Definition of the size of the variables
h = zeros(1,5); lambda = zeros(1,5); a = zeros(n,5); T = zeros (n,5);
vec_b = zeros(n,5); vec_Q = zeros(n,5); b = zeros(1,n); Q = zeros(1,n);
T_begin = zeros(1,n); dif = zeros(1,n); Biot = zeros(1,n); save_T = zeros(1,n);
old_T = zeros(1,n); save_lim = zeros(1,n); viz = zeros(11,n);


%_____ STEP 4 _____


%Process Variables
T_L = 270;          %Extrusion temperature (°C)
T_E = 70;           %Temperature of the envelope (°C)
v = 0.02;           %Velocity of the extrusion head (m/sec)
for lin = 1:n       %Temperature of support (°C)
   T(lin,1) = T_E;
end

%Filament dimensions
w = 0.0003;         %Layer Thickness (meters)
L = 0.02;           %Length of the filament (meters)
area = pi * (w/2)^2; %Area of the cross section of filament (meters^2)
per = pi * w;       %Perimeter of the cross section of filament (meters)
vol = area*L;       %Volume of the filament
A_p = per*L;        %Superficial area of the filament

% Material Properties

%Thermal conductivity (W/m.K)
conductivity(1) = 0.1768; % material A
conductivity(2) = 0.5;    % material B
%Density (kg/m^3)
ro(1) = 1050;             % material A
ro(2) = 1500;             % material B
%Specific heat (J/kg.K)
C(1) = 2019.7;            % material A
C(2) = 2500.7;            % material B

%_____ STEP 5 _____
% Heat transfer coefficient (lost of heat by natural convection)
h_conv = 45;

%Thermal contact conductances between
h(1,1) = 200;        % filament and left adjacent filament
h(1,2) = 200;        % filament and down adjacent filament
h(1,3) = 200;        % filament and right adjacent filament
h(1,4) = 200;        % filament and top adjacent filament
h(1,5) = 10;         % filament and support

%Fraction of perimeter contact between
lambda(1,1) = 0.2;   % filament and left adjacent filament
lambda(1,2) = 0.25;  % filament and down adjacent filament
lambda(1,3) = 0.2;   % filament and right adjacent filament
lambda(1,4) = 0.25;  % filament and top adjacent filament
lambda(1,5) = 0.25;  % filament and support
```

Fig. 7. Definition of the variables.

The parameters used in Equation (5) and those necessary to compute variables b and Q (in Eq. (3)) must also be defined. Finally, the time increment between two consecutive contacts is calculated taking into consideration the type of deposition sequence (Figure 8).

```
%_____ STEP 6 _____
%Definition of the parameters influenced by the contacts
for col = 1:5
    for lin = 1:n
        vec_b(lin,col)  = h(1,col)*lambda(1,col);
        vec_Q(lin,col)  = vec_b(lin,col)*T(lin,col);
    end
end
```

```
%_____ STEP 7 _____
%Definition of the parameters influenced by the material properties
contar = 0;
number_filament = 0;
for i = matrix_lin:-1:1
    contar = contar + 1;
    if isodd(contar) == 1
        for j = 1:matrix_col
            if matrix(i,j) ~= 0
                number_filament = number_filament + 1;
                escalar(number_filament) = -per/(ro(matrix(i,j))*area*C(matrix(i,j)));
                esc(number_filament) = h_conv/(ro(matrix(i,j))*L*C(matrix(i,j)));
                kt(number_filament) =  conductivity(matrix(i,j));
            end
        end
    else
        for j = matrix_col:-1:1
            if matrix(i,j) ~= 0
                number_filament = number_filament + 1;
                escalar(number_filament) = -per/(ro(matrix(i,j))*area*C(matrix(i,j)));
                esc(number_filament) = h_conv/(ro(matrix(i,j))*L*C(matrix(i,j)));
                kt(number_filament) =  conductivity(matrix(i,j));
            end
        end
    end
end
```

```
%_____ STEP 8 _____
%Definition of the periods of time between two successive contacts
for i = 1:(n+2)
    if isodd(i) == 1
        limite(i,1) = (i*L-x)/v;
        limite(i,2) = (i*L+x)/v;
    else
        limite(i,1) = limite(i-1,2);
        limite(i,2) = ((i+1)*L-x)/v;
    end
end
for road = 1:n
    linha = 0;
    for i = 0:passo:limite(n,2)
        linha = linha + 1;
        temp(linha,road) = T_L;
    end
end
```

Fig. 8. Definition of the parameters to be used for the computation of temperatures and time between two consecutive contacts.

4.2 Computation of the temperatures for the first filament of the first layer

Computation of the temperatures starts with the activation of the contact between the first filament and the support. Parameters b and Q (equation (3)) are calculated (Figure 9).

The temperatures are computed at each time increment; confirmation of the value of Biot number (Eq. (6)) is also made: if greater than 0.1, the code devolves a warning message (Figure 10).

```
for layer = 1:m
    if layer == 1
        for num = 1:vector(layer,1)
            if num == 1
%_____ STEP 9 _____
                a(num,5) = 1;      %Activation of the contact with support

%_____ STEP 10 _____
                %Definition of the variables b and Q defined in equation Eq. 7
                b(num) = h_conv*(1-lambda*a(num,:)') + vec_b(num,:)*a(num,:)';
                Q(num) = (h_conv*(1-lambda*a(num,:)')*T_E +
vec_Q(num,:)*a(num,:)')/b(num);
```

Fig. 9. Activation of the contacts and computation of b and Q for the first filament.

```
%_____ STEP 11 _____
                p = 0;
                for t = 0:passo:limite(num,1)
                    p = p+1; abcissa(p) = t;
                end

%_____ STEP 12 _____
                %Computation of the temperatures of the first filament
                for t = (limite(num,1)+passo):passo:limite_final
                    p = p+1; abcissa(p) = t;
                    temp(p,num)=(T_L-Q(num))*exp(escalar(num)*b(num)*(t-limite(num,1)))
                    +Q(num);
                end
                %Saving the last temperature of the period time of cooling down
                T_begin(num) = temp(p,num);

%_____ STEP 13 _____
                %Verification of the value of Biot Number
                Biot(num) = (vol/A_p)*(b(num)/kt(num));
                if Biot(num)>=0.1
                    'WARNING! We cannot use a Lumped System'
                End
```

Fig. 10. Computation of the temperatures for the first filament and verification of the value of the Biot number.

4.3 Computation of the temperatures for the remaining filaments of the first layer

Before proceeding to the remaining filaments of the first layer, the lateral and support contacts for each filament being deposited must be defined, as well as for the previous one. Consequently, the variable b in expression Eq. (3) is up-dated (Figure 11).

At this point, only the lateral and support contacts must be defined, since only the first layer is being computed. For the remaining layers, other contacts (such as the vertical ones) must be considered. Once each filament is deposited, the code checks whether the part has been completed. If so, it remains in the same conditions during a pre-defined time, in order to reach the equilibrium temperature (Figure 12).

```
%_____ STEP 14 _____
        else
            %Activation of the contacts
            a(num-1,3) = 1; a(num,1) = 1; a(num,5) = 1;

%_____ STEP 15 _____
        %Up-dating of the variable b
        for j = 1:num
            b(j) = h_conv*(1-lambda*a(j,:)') + vec_b(j,:)*a(j,:)';
        end
```

Fig. 11. Activation of the contacts for the current and previous filaments and up-dating of variable *b*.

```
%_____ STEP 16 _____
    if m == 1
        if num == vector(layer,1)
            limite_final = limite(num,2) + temp_mais;
        else
            limite_final = limite(num,2);
        end
    else
        limite_final = limite(num,2);
    end
```

Fig. 12. Definition of an additional time for the last filament.

Finally, the temperatures of the remaining filaments are computed. At each time increment, the temperatures of the adjacent filaments are saved and parameter Q (Eq. (3) is up-dated. The value of the Biot number is checked before the deposition of a new filament (Figure 13).

```
    for t = (limite(num,1)+passo):passo:limite_final
        p = p+1; abcissa(p) = t;
        last = p-1;
        for j = 1:num
            save_T(j) = temp(last,j);
        end

%_____ STEP 17 _____
        %Iterative process
        for q = 1:100000

            %Saving contacts and temperatures of adjacent filaments
            for j = 1:num
                if j == 1
                    T(j,3) = save_T(j+1);
                    viz(3,j) = j+1;
                end
                if j > 1 & j < num
                    T(j,1) = save_T(j-1);
                    viz(1,j) = j-1;
                    T(j,3) = save_T(j+1);
                    viz(3,j) = j+1;
                end
                if j == num
                    T(j,1) = save_T(j-1);
                    viz(1,j) = j-1;
                end
                for k = 1:5
                    if T(j,k) ~= 0 & k ~= 5
```

```matlab
                                vec_Q(j,k) = vec_b(j,k)*T(j,k);
                            end
                        end

                        %Up-dating of the variable Q
                        Q(j) = (h_conv*(1-lambda*a(j,:)')*T_E +
vec_Q(j,:)*a(j,:)')/b(j);
                        old_T(j) = save_T(j);
                    end
                    %Computation of the temperatures
                    if num == 2
                        save_T(1) = (T_begin(1)-Q(1))*exp(escalar(1)*b(1)*
                                    (t-limite(1,1)))+Q(1);
                        save_T(2) = (T_L-Q(2))*exp(escalar(2)*b(2)*(t-
limite(1,1)))+Q(2);

                        save_lim(1,1) = limite(num,1);
                        save_lim(1,2) = limite(num,1);
                    else
                        for j=1:num-2
                            save_T(j) = (T_begin(j)-Q(1))*exp(escalar(j)*b(j)*
                                        (t-save_limite(1,j)))+Q(j);
                        end
                        save_T(num-1) = (T_begin(num-1)-Q(num-1))*
                                    exp(escalar(num-1)*b(num-1)*(t-limite(num,1)))+Q(num-
1);

                        save_T(num) = (T_L-Q(num))*
                                    exp(escalar(num)*b(num)*(t-limite(num,1)))+ Q(num);
                        save_lim(1,num-1) = limite(num,1);
                        save_lim(1,num) = limite(num,1);
                    end
                    for j = 1:num
                        dif(j) = abs(save_T(j)-old_T(j));
                    end
                    try = 1;
                    stop = 0;
                    for j = 1:num
                        if dif(try) < erro
                            try = try+1;
                        end
                        if try == num+1;
                            stop = 1;
                        end
                    end
                    if stop == 1
                        for j = 1:num
                            temp(p,j) = save_T(j);
                        end
                        break;
                    end
                end
            end
            T_begin(num) = temp(p,num);
            %End of iterative process

%_____ STEP 18 _____
            %Verification of the Biot Number
            for j=1:num
                Biot(j) = (vol/A_p)*(b(j)/kt(j));
                if Biot(j)>=0.1
                    'WARNING! We can not use a Lumped System'
                    j
                    Biot(j)
                end
            end
        end
    end
```

```
    end
end
```

Fig. 13. Computation of the temperature of the filaments of the first layer and verification of the Biot number.

5. Results

In order to demonstrate the usefulness of the code developed, two case studies will be discussed. The first deals with a part constructed with two distinct materials, while the second illustrates the role of the deposition sequence.

5.1 Case study 1
Consider the small part with the geometry presented in Figure 14, to be manufactured under the processing conditions summarized in Table 1.

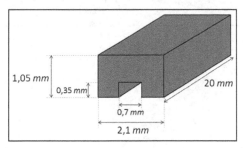

Fig. 14. Geometry of the part.

Property	Value
Extrusion temperature (°C)	270
Environment temperature (°C)	70
Extrusion velocity (m/s)	0.025
Filament length (m)	0.02
Cross section x (m)	0.01
Geometric form of cross section	circle
Cross section diameter (m)	0.00035
Contact ratio	88%
Heat transfer coefficient (convection) (W/m²°C)	60
Thermal contact conductance with filaments (W/m²°C)	180
Thermal contact conductance with support (W/m²°C)	10
Thermal conductivity (W/m°C) materials A / B	0.1768 / 0.5
Specific heat (J/kg°C) materials A / B	2019.7 / 2500.7
Density materials A / B	1.05 / 1.5

Table 1. Processing conditions

The production of this part requires the use of a support material. Figure 15 shows the deposition sequence and corresponding material matrix, while Figure 16 presents the evolution of temperature of every filament with deposition time. As expected, once a new filament is deposited, the temperature of the preceding adjacent filaments increases and their rate of cooling decreases.

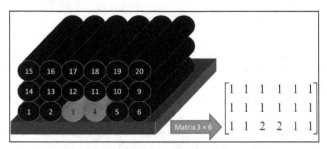

Fig. 15. Filaments deposition sequence and corresponding material matrix.

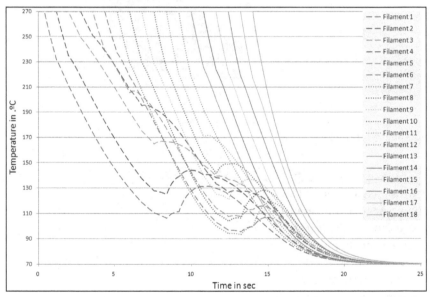

Fig. 16. Temperature evolution with time (at x = 0.01 m), for the deposition sequence illustrated in Figure 15.

5.2 Case study 2

Consider now the parallelepipedic part depicted in Figure 17, to be built using unidirectional and aligned and perpendicular sequences, respectively, under the processing conditions summarized in Table 2.

Figures 18 and 19 depict the deposition sequence and corresponding temperatures (this required an additional part of the code together with the use of the Tecplot software). At each time increment, a 1 mm or a 0.35 mm filament portion was deposited, for unidirectional and aligned and perpendicular filaments, respectively. This lower value is related with the lower contact area arising from this deposition mode. Consequently, the total computation time was circa 7 minutes for unidirectional and aligned deposition and more than two and a half hours for perpendicular filaments for a conventional portable PC. As the manufacture is completed (t = 14.4 sec), the average part temperature is approximately 120 °C or 90 °C depending on the deposition mode. This information is relevant for practical purposes, such as evaluating the quality of the adhesion between adjacent filaments, or the extent of deformation.

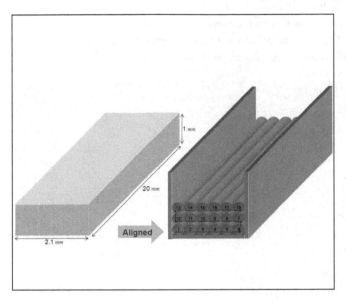

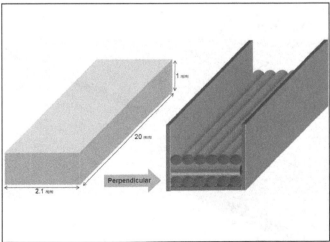

Fig. 17. Geometry of the part and corresponding deposition sequence: top: unidirectional and aligned; bottom: perpendicular.

Property	Value
Extrusion temperature (°C)	270
Environment temperature (°C)	70
Extrusion velocity (m/s)	0.025
Filament length (m)	0.02
Geometric form of cross section	circle
Cross section diameter (m)	0.00035
Contact ratio	88%
Heat transfer coefficient (convection) (W/m²°C)	70
Thermal contact conductance with filaments (W/m²°C)	200
Thermal contact conductance with support (W/m²°C)	15
Thermal conductivity (W/m°C)	0.1768
Specific heat (J/kg°C)	2019.7
Density	1.05

Table 2. Processing conditions

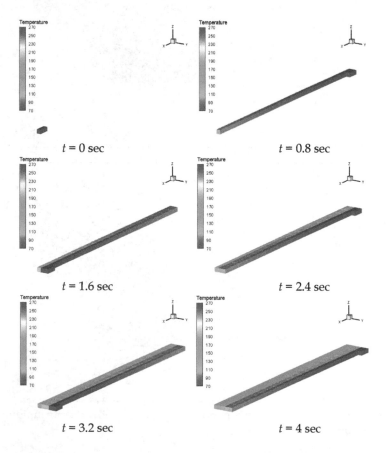

$t = 0$ sec

$t = 0.8$ sec

$t = 1.6$ sec

$t = 2.4$ sec

$t = 3.2$ sec

$t = 4$ sec

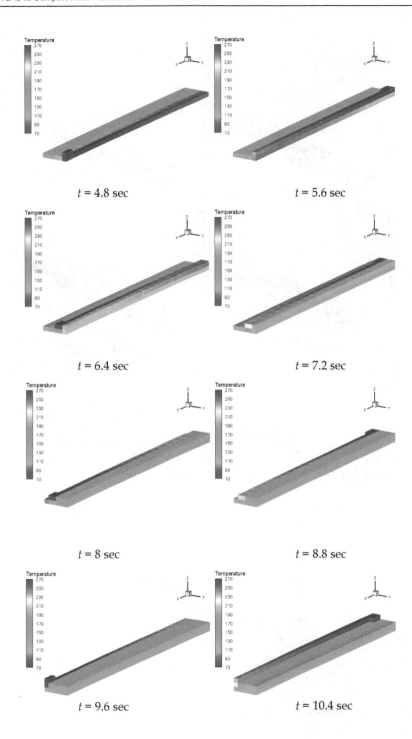

$t = 4.8$ sec $t = 5.6$ sec

$t = 6.4$ sec $t = 7.2$ sec

$t = 8$ sec $t = 8.8$ sec

$t = 9.6$ sec $t = 10.4$ sec

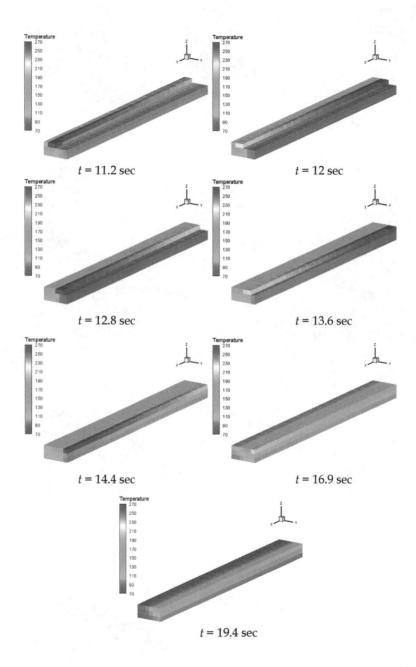

Fig. 18. Deposition sequence of the part of Figure 17 (unidirectional and aligned filaments).

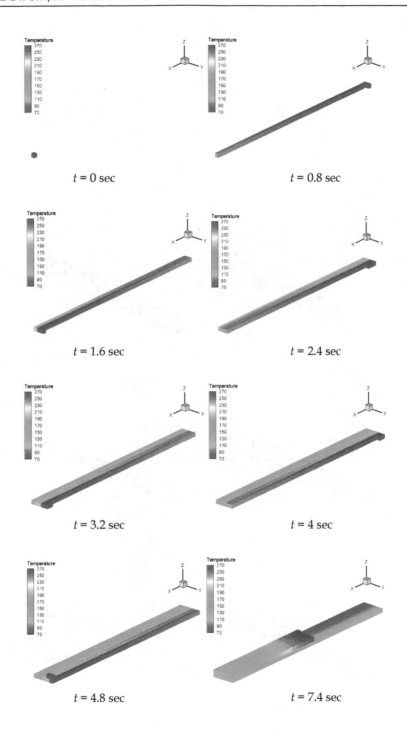

$t = 0$ sec

$t = 0.8$ sec

$t = 1.6$ sec

$t = 2.4$ sec

$t = 3.2$ sec

$t = 4$ sec

$t = 4.8$ sec

$t = 7.4$ sec

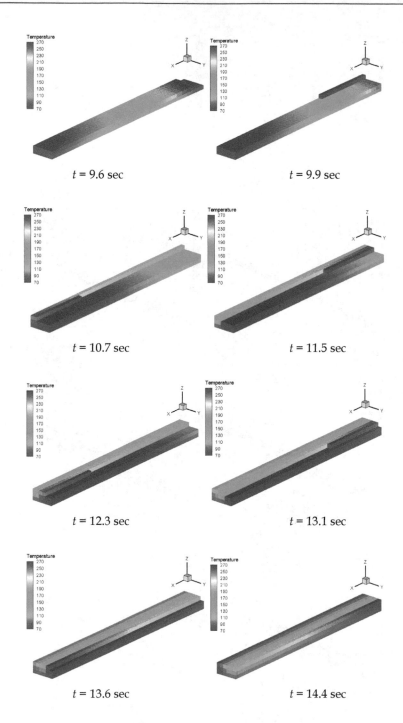

t = 9.6 sec t = 9.9 sec

t = 10.7 sec t = 11.5 sec

t = 12.3 sec t = 13.1 sec

t = 13.6 sec t = 14.4 sec

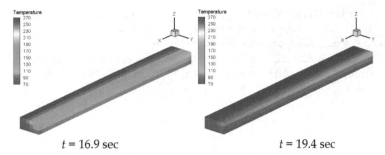

$$t = 16.9 \text{ sec} \qquad\qquad t = 19.4 \text{ sec}$$

Fig. 19. Deposition sequence of the part of Figure 17 (perpendicular filaments).

6. Conclusion

In Free Form Extrusion, FFE, a molten filament is deposited sequentially to produce a 3D part without a mould. This layer by layer construction technique may create problems of adhesion between adjacent filaments, or create dimensional accuracy problems due to excessive deformation of the filaments, if the processing conditions are not adequately set.

This chapter presented a MatLab code for modelling the heat transfer in FFE, aiming at determining the temperature evolution of each filament during the deposition stage. Two case studies illustrated the use of the programme.

7. References

Rodriguez, J. F. (1999). *Modelling the mechanical behaviour of fused deposition acrylonitrile-butadiene-styrene polymer components*, Ph.D. Dissertation, Department of Aeorospace and Mechanical Engineering, University of Notre Dame, Notre Dame, USA

Thomas, J. P. & Rodríguez, J. F. (2000). *Modeling the fracture strength between fused deposition extruded roads*, Solid Freeform Fabrication Symposium Proceeding, Austin.

Yardimci, M. A. & Guceri, S. I. (1996). *Conceptual framework for the thermal process modelling of fused deposition*, Rapid Prototyping Journal, 2, 26-31.

Li, L.; Sun, Q.; Bellehumeur, C. & Gu, P. (2003). *Modeling of bond formation in FDM process*, Trans. NAMRI/SME, 8, 613-620.

Sun, Q.; Rizvi, G.C.; Bellehumeur, C. & Gu, T. P. (2004). *Experimental study and modeling of bond formation between ABS filaments in the FDM process*, Proc. SPE ANTEC'2004.

Costa, S.; Duarte, F. & Covas, J. A. (2008). *Towards modelling of Free Form Extrusion: analytical solution of transient heat transfer*, Esaform 2008, Lyon, France.

Bejan, A. (1993). *Heat Transfer*, John Wiley & Sons, Inc., New York.

Marsan, A.; Dutta, D. (2000). *A review of process planning techniques in layered manufacturing*, Rapid Prototyping Journal, Vol.6, No.1, pp. 18-35, ISSN 1355-2546.

Pérez, C. J. L. (2002). *Analysis of the surface roughness and dimensional accuracy capability of fused deposition modelling processes*, International Journal of Production Research, Vol.40, Issue 12, pp. 2865 – 2881, ISSN 1366-588X.

Ahn, S. H. (2002). *Anisotropic material properties of fused deposition modeling ABS*, Rapid Prototyping Journal, Vol.8, No.4, pp. 248–257, ISSN 1355-2546.

Ziemian, C. W. & Crawn, P. M. (2001). *Computer aided decision support for fused deposition modeling*, Rapid Prototyping Journal, Vol.7, No.3, pp. 138-147, ISSN 1355-2546.

Agarwala, M. K.; Jamalabad, V. R.; Langrana, N. A.; Safari, A.; Whalen, P. J. & Danthord, S.
    C. (1996). *Structural quality of parts processed by fused deposition*, Rapid Prototyping
    Journal, Vol.2, No.4, pp. 4-19, ISSN 1355-2546.
Bellini, A.; Shor, L. & Guceri, S. (2005). *New developments in fused deposition modeling of
    ceramics*, Rapid Prototyping Journal, Vol.11, No.4, pp. 214-220, ISSN 1355-25.

4

Visual and Thermal Image Fusion for UAV Based Target Tracking

K. Senthil Kumar[1], G. Kavitha[2],
R. Subramanian[3] and G. Ramesh[4]
[1]Division of Avionics, Department of Aerospace Engineering,
Madras Institute of Technology, Anna University,
[2]Department of Electronics and Communication Engineering,
Madras Institute of Technology, Anna University
[3]Division of Avionics, Department of Aerospace Engineering,
Madras Institute of Technology, Anna University
[4]National Aerospace Laboratories (NAL) Bangalore,
India

1. Introduction

Unmanned aerial vehicles (UAVs) are aircrafts which have the capability of flight without an onboard pilot. These vehicles are remotely controlled, semi-autonomous, autonomous, or have a combination of these capabilities. UAV's has its applications in a whole lot of domains. Image processing applications with specific importance to surveillance and reconnaissance is of immense interest.

UAVs are equipped with imaging sensor platform, which operates remotely controlled, semi-autonomously or autonomously, without a pilot sitting in the vehicle. The platform may have a small or medium size still-video or video camera, thermal or infrared camera systems, airborne light detection and ranging (LIDAR) system, or a combination thereof. All these different kinds of cameras are an effective sensor tool which is portable, light weight and airborne in a platform on the UAV.

Thermal images have a valuable advantage over the visual images. Thermal images do not depend on the illumination, the output is the projection of thermal sensors of the emissions of heat of the objects. This unique merit gives rise for effective segmentation of objects. Ultimately, surveillance measure using an UAV gets improved.

With the development of new imaging sensors arises the need of a meaningful combination of all employed imaging sources. Image fusion of visual and thermal sensing outputs adds a new dimension in making the target tracking more reliable. Target tracking at instances of smoke, fog, cloudy conditions gets improved. With conditions of same background colour perception of target unnoticed getting eliminated with thermal image inclusion, image fusion gives complementary information. A holistic system which represents the combined fused data is perceived at the control level of the UAV's.

2. Thermal imaging

Thermography which uses black body radiation law makes it to have information gathering without visible illumination. Thermal imaging cameras detect radiation in the infrared (IR) range of the electromagnetic spectrum (3-6 μm and 8–14 μm).

The charge coupled device (CCD) and complementary metal oxide semiconductor (CMOS) sensors are used for visible light cameras. These can detect only the non thermal part of the infrared spectrum called near-infrared (NIR). On the other hand, thermal imaging cameras make use specialized focal plane arrays (FPAs) that respond to longer wavelengths (mid- and long-wavelength infrared).

There is also a difference between how far one can see with a cooled and with an uncooled thermal imaging camera. Cooled camera systems are more expensive, but generally have a longer range than uncooled systems under many conditions. Extremely long range thermal imaging applications are best served by cooled camera systems. This is particularly true in the midwave band in humid atmospheric conditions.

The heat radiation is focused onto special receptors in the camera which convert it into a format which is displayed on a monitor in monochrome which is recognisable by the human eye. The objects emitting the greatest intensity of heat are usually presented as the darkest (black) in the greyscale, i.e. known as 'black-hot'. Many cameras have a function whereby the functionality can be switched from 'blackhot' to 'white-hot' and back again at the operator's wish. Probably the greatest 'enemy' of thermal imaging is extended rainfall since that has the effect of cooling all inanimate objects and severely reducing contrast.

Thermal imaging makes it possible of real time target tracking. Detection of targets in dark and low light conditions can be done. All weather operation and dull, dirty and dangerous (DDD) roles are possible.

Thermal imaging cameras produce a clear image in the darkest of nights, in light fog and smoke and in the most diverse weather conditions. There has also been an increased interest in thermal imaging for all kinds of security applications, from long-range surveillance at border crossings, truck and shipping container inspection, to the monitoring of high-security installations such as nuclear power stations, airports, and dams. But thermal imaging has a lot more to offer than just a night vision solution for security applications.

Car manufacturers are integrating night vision modules for driver vision enhancement into cars. By helping drivers to see at night, accidents can be avoided. Boats and yachts are being equipped with thermal imaging cameras for night time navigation and other maritime applications like man overboard searches.

Often the thermal imager is just a small part of the complete system as in an UAS, so it needs to be as small, light and inexpensive as possible. Low-cost thermal imager is used as a pilot's night vision enhancement. It helps pilots by enhancing the ability to see terrain and other aircraft at long ranges, even in total darkness, light fog, dust and smoke. Thermal imaging is a technology that enables detection of people and objects in total darkness and in very diverse weather conditions.

A typical application for thermal imaging is border security, where most threats occur at night. Thermal imaging allows the aircraft to fly in total darkness and detect targets through smoke. The same aircraft can also be used to detect such things as forest fires. Areas which are hotter than the surroundings can indicate the start of a fire and can clearly be seen on a thermal image.

3. Image segmentation

Segmentation is the key and the first step to automatic target recognition, which will directly affect the accuracy of the following work. As a result, the division methods and its precision degree are essential. Infrared heat wave image is different from the visible light images. It reflects the distribution of the object surface temperature and latent characteristics of material form.

The infrared heat radiation, due to the imperfections of the system, will bring a variety of noise in the imaging process. The noise of complex distribution of infrared images makes the signal to noise ratio lower than visible light images.

3.1 2D OTSU algorithm

The two dimensional Otsu algorithm is given as follows. Suppose an image pixel size is M × N, gray-scale of the image ranges from 0 to L-1. The neighborhood average gray g (m, n) of the coordinate definition (m, n) pixel point is as follows:

$$g(m,n) = \frac{1}{k \times k} \sum_{i=-(k-1)/2}^{(k-1)/2} \sum_{j=-(k-1)/2}^{(k-1)/2} f(m+i, n+j) \tag{1}$$

Calculating the average neighbourhood gray of each pixel point, a gray binary group (i, j) may form. We use C_{ij} to represent the occurrence frequency of (i, j). Then the probability P_{ij} of vector (i, j) may be determined by the formula:

$$P_{ij} = \frac{C_{ij}}{M \times N} \tag{2}$$

Here, $0 \le I, j < L$, and $\sum_{i=0}^{L-1} \sum_{j=0}^{L-1} P_{ij} = 1$.

Assuming the existence of two classes C_0 and C_1 in Two dimensional form, the histogram represents their respective goals and background, and with two different probability density distribution function. If making use of two-dimensional histogram threshold vector (s, t) to segment the image (of which $0 \le s, t < L$), then the probability of two classes are respectively: The probability of background occurrence is:

$$\omega_0 = P(C_0) = \sum_{i=0}^{s} \sum_{j=0}^{t} P_{ij} = \omega_0(s,t) \tag{3}$$

The probability of object occurrence is:

$$\omega_1 = P(C_1) = \sum_{i=s+1}^{L-1} \sum_{j=t+1}^{L-1} P_{ij} = \omega_1(s,t) \tag{4}$$

The definition of dispersion matrix:

$$\sigma B = \omega 0 [(\mu 0-\mu\tau)(\mu 0-\mu\tau)T] + \omega 1 [(\mu 1-\mu\tau)(\mu 1-\mu\tau)T] \tag{5}$$

When the track of the above-mentioned dispersion matrix gets the maximum, the corresponding threshold of segmentation is the optimal threshold (S, T), namely:

$$tr(\sigma_B(S,T)) = max_{0 \le s,t < L} \{tr(\sigma_B(S,T))\} \tag{6}$$

We know that 2-D thermal images with noise segmented by Otsu way may get better results compared to one dimensional threshold segmentation methods. However, the computation cost gets huge, which is because the determination of the optimal threshold need to travel all the s and t, of which $0 \le s, t < L$. That is to say, the more gray scale value of images is, the longer choice time of the threshold is.

The segmentation of various thermal images is illustrated here. The segmentation results can be made more efficient in identification of targets and optimized by a number of methods. These segmentation results are used in fused image target tracking. One such method will be determining optimum threshold using histogram analysis. The method of using chaos based genetic algorithm makes the process time lower. The chaos based genetic algorithm uses Otsu algorithm as fitness function and proceeds for segmentation.

The so-called chaos refers to the uncertainty in the system appearing in seemingly without rules. From the mathematical sense, for determined series initial values, it is possible to predict the long-term behaviour of the system, even know its past behaviour and state by the power system. It is a unique phenomenon of non-linear systems. Chaos has randomicity, ergodicity and regularity. Based on these characteristics of chaos, using chaotic variables to optimize search is no doubt better than random search. Logistic map is the most basic chaotic map. The chaos equation of the Logistic definition can be described as follows:

$$x_{(n+1)} = u\, x_n\, (1 - x_n) \; ; \; 0 < u \le 4 \tag{7}$$

x_n lies between 0 and 1. n varies from 0,1,2, etc.

Fig. 1. Thermal Image

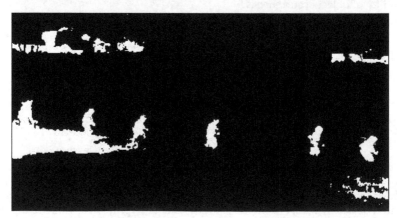

Fig. 2. Segmented Image

When u = 4, the system is the chaos state of the biggest ergodicity. Genetic algorithm is a kind of random search algorithm drawn from natural selection and natural genetic mechanisms of biology, which is particularly well suited to deal with the complex and nonlinear problems that traditional search methods are difficult to resolve.

Fig. 3. Thermal Image

Fig. 4. Segmented Image

The segmentation results are shown in Fig. 1 to Fig. 4 with the segmented image of the thermal image.

4. Image fusion process

Image fusion is the process by which two or more images are combined into a single image retaining the important features from each of the original images. The fusion of images is often required for images acquired from different instrument modalities or capture techniques of the same scene or objects. Important applications of the fusion of images include medical imaging, microscopic imaging, remote sensing, computer vision, and robotics. Fusion techniques include the simplest method of pixel averaging to more complicated methods such as principal component analysis (PCA) and wavelet transform (WT) based fusion.

Image fusion is the process of relevant information extraction from two or more images. The resulting image will encompass more information than any of the given input images. A multi sensor, multi temporal and multi view information techniques are required which overcome the limitations of using single senor information. The benefits of image fusion are extended range of operation, extended spatial and temporal resolution and coverage, reduced uncertainty, higher accuracy, reliability and compact representation.

Various kinds of image fusion for visual, Infrared and Synthetic Aperture Radar (SAR) images exist. Some of the primitive fusion process algorithms also have disadvantages. Direct fusion method makes the image blurred. The pixel based image fusion is computationally complex for large and high resolution images. The image averaging method produces a reduced contrast of information. The requirement is thus a novel and efficient information fusion process. Image fusion has a significant role of recognition of targets and objects. Target identification, localisation, filtering and data association forms an important application of the fusion process. Thus an effective surveillance and reconnaissance system can be formed.

There is information which is redundant and at the same time complementary too. The following summarize several approaches to the pixel level fusion of spatially registered input images. A generic categorization of image fusion methods in the following:

- Linear Superposition, Nonlinear Methods, Expectation Maximisation, Image Pyramids, Wavelet Transform, Generic Multiresolution Fusion Scheme, Optimization Approaches, Artificial Neural Networks, Fuzzy Techniques

Some of the prominent applications of image fusion are:

- Concealed Weapon Detection, Night Time Surveillance, Automatic Landing System, Digital Camera Applications, Medical Diagnosis, Defect Inspection and Remote Sensing

4.1 Wavelet transform

A signal analysis method similar to image pyramids is the discrete wavelet transform. The main difference is that while image pyramids lead to an over complete set of transform coefficients, the wavelet transform results in a nonredundant image representation. The discrete two dimensional wavelet transform is computed by the recursive application of low pass and high pass filters in each direction of the input image (i.e. rows and columns) followed by sub sampling.

These basis functions or baby wavelets are obtained from a single prototype wavelet called the mother wavelet, by dilations or contractions (scaling) and translations (shifts). They have advantages over traditional Fourier methods in analyzing physical situations where the signal contains discontinuities and sharp spikes.

Image fusion process is achieved by multiresolution decomposition at fourth level. The multiwavelet decomposition coefficients of the input images are appropriately merged and a new fixed image is obtained by reconstructing the fused multiwavelet coefficients. The theory of multiwavelets is also based on the idea of multiresolution analysis (MRA) as shown in Fig. 5. During a single level of decomposition using a scalar wavelet transform, the two-dimensional (2-D) image data is replaced with four blocks corresponding to the subbands representing either low-pass or high-pass filtering in each direction.

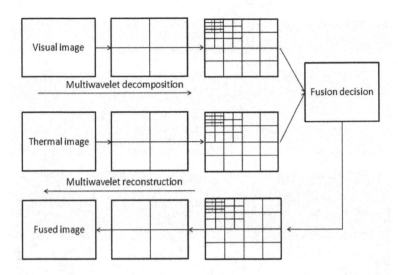

Fig. 5. Wavelet Multi Resolution Analysis

The Haar wavelet is a certain sequence of rescaled "square-shaped" functions which together form a wavelet family or basis. Wavelet analysis is similar to Fourier analysis in that it allows a target function over an interval to be represented in terms of an orthonormal function basis. The Haar wavelet is also the simplest possible wavelet.

4.2 FIS based image fusion

Neural Network and Fuzzy Logic approach can be used for sensor fusion. Such a sensor fusion could belong to a class of sensor fusion in which case the features could be input and decision could be output. The system can be trained from the input data obtained from the sensors.

The basic concept is to associate the given sensory inputs with some decision outputs. The following algorithm for pixel level image fusion using Fuzzy Logic illustrate the process of defining membership functions and rules for the image fusion process using FIS (Fuzzy Inference System) editor of Fuzzy Logic toolbox in MATLAB. The process flow of the process is as follows:

1. The visual and thermal image forms the inputs for the fusion system. The inputs must be with the same field of view.
2. With a gray level conversion applied, the two images are transformed to a column form.
3. The number and type of membership functions for both the input images are given to the FIS. The rule base for FIS decides how the output fused image should be.
4. The fused image is converted back to matrix format from column form.

The fuzzy system considered here is Mamdani type and its' FIS model in MATLAB is shown in Fig. 6. The Mamdani rule base is a crisp model of a system, i.e. it takes crisp inputs and produces crisp outputs. It does this with the use of user-defined fuzzy rules on user-defined fuzzy variables.

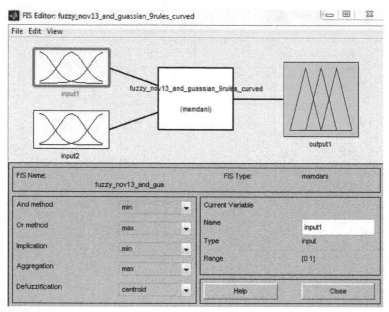

Fig. 6. FIS Model

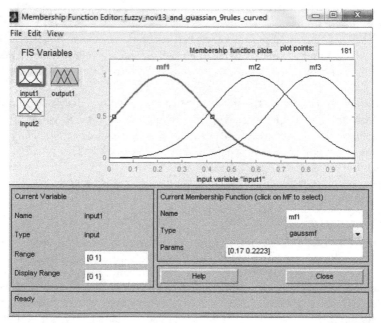

Fig. 7. FIS Membership Function

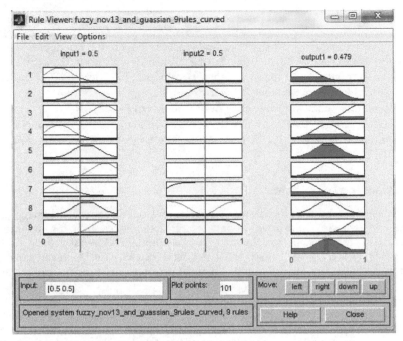

Fig. 8. Rule Base of FIS

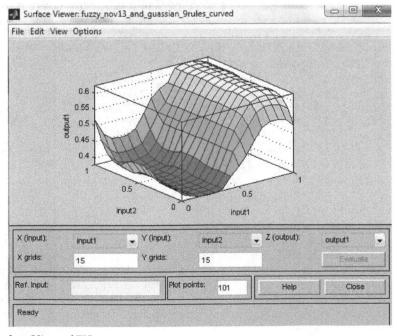

Fig. 9. Surface View of FIS

The idea behind using a Mamdani rule base to model crisp system behavior is that the rules for many systems can be easily described in terms of fuzzy variables. Thus we can effectively model a complex non-linear system, with common-sense rules on fuzzy variables.

The operation of the Mamdani rule base can be broken down into four parts: 1) mapping each of the crisp inputs into a fuzzy variable (fuzzification), 2) determining the output of each rule given its fuzzy antecedents, 3) determining the aggregate output of all of the fuzzy rules; 4) mapping the fuzzy output to crisp output (defuzzification).

The membership function used is Guassian as shown in Fig. 7. The rule base is formed for the fusion process as shown in Fig. 8. The surface view of the two inputs and one output is represented in Fig. 9.

5. Target tracking of objects

Automatic detection and tracking of interested targets from a sequence of images obtained from a reconnaissance platform is an interesting area of research for defence related application. The video images are obtained from an unmanned aerial vehicle (UAV) with on-board guidance and navigation system. The aircraft carries a multispectral camera which acquires images of the territory and sends the information to a ground control station (GCS) in real time.

During flight, the pilot in the ground control station may identify a region of interest as a target. This identification can be click and target type or an intelligent perception type.

The target which appears on a small window could be tracked by engaging track mode. Optical flow is an approximation of the local image motion based upon local derivatives in a given sequence of images. That is, in 2D it specifies how much each image pixel moves between adjacent images while in 3D in specifies how much each volume voxel moves between adjacent volumes. The 2D image sequences used are formed under perspective projection via the relative motion of a camera and scene objects.

The differential methods for determining the optical flow are Lucas-Kanade, Horn-Schunck, Buxton-Buxton, Black-Jepson and variational methods.

Lucas–Kanade method is a widely used differential method for optical flow estimation developed by Bruce D. Lucas and Takeo Kanade. The assumption in this method is that the flow is essentially constant in a local neighbourhood of the pixel under consideration, and solves the basic optical flow equations for all the pixels in that neighbourhood, by the least squares criterion.

Horn–Schunck method of estimating optical flow is a global method which introduces a global constraint of smoothness to solve the aperture problem. The Horn-Schunck algorithm assumes smoothness in the flow over the whole image. Thus, it tries to minimize distortions in flow and prefers solutions which show more smoothness.

5.1 Tracking of objects in fused images

A brief representation of the process used is as represented in Fig. 10. The visual and thermal video is first obtained from an airborne camera. The cameras used must be of acceptable resolution with good preprocessing features. A high resolution, light weight, rugged, portable, stabilized platform sensing element is required to be mounted on the airframe. The images are preprocessed for ego-sensory motion, atmospheric disturbances and inherent noise. Then a fusion process of thermal and visual images is adapted. The algorithms for such a fusion process would involve processing of information separately and then fusing the data. The other way is to fuse and process the data available.

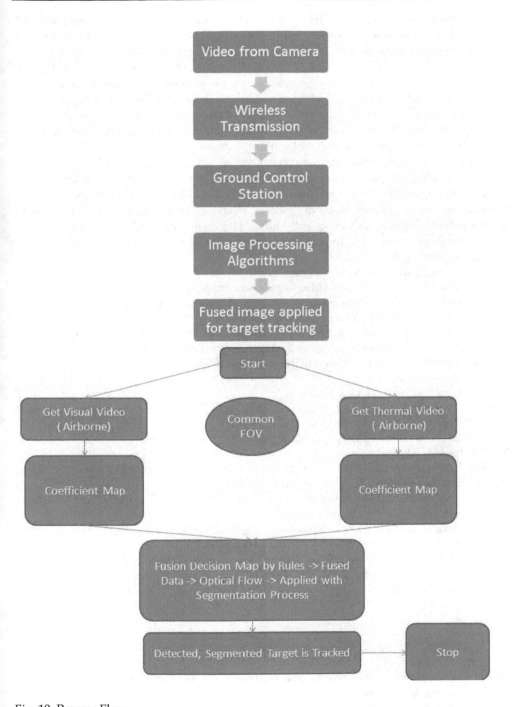

Fig. 10. Process Flow

The transmission of information from on board real time processing and display of all required data are done in the ground station. The control interaction with UAV is done by wireless communication transfer.

The video file obtained from the camera is loaded as an avi file. It is processed in MATLAB. It aids in real time and efficient implementation of the algorithm. The video is processed for detection of targets in a sequence of frames. The target detection and localisation process commences from applying the frames to an optical flow pattern which generates vectors. The target detection is done with respect to feature matching and extraction from the initial frame. The target which is the region of interest is separated out effectively. By using this novel technique, an optimized search process for an effective segmented image with less noise effects when compared to other algorithms is obtained. The targets are thus effectively located and segmented. The output frames are integrated to form a video file. Then effective tracking algorithms are applied for the process. Filtering and the required data association for the output obtained are subsequently done. The inputs needed for processing include that of two images (Visual and thermal) for image fusion. The steps involved are:

1. The airborne video is obtained from the UAV with
   a. A visual and thermal camera onboard the UAV.
   b. Wireless transmission of video to ground control station.
2. The inputs needed are two videos (visual and thermal) which are split into images with respect to frames. The factors to be considered are:
   a. Two videos are to be of same resolution and frame rate.
   b. Two images are to be considered with the same field of view (FOV).
3. Segmentation process is applied to the images and the targets are segmented.
4. For the fusion process:
   a. Consider two images at a time.
   b. Apply wavelet based image fusion with Haar transform with four level decomposition of the image.
   c. An inverse transform is applied to get back the fused image.
5. For tracking algorithm:
   a. The tracking algorithm is implemented in SIMULINK in MATLAB. The fused images are stitched to form a video of the same frame rate.
   b. The fused image is applied to an optical flow technique. The optical flow technique is based on Horn-Schunck method.
   c. Further segmentation accompanied with thresholding principles is applied for the output obtained after computing optical flow.
   d. Blob detection principles accompany the process for spotting the targets in the frame of concern. Thus the targets are given a rectangular boundary of identification.

6. Results

Image fusion results based on wavelet transform are discussed. Two images (Visual and thermal) are taken as shown in Fig. 11 and Fig. 12.

The visual image gives a realistic human sensing view. The thermal image identifies the target with the temperature difference coming into the picture with objects possessing different emissivity values.

Fig. 11. Visual Image

Fig. 12. Thermal Image

The fused image is given as Fig. 13. The fusion process is applied for a concealed weapon detection process. The results for such an application are given below in Fig. 14 to Fig. 15. The visual and thermal images are fused and the fused image gives combined information in one representation.

Fig. 13. Fused Image

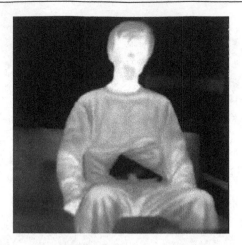

Fig. 14. Thermal Image

Fig. 15. Fused Image

The thermal images clearly give the information about concealed weapons. The fused image gives both the RGB based information present in visual image and the concealed weapon information present in thermal image. The fused image is thus capable of giving enhanced detection capabilities.

6.1 Target tracking results

For target tracking, the database of thermal and visual images is considered. The video obtained is converted to a series of frames. Each thermal and visual image is fused and at the end the fused images are combined to form a video which is given for target tracking process.

One such visual and thermal image from the sequence of frames is shown in Fig. 16 and Fig. 17. The fused image obtained as a result of wavelet transform using Haar wavelet is shown in Fig. 18.

Fig. 16. Visual Image

Fig. 17. Thermal Image

Fig. 18. Fused Image

The target tracking results including segmentation, optical flow and identification of targets in their corresponding frame are shown in Fig. 19, Fig. 20 and Fig. 21.

For the four sample frames considered, the segmentation results and tracking results are illustrated. The segmentation shows that of humans being segmented according to the threshold values.

Fig. 19. Segmented Image

Fig. 20. Optical Flow Detection

The optical flow which is found out from the images gives the movement of the humans which is being tracked and given a rectangular representation.

Fig. 21. Target Detected Image

The following results correspond to taking the thermal images alone and doing target tracking. The target tracking for aerial aircrafts' motion is shown in Fig. 22 and Fig. 23. These images correspond to the optical flow and the target detection from a real time video sequence. The target tracking for identification of humans is given in Fig. 24. The targets are tracked with respect to the movement of objects identified with optical flow. In this frame, an airborne flight is being tracked. This aids to the visual perception other than usage of RADAR.

Fig. 22. Optical Flow Detection

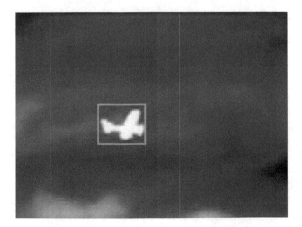

Fig. 23. Target Detected Image

Further sample results for tracking of objects in thermal video is shown in Fig. 24. This is an airborne thermal video which is tracked for vehicles and humans if present. The ego sensory motion is present in this kind of a dynamic moving platform. They have to be compensated for a stabilized video and for the tracking process has to be improved for a multiple target tracking environment.

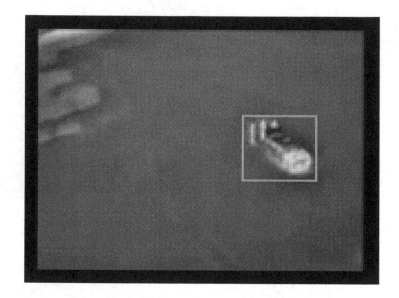

Fig. 24. Target Detection in Aerial Image

7. Conclusion

The airborne images obtained from an UAV are analysed in ground control station. By using the thermal images, all weather and night operation are possible. Visual and thermal image fusion is done and the fused image is given for target tracking.

This system has the benefit of enhanced target tracking application wherein only visual or thermal target tracking would not provide sufficient efficiency. Thus the image fusion process augments information leading to an improved system as a whole. The overall system incorporates segmentation, fusion and target tracking principles.

8. Acknowledgements

The authors are grateful to **The Vice Chancellor**, Anna University and **The Dean,** Madras Institute of Technology, Anna University for providing organizational facilities for carrying out this research work at Madras Institute of Technology. We would like to express our sincere thanks & gratitude to **The Director NAL** for providing sufficient funds for successful completion this sponsored research work. We also express special thanks to V.S.Chandrasekhar, B.P.Shasidhara and K.V.Srinivasan, Scientists, Aeronautical Development Establishment(ADE), DRDO, Bangalore. for their inspiration and encouragement. We would like to convey our thanks and wishes to all the **Avionics students.**

9. References

Y.Chena and C.Han, "Night-time Pedestrian Detection by Visual-Infrared Video Fusion," Proceedings of 7th World congress on Intelligent Control and Automation, China, 2008.

Anjali Malviya and S. G. Bhirud, "Visual Infrared Video Fusion for Night Vision using Background Estimation", Journal of Computing, Vol.2, April 2010.

Alex Leykin, Yang Ran and Riad Hammoud, "Thermal-Visible Video Fusion for Moving Target Tracking and Pedestrian Classification", IEEE Conference on Computer Vision and Pattern Recognition, Minneapolis, 2007.

Zhang Jin-Yu, Chen Yan and Huang Xian-Xiang, "IR Thermal Image Segmentation Based on Enhanced Genetic Algorithms and Two-Dimensional Classes Square Error", Second International Conference on Information and Computing Science, 2009.

Yi Wang, Aldo Camargo, Ronald Fevig, Florent Martel and Richard.R.Schultz, "Image Mosaicking from Uncooled Thermal IR Video Captured by a Small UAV", Proceedings of the IEEE Southwest Symposium on Image Analysis and Interpretation, 2008.

Daniel Olmeda, Arturo de la Escalera and Jos M Armingol, "Detection and Tracking of Pedestrians in Infrared Images", International Conference on Signals, Circuits and Systems, 2009.

Wai Kit Wong, Poi Ngee Tan, Chu Kiong Loo and Way Soong Lim, "An Effective Surveillance System Using Thermal Camera", International Conference on Signal Acquisition and Processing, 2009.

H.Wang, J.Peng and W.Wu, "Fusion algorithm for multisensory images based on discrete multiwavelet transform", Vision, Image and Signal Processing, Proceedings of the IEEE, Vol.149, no.5, 2002.

H.B.Mitchell, Image Fusion: Theories, Techniques and Applications, Springer, 2010. www.imagefusion.org

Wai Kit Wong, Hong Liang Lim, Chu Kiong Loo and Way Soong Lim, "Home alone faint detection surveillance system using thermal camera", Second International Conference on Computer Research and Development, Kuala Lumpur, 2010.

Ju Han and Bir Bhanu, "Fusion of color and infrared video for moving human detection,"
    ACM Portal, Pattern Recognition, pp 1771-1784.

5

Research of Fuzzy-Systems of Automatic Frequency and Phase Control on Basis of MATLAB

Vladimir Gostev
State University of Information and Communication Technologies
Ukraine

1. Introduction

Systems of phase auto fine tuning (phase locked loop – PLL-system) are one of the most widespread functional knots of various electronic systems. A phase-locked loop (PLL) is a closed-loop feedback control system that generates and outputs a signal in relation to frequency and phase of an input "reference" signal. They are used in digital networks for synchronization of some exact setting generators on the reference generator, in frequency synthesizers for multichannel communication systems with frequency consolidation where the grid of carrier frequencies for division of channels is required, for example, in broadcasting and TV, in schemes of restoration bearing and clock frequencies in synchronous communication systems, as discriminators for demodulation is frequency - and phase-modulated bearing, as voice-frequency decoders in telephone switchboards for decoding of figures from accepted voice-frequency combinations. In the given chapter fuzzy-systems of frequency and phase auto fine tuning (PLL-system with the digital fuzzy controllers working on the basis of fuzzy logic) are investigated. Research of fuzzy-systems PLL is spent by mathematical modeling with use of the interactive environment for scientific and engineering calculations MATLAB and a powerful tool of modelling and research of control systems with feedback Simulink.

2.1 Fuzzy-systems of Phase Locked Loop –PLL

Let's consider widely used system of the PLL frequency control which function diagram is resulted on fig. 2.1.

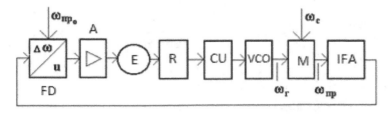

Fig. 2.1. System of the PLL frequency control.

A open-ended circuit of system is consists of serial connection of frequency discriminator FD, an amplifier A, an engine E with a reducer R, a controlling unit CU, a voltage-controlled oscillator VCO, a mixer M and intermediate – frequency amplifier IFA. System operation detail is described in [1]. A frequency discriminator can be presented by the series connection of a device of comparing, nonlinearity $K(\omega)$ and the low-pass filter LPF. An elementary low-pass filter is described by transfer function $G_F(s) = K_F(T_F s + 1)^{-1} = k / (s + b)$, where $k = K_F / T_F$, $b = 1 / T_F$, K_F - gain factor T_F - a constant of time of the filter on the output of discriminator. We accept $\omega_{np_0} = const$ and $\omega_c = const$. Inertial properties of intensive elements can be neglected. An engine is used as an integrating element for giving to system astaticism the first order that allows to reduce a dynamic error. It is possible to use the electronic integrator instead of the electromechanical engine. Therefore transfer function of control object may be written down in a type $G_0(s) = \alpha[s(s + a)]^{-1}$, where $a = 1 / T_G$, T_G - constant of time of the generator with a controlling unit.

The block diagram of system of the PLL frequency control in interactive system MATLAB we will present in a kind fig. 2.2. For maintenance of demanded dynamics of system it is used Fuzzy controller or PID-controller.

A curve $K(\omega)$ is called the static discrimination characteristic. The fluctuation component on an output of discriminator is described by spectral density S_n and dependence $S_n(\omega)$ is called of fluctuation characteristic of discriminator. At simulation fluctuation component can considered as voltage $V(t)$ - random disturbance applied to the output of the discriminator. A mathematical model of nonlinearity $K(\omega)$ we are describing expression

$$K(\omega) = K_d \omega \exp\{-\frac{\omega^2}{\Delta^2}\} \tag{2.1}$$

where K_d - a conversion coefficient of the discriminator, and Δ - a half-width of the discrimination characteristic, determines resolution capacity of the discriminator, $\omega \equiv \Delta \omega_{np}$ - detuning concerning nominal intermediate frequency $\omega_{np_0} = const$. Graphically a nonlinearity $K(\omega)$ at $\omega \equiv e$ is presented at the fig. 2.3

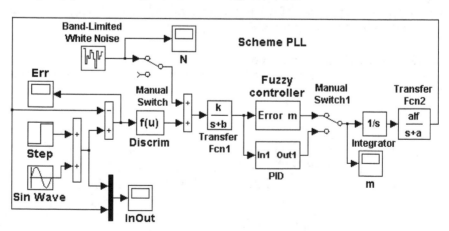

Fig. 2.2. The block diagram of system of the PLL frequency control.

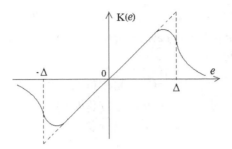

Fig. 2.3. A nonlinearity $K(\omega)$ at $\omega \equiv e$

It should be emphasized, that on an output of the unit of nonlinearity on the block diagram the mismatch error is defined as $K[\omega(t)] \equiv K[e(t)]$. The mismatch error on the input a frequency discriminator is defined as $\omega(t) \equiv e(t)$.

At the description of the discrimination characteristic represented on fig. 2.3, usually used approximation in a type

$$K(e) = K_d e \exp(-ae^2). \tag{2.2}$$

For determine the parameter a at the given half-width of the discrimination characteristic Δ area, bounded by a branch of function (2.2), which is defined as

$$K_d \int_0^\infty e \exp(-ae^2) de = \frac{K_d}{2a},$$

replace an area of a right triangle (fig. 2.3) with length of legs Δ and $K_d\Delta$ which is defined as $K_d\Delta^2 / 2$.

From here we have $a = 1 / \Delta^2$ also expression (2.2) at $\omega \equiv e$ it will be transformed to expression (2.1).

A frequency discriminator FD (see fig. 2.1) in a figure 2.2 is presented by the comparing circuit from the adder and characteristic of discrimination Discrim -- $K(\omega)$. A low-pass filter LPF is described by link TransferFcn1 with transfer function $G_F(s)$. The object of control - an integrator and the clock oscillator with a controlling unit - with transfer function $G_0(s)$ is presented by links Integrator and Transfer Fcn2.

The digital fuzzy controller (Fuzzy controller on fig. 2.2) is fulfilled under the block diagram with the identical triangular membership function erected in degree and consists of the block of the shaper of sizes A (t) and B (t), the block of comparing of sizes A and B and calculation u_c and the block of normalization variable [2]. The mismatch error $\theta(t)$ from an output of a low-pass filter arrives on a analog-digital converter (AD converter) (Zero-Order Hold), included at the input of a fuzzy controller . A quantization step of AD converter h =0,01s. At the output of a fuzzy controller is included the digital to analog converter (Zero-Order Hold1).

For simplification of normalization (recalculation of values of signals in values of elements of universal set) ranges of change input and output signals (parameters of a fuzzy controller) we is accepting by symmetric:

$$\theta_{max} = -\theta_{min}; \ \dot{\theta}_{max} = -\dot{\theta}_{min}; \ \ddot{\theta}_{max} = -\ddot{\theta}_{min}; \ m_{max} = -m_{min}.$$

Then recalculation of values of signals in values of elements of universal set perform according to the formulas

$$u_1^* = (\theta^* + A_m)/(2A_m); \\ u_2^* = (\dot{\theta}^* + B_m)/(2B_m); \\ u_3^* = (\ddot{\theta}^* + C_m)/(2C_m).$$

Values of ranges $(Am = \theta_{max} = -\theta_{min}; \quad Bm = \dot{\theta}_{max} = -\dot{\theta}_{min}; \quad Cm = \ddot{\theta}_{max} = -\ddot{\theta}_{min}; \\ Dm = m_{max} = -m_{min})$ at adjustment of a fuzzy controller steal up either manually, or automatically by the decision of the optimization task.

If studying of system (see fig. 2.2) the method of mathematical simulation selection following parameters:

$$k = 1; a = 10 \, c^{-1}; b = 12,5 \, c^{-1}; c = 1; \ a = \mathrm{alf} = 15; \ \Delta = 1; K_d = 1.$$

The system was studied when exposed on input an equivalent harmonic signal

$$u(t) = 1 + 0,5\sin 2\pi Ft,$$

with carrier frequency $F = 0,1Hz$.

The adjustment of a fuzzy controller is carried out by criterion of a minimum of a dynamic error. Is received following optimal parameters of a fuzzy controller :

$$Am = \theta_{max} = 0,05; \ Bm = \dot{\theta}_{max} = 0,4; \ Cm = \ddot{\theta}_{max} = 10; \ Dm = m_{max} = 150.$$

Processes in system of the PLL frequency control (see fig. 2.2) with a fuzzy controller are shown on fig.2.4 where $u(t)$ - an input action, $x(t)$ - an output a system (see fig. 2.4,a), $e(t) \equiv \mathrm{Err}$ – a mismatch error on a discriminator input (see fig. 2.4, b), $m(t)$ - an output of a fuzzy controller (see fig. 2.4, c).

The maximum dynamic error (except for initial burst at the moment of signal capture) does not exceed 0,7 % from amplitude of a sinusoid.

At the fig. 2.4, d transition is presented process of system of the PLL frequency control - response to unit step action. The system fulfills input influence in time, not exceeding 0,16 s, without overshoot.

Thus, the digital fuzzy controller provides not only greater accuracy castings input influence, but and high system performance by an step action.

It should be noted that the research system with the above parameters, without the regulator shows that the system lacks stability.

The system (see fig. 2.2) with a digital fuzzy controller it is researched also in the presence of a stationary white noise (Band-Limited White Noise) on a frequency discriminator output. Implementation of a white noise $v(t)$ is shown at the fig. 2.5, a. A mismatch error on an input of the slope detector $e(t)$ and an output of a fuzzy controller $m(t)$ thus are casual processes (see fig. 2.5, b and c).

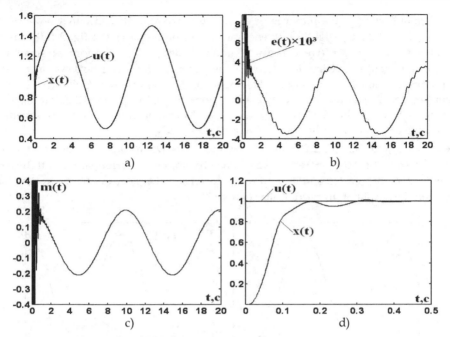

Fig. 2.4. Processes in system of PLL frequency control.

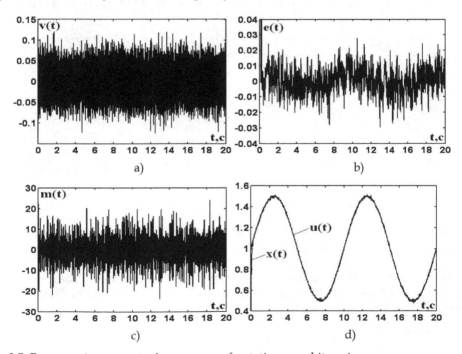

Fig. 2.5. Processes in system in the presence of a stationary white noise

Researches of system in the presence of a stationary white noise show that noise of such intensity (see fig. 2.5 a,) slightly influences a system output $x(t)$ (see fig. 2.5,d), however error of system increases (we compare fig. 2.4, b and 2.5b), therefore at small input influences (at small frequency deviations of the generator from set) noise on a frequency detector output will make the considerable impact on a dynamic error of system.

System (see fig.2.2) was also studied by using a more simple fuzzy controller. Parameter a in the fuzzy controller is chosen to be 0.2, and ranges of variation of input and output variables left unchanged: Am = 0,05; Bm = 0,4; Cm = 10; Dm = 150 .

Processes in system (see fig. 2.2) with a fuzzy controller where $u(t)$ – an input , $x(t)$ – an output of system (fig.2.6,a), $e(t) \equiv$ Err – a mismatch error on a discriminator input (fig.2.6,b). $x(t)$ and $m(t)$ - response to a unit jump of the input signal $u(t)$ respectively, at the system output and the output of fuzzy controller (see fig.2.6,c,d).

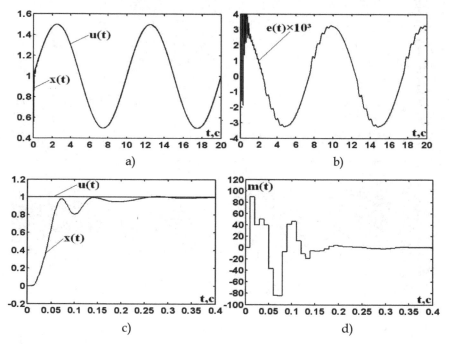

a)   b)

c)   d)

Fig. 2.6. Processes in system with a fuzzy controller

The maximum dynamic error (except for initial burst at the moment of signal capture) does not exceed 0,64 % from amplitude of a sinusoid. The system fulfills input influence in time, not exceeding 0,13s, without overshoot.

Of interest to examine the processes in the system (see Fig.2.2), by using instead of a fuzzy controller of the traditional PID controller. The block diagram of digital PID controller shown in fig.2.2. The transfer function of the regulator

$$W(z) = G_1 + G_2 \frac{z+1}{z-1} + G_3 \frac{z-1}{z} ,$$

where $G_1 = K$, $G_2 = \dfrac{K_i h_0}{2}$, $G_3 = \dfrac{K_d}{h_0}$, h_0 – digitization step.

As a result of tuning of PID-controller at the indicated higher parameters of the system and input an equivalent harmonic signal $u(t) = 1 + 0,5\sin 2\pi F t$, with carrier frequency $F = 0,1Hz$, is received following optimal parameters of a PID-controller, at the h_0 =0.01s: $G_1 = 171,2$; $G_2 = 0,48$; $G_3 = 1800$.

Processes in system (see fig. 2.2) with a PID-controller are shown at the fig. 2.7 where $u(t)$ - an input action, $x(t)$ - an output a system (see fig. 2.7, a), $e(t) \equiv$ Err – a mismatch error on a discriminator input (see fig. 2.7,b). $m(t)$ - an output of a fuzzy controller (see fig. 2.7,c). The maximum dynamic error on system of the of the PLL frequency control with a PID-controller (except for initial burst at the moment of signal capture) does not exceed 2,4 % from amplitude of a sinusoid. The maximum dynamic error on system of the PLL frequency control with a PID-controller in 3,5 times more than the maximum dynamic error in system of the PLL frequency control with a fuzzy controller and in 3,75 times with a fuzzy controller.

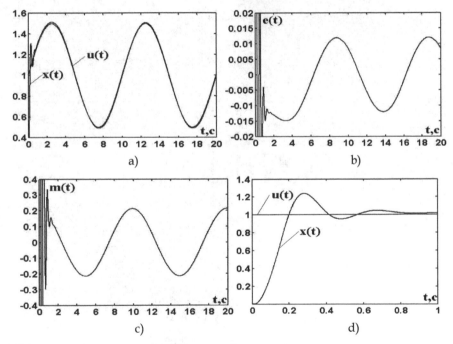

Fig. 2.7. Processes in system with a PID-controller

At the fig. 2.4, d transition is presented process of system with a PID-controller - response to unit step action. The transitional process - the oscillating with the overshoot of more than 20%. The system fulfills input influence in time, exceeding 0,4 s. The regulation time in system of the PLL frequency control with the PID-controller approximately in 2,5 times is more than regulation time in system with a fuzzy controller and in 3 times with an simple fuzzy controller.

Thus, the fuzzy controllers provide accuracy fulfills of input influences and high-speed performance of system of the PLL frequency control it is much better, then the PID-controller.

The system (see fig. 2.2) with a digital PID-controller it is researched also in the presence of a stationary white noise (Band-Limited White Noise) on a frequency discriminator output. Implementation of a white noise $v(t)$ is shown at the fig. 2.8,*a*.

Researches of system in the presence of a stationary white noise show that noise of such intensity (see fig. 2.8 a,) slightly influences a system output $x(t)$ (see fig. 2.5,d) however error of system increases (we compare fig. 2.7, b and 2.8b) therefore at small input influences (at small frequency deviations of the generator from set) noise on a frequency detector output will make the considerable impact on a dynamic error of system.

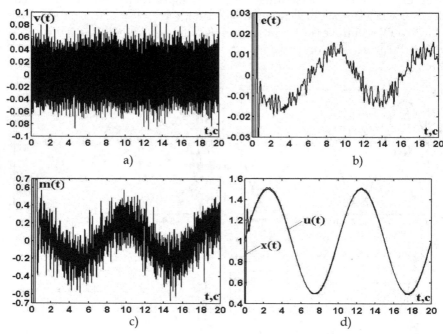

Fig. 2.8. Processes in system in the presence of a stationary white noise

Let's consider a mathematical model (block diagram) of system of the of the PLL frequency control in interactive system MATLAB (see fig. 2.9), with the low-pass filter of the second order which has transfer function in a numerical type

$$G(s) = \frac{k}{a_0 s^2 + a_1 s + 1} = \frac{0,008}{0,008 s^2 + 0,18 s + 1}.$$

A frequency discriminator FD at the fig. 2.9 is presented by the comparator circuit on the adder and the discrimination characteristic (Discrim)

$$K(e) = K_d e \exp\{-\frac{e^2}{\Delta^2}\} = e \exp\{-\frac{e^2}{0,64}\},$$

where conversion coefficient of the discriminator $K_d = 1$, and the half-width of the discrimination characteristic defining resolution capability of the discriminator, $\Delta = 0{,}8$.
The object of control - the integrator and the without inertia clock generator - with transfer function $G_0(s) = alf / s$, $alf = 25$, is presented by link Transfer Fcn1.

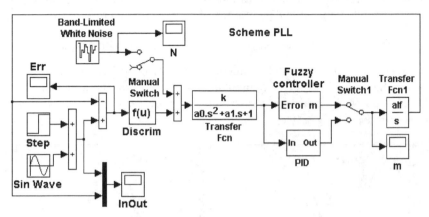

Fig. 2.9. The block diagram of system of the PLL frequency control

In system is used the elementary digital fuzzy controller (Fuzzy controller at the fig. 2.9) is fulfilled under the block diagram. The controller consists of the block of the shaper of sizes A (t) and B (t), the block of comparing of sizes A and B and calculation u_c and the block of normalization output variable[2].

The mismatch error $\theta(t)$ from an output of a low-pass filter arrives on a analog-digital converter (AD converter) (Zero-Order Hold), included at the input of a fuzzy controller. A quantization step of AD converter $h = 0{,}01s$. On an output of a fuzzy controller is included the digital/analog converter DAC (Zero-OrderHold1).

For simplification of normalization (recalculation of values of signals in values of elements of universal set) ranges of change input and output signals (parameters of a fuzzy controller) we is accepting by symmetric:

$$\theta_{max} = -\theta_{min}; \quad \dot\theta_{max} = -\dot\theta_{min}; \quad \ddot\theta_{max} = -\ddot\theta_{min}; \quad m_{max} = -m_{min}.$$

Then recalculation of values of signals in values of elements of universal set perform according to the formulas

$$\left. \begin{aligned} u_1^* &= (\theta^* + A_m) / (2A_m); \\ u_2^* &= (\dot\theta^* + B_m) / (2B_m); \\ u_3^* &= (\ddot\theta^* + C_m) / (2C_m). \end{aligned} \right\}.$$

Values of ranges ($Am = \theta_{max} = -\theta_{min}$; $Bm = \dot\theta_{max} = -\dot\theta_{min}$; $Cm = \ddot\theta_{max} = -\ddot\theta_{min}$; $Dm = m_{max} = -m_{min}$) at adjustment of a fuzzy controller steal up either manually, or automatically by the decision of the optimization task.

The system was studied when exposed on input an equivalent harmonic signal

$$u(t) = 1 + 0,5\sin 2\pi Ft$$
,

with carrier frequency $F = 0,1Hz$.
The adjustment of a fuzzy controller is carried out by criterion of a minimum of a dynamic error. Is received following optimal parameters of a fuzzy controller:

$$Am = \theta_{max} = 0,05; \quad Bm = \dot{\theta}_{max} = 0,4; \quad Cm = \ddot{\theta}_{max} = 10; \quad Dm = m_{max} = 150 .$$

Processes in system of the of the PLL frequency control (see fig. 2.9) with a fuzzy controller are shown on fig. 2.10 where $u(t)$ - an input action, $x(t)$ - an output a system (see fig. 2.10 a,), $e(t) \equiv \text{Err}$ – a mismatch error on a discriminator input (see fig. 2.10,b). $m(t)$ - an output of a fuzzy controller (see fig. 2.10,c).

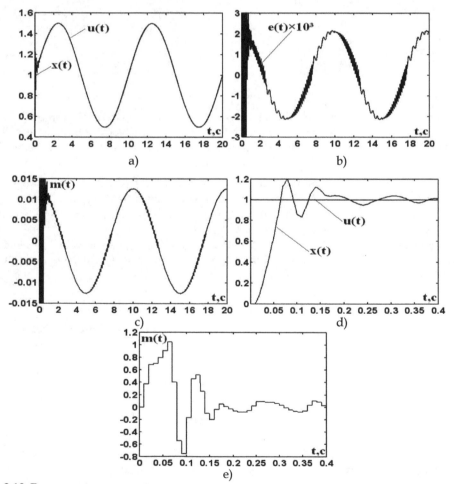

Fig. 2.10. Processes in system

The maximum dynamic error (except for initial burst at the moment of signal capture) does not exceed 0,4 % from amplitude of a sinusoid.

At fig. 2.10,d,e are presented reactions to unit step of input signal $u(t)$ respectively, at the output of system $x(t)$ and at the output of a fuzzy controller $m(t)$. The transition process – the oscillation, which the overshoot of more then 20%. The system fulfills input influence in time, not exceeding 0,25 s.

At usage in system (fig. 2.9 see) a digital PID- controller it is received following results.

Tuning of PID-controller at the indicated higher parameters of the system and input an equivalent harmonic signal $u(t) = 1 + 0,5\sin 2\pi Ft$, with carrier frequency $F = 0,1Hz$, is received following earlier optimal parameters of a PID-controller, at the h_0 =0.01s: $G_1 = 171,2$; $G_2 = 0,48$; $G_3 = 1800$.

Therefore processes in system (see fig. 2.9) with a digital PID-controler same what are shown at the fig. 2.7.

The maximum dynamic error in system of the of the PLL frequency control with the PID-controller (except for initial burst at the moment of signal capture) does not exceed 2,4 % from amplitude of a sinusoid. Transfer process - oscillatory, with overshoot more than 20 %. The system fulfills input influence for time exceeding 0,4 with. The maximum dynamic error in system of the of the PLL frequency control (fig. 2.9) with the PID-controller in 6 times more the maximum dynamic error in system of the of the PLL frequency control with a fuzzy controller see, and regulation time in system of the of the PLL frequency control with the PID- controller approximately in 1,6 times is more than regulation time in system with a fuzzy controller.

Thus, the fuzzy controller is provided with accuracy of working off of input influences and high-speed performance of system of the frequency self-tuning it is much better, than the PID-controller.

2.2 Fuzzy systems of clock synchronization

Systems of clock synchronization CS found a wide circulation in various areas of technique, in particular on digital networks and transmission systems of information DTSI. The modern development of technique demands requires the CS to meet the new higher quality of indicators.

At the fig. 2.11 shows a typical function diagram of CS DTSI. Diagram includes leading and slave clock oscillator - LCO and SCO accordingly; the input device of regenerator - IDR; the extractor of clock synchro signal (ECS); a solver - S; a phase detector – PD; a low-pass filter LPF; a manager -M; a communication line - a CL.

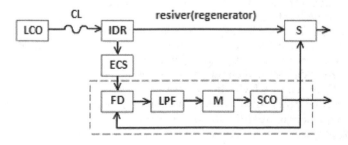

Fig. 2.11. System of clock synchronization

Clock synchronization of digital signals of telecommunication DST is a process of establishment and maintaining the required phase relations between the significant moments of a digital signal of telecommunication DST and a clock synchro signal. Thus, into the decision of the task of clock synchronization include: 1) formation of the clock synchro signal solver of the receiver or a regenerator; 2) "binding" of a phase of the specified synchro signal to a phase of the significant moments DST, accepted from a communication line; 3) monitoring of the given phase relationship between the timing signal accepted from a communication line and a synchro signal submitted on solver of the receiver; 4) framing of controlling influence in the presence of an error at violation of the specified phase relationship; 5) base service of a phase error according to the worked out control action.

The solution of these problem is possible, first of all, creation of system of automatic control of a phase of a clock synchronize of the receiver or regenerator DST. Clearly that inphase operation of the transmitter and receiver DST is inconceivable without presence synhro information (upsetting control of system of automatic control). Clock synchro signal are worked out by clock oscillator CO. Consequently, it is necessary to carry out generating of a clock synchro signal on transmission and on reception that in turn causes of presence TG on transmission and on reception. Thus, the first stage of solving the problem of clock synchronization in practice is implemented by presence TG in a regenerator or a receiving part of the equipment DST, and clock synchronization can be shown to synchronization CO, i.e. process of establishment and maintenance of demanded phase relationships between clock synchro signal two or several CO. Thus CO of transmitter is leading, he works out *setting action*; and CO the receiver or a regenerator - slave, the phase of his synchro signal is a measured variable of automatic system of PLL of a phase. This circumstance is an important feature of the synchronization system , which becomes a telemechanical system.

Setting action - a phase of a clock synhro signal of leader CO in the general case, due to random distortions when moving the synhro signal from the transmitter to the receiver, instability of generating of pulses by leader CO, and other is unknown function of time, i.e. $\varphi_{TG}(t) = \text{var}$. This position gives the grounds to classify system of clock synchronization as follow-up systems of automatics, and at $\varphi_{TG}(t) = const$ – as stabilizing systems.

Basic element of system of clock synchronization is the system PLL which is selected by a dotted line for fig. 2.11

In phase-locked loop systems the coordination of phases of two oscillations is carried out - the current phase of controlled oscillations is set up under a current phase of setting oscillations so that ideally the phase difference of these oscillations saves constant value. As persistence of a phase difference is possible only at equality of oscillation frequencies in PLL systems frequency of controlled oscillations ideally is installed to equal frequency of setting oscillations. This property of PLL systems defines their double assignment - as systems of self-locked of frequency and as systems of self-locked of a phase.

In the first case the immediate aim of application of system is establishment of demanded correspondence between frequencies of two oscillations, and in the second - establishment of demanded correspondence between phases of two oscillations.

The phase-locked systems which immediate aim is establishment of demanded correspondence between frequencies of two oscillations, received a title of phase-locked loop systems of frequency control (PLL frequency control).

If the immediate purpose of functioning of system is the coordination of phases of two oscillations it name the same as also all class of considered systems - the phase-locked loop system (PLL).

Distinction of titles reflects only distinction in immediate mission and does not mean distinctions in principles of actions. Principles of action of systems PLL OF and PLL are identical.

System PLL defines accuracy and high-speed performance of all system of clock synchronization. Object of control in system PLL is the clock VCO which taking into its inertial can be described transfer function

$$G(s) = \alpha[s(s+a)]^{-1}$$

(If an output variable of the generator is the phase of oscillations), or transfer function

$$G(s) = \alpha / (s+a)$$

(If an output variable of the generator is oscillation frequency), where $\alpha = K_G / T$, $a = 1/T$, K_G - transmission factor, $rad / (s \cdot V)$, T - time constant VCO. Assuming, that the VCO is without inertial element of system PLL, its transfer function can be defined as

$$G(s) = \alpha / s$$

(If an output variable of the generator is the phase of oscillations), or the transfer function

$$G(s) = \alpha$$

(If an output variable of the generator is oscillation frequency), where $\alpha = K_G$, K_G - transmission factor VCO, $rad / (s \cdot V)$.

The mathematical model of the phase detector can be present series connection of the device of comparing, non linearity $K(\varphi)$ and low-pass filter LPF. The simplest LPF is described by the transfer function

$$G_F(s) = K_F / (T_F s + 1) = k / (s+b),$$

where $k = K_F / T_F$, $b = 1/T_F$, K_F - an amplification factor, T_F - the constant of the filter phase detector.

Curve $K(\varphi)$ is called the static discrimination characteristic. Mathematical model of the nonlinearity of the type "discrimination feature" can be described by

$$K(\varphi) = K_d \sin \varphi,$$

where K_d - gain of phase detector, $\varphi(t) \equiv e(t)$ - a mismatch error on an input of phase detector, or expression at the "linear discrimination characteristic

$$K(\varphi) = \begin{cases} K_d\varphi & \text{at } -\Delta \le \varphi \le \Delta, \\ 0 & \text{at } \quad |\varphi| \rangle \Delta. \end{cases}$$

Usually the half-width Δ "linear" discrimination characteristic of phase detector is equal $\pi / 2$, π or 2π.

Discrimination characteristic of phase-frequency detector can be described by the expression

$$K(\varphi) = \begin{cases} K_0 & \text{at} \quad \varphi \langle -2\pi, \\ -K_d\varphi & \text{at} \quad -2\pi \leq \varphi \leq 2\pi, \\ K_0 & \text{at} \quad \varphi \rangle 2\pi. \end{cases}$$

Let's consider a block diagram (a mathematical model) of system of the PLL presented in interactive system MATLAB, in fig.2.12 [3,4]. To ensure the dynamics of the system using fuzzy and PID-controllers (Fuzzy controller and PID at the fig.2.12).

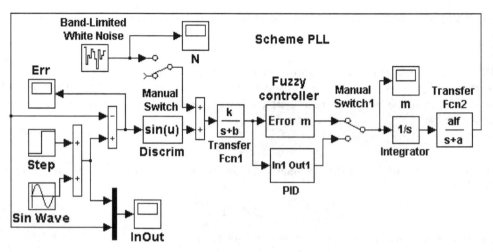

Fig. 2.12. System of the PLL.

Phase detector FD (see fig. 2.11) in fig.2.12 is presented by the compare circuit on the adder and discrimination characteristic Discrim – $K(\varphi) = K_d \sin \varphi$. The low-pas filter LPF is described by link Transfer Fcn1 with transfer function $G_F(s)$. The clock generator with transfer function $G(s)$ is described by links Integrator and Transfer Fcn2.

The digital fuzzy controller (fuzzy controller at the fig. 2.12) is fulfilled under the block diagram, with the identical triangular membership function erected in degree and consists of the block of the shaper of sizes A (t) and B (t), the block of comparing of sizes A and B and calculation u_c and the block of normalization output variable[2]. The mismatch error $\theta(t)$ from an output of a low-pass filter arrives on a analog-digital converter (AD converter) (Zero-Order Hold), included at the input of a fuzzy controller . A quantization step of AD converter h =0,01s. On an output of a fuzzy controller is included the digital/analog converter (Zero-Order Hold1).

For simplification of normalization (recalculation of values of signals in values of elements of universal set) ranges of change input and output signals (parameters of a fuzzy controller) we is accepting by symmetric:

$$\theta_{\max} = -\theta_{\min}; \ \dot{\theta}_{\max} = -\dot{\theta}_{\min}; \ \ddot{\theta}_{\max} = -\ddot{\theta}_{\min}; \ m_{\max} = -m_{\min}.$$

Then recalculation of values of signals in values of elements of universal set perform according to the formulas

$$
\left.\begin{array}{l}
u_1^* = (\theta^* + A_m) / (2A_m); \\
u_2^* = (\dot{\theta}^* + B_m) / (2B_m); \\
u_3^* = (\ddot{\theta}^* + C_m) / (2C_m).
\end{array}\right\}.
$$

Values of ranges ($Am = \theta_{max} = -\theta_{min}$; $Bm = \dot{\theta}_{max} = -\dot{\theta}_{min}$; $Cm = \ddot{\theta}_{max} = -\ddot{\theta}_{min}$; $Dm = m_{max} = -m_{min}$) at adjustment of a fuzzy controller steal up either manually, or automatically by the decision of the optimization task.

Let's notice that mathematical models of systems at the fig. 2.12 and fig. 2.2 differ only discrimination characteristics, therefore at identical parameters of other elements it is necessary to expect identical or close results at research of these systems. If studying of system (see fig. 2.12) the method of mathematical simulation selection following parameters: $k = 1; a = 10\,c^{-1}; b = 12,5\,c^{-1}; c = 1; a = alf = 15$. The system was studied when exposed on input an equivalent harmonic signal $u(t) = 1 + 0,5\sin 2\pi Ft$ with carrier frequency $F = 0,1Hz$.

The adjustment of a fuzzy controller is carried out by criterion of a minimum of a dynamic error. Is received following optimal parameters of a fuzzy controller: $Am = 0,05$; $Bm = 0,4$; $Cm = 10$; $Dm = 150$.

Processes in system (see fig. 2.12) are shown at the fig. 2.13 where $u(t)$ - an input action, $x(t)$ - an output a system (see fig. 2.13,a), $e(t) \equiv Err$ – a mismatch error on a discriminator input (see fig. 2.13). $m(t)$ - an output of a fuzzy controller (see fig. 2.13c,). The maximum dynamic error (except for initial burst at the moment of signal capture) does not exceed 0,7 % from amplitude of a sinusoid. At the fig. 2.13,d transition is presented process of system - response to unit step action. The system fulfills input influence in time, not exceeding 0,22s, with overshoot not more than 10%.

Thus, the fuzzy controllers provide accuracy fulfills of input influences, but and high-speed performance of system at the jump action. It should be noted that the study of the system without the controller shows, that the system does not have the stability.

The system (see fig. 2.12) with a fuzzy controller it is researched also in the presence of a stationary white noise (Band-Limited White Noise) on an output of frequency discriminator [5]. Implementation of a white noise $v(t)$ is shown at the fig. 2.14,a. A mismatch error on an input of the slope detector $e(t)$ and an output of a fuzzy controller $m(t)$ thus are casual processes (see fig. 2.14, b and c). Researches of system in the presence of a stationary white noise show that noise of such intensity slightly influences a system output $x(t)$ (see fig. 2.14 d) however error of system increases (we compare fig. 2.4b and 2.5b) therefore at small input influences (at small frequency deviations of the generator from set) noise on a detector output will make the considerable impact on a dynamic error of system.

It is of interest to consider the processes in the system of PLL (see fig.2.12)if using instead of the fuzzy controller the PID-controller [6]. The transfer function of the digital PID (PID on fig.2.12) controller

$$
W(z) = G_1 + G_2 \frac{z+1}{z-1} + G_3 \frac{z-1}{z},
$$

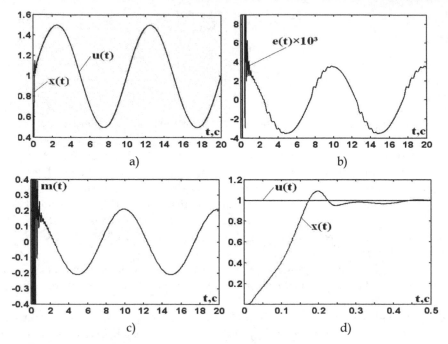

Fig. 2.13. Processes in system

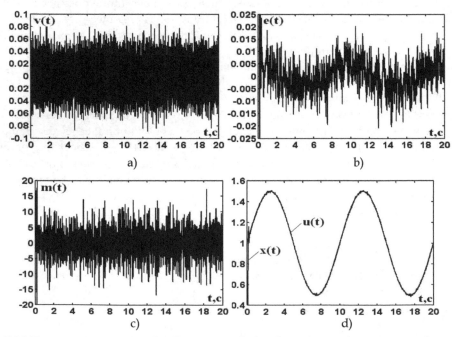

Fig. 2.14. Processes in system with a fuzzy controller in the presence of a stationary white noise

where $G_1 = K$, $G_2 = \dfrac{K_i h_0}{2}$, $G_3 = \dfrac{K_d}{h_0}$, h_0 – a digitization step.

As a result of tuning a controller at the indicated higher parameters of the system and input an equivalent harmonic signal is received following optimal parameters of a PID – controller, at the $h_0 = 0.01c$: $G_1 = 130$; $G_2 = 0,48$; $G_3 = 2000$. Processes in system (see fig. 2.12) with a PID-controller are shown on fig. 2.15 where $u(t)$ - an input action, $x(t)$ - an output a system (see fig. 2.15,a), $e(t) \equiv \text{Err}$ – a mismatch error on a discriminator input (see fig. 2.15,b). $m(t)$ - an output of a fuzzy controller (see fig. 2.15,c).

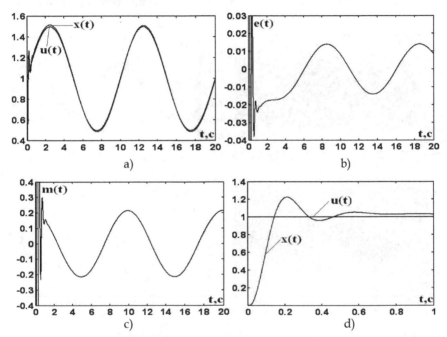

Fig. 2.15. Processes in system with a PID-controller

The maximum dynamic error in system of PLL with a PID – controller (except for initial burst at the moment of signal capture) attains of 2,8% from amplitude of a sinusoid. The maximum dynamic error in system of PLL with a PID–controller in 4 times more than the maximum dynamic error in system of PLL with a fuzzy controller.

On fig. 2.15,d transition is presented process of system with a PID-controller - response to unit step action. The transitional process - the oscillating with the overshoot of more than 20%. The system fulfills input influence in time, exceeding 0,31 s. The overshoot in system of PLL with the PID-controller in 2 times, and the regulation time in 1,4 times more than the appropriate parameters in system of PLL with a fuzzy controller.

When reducing the dynamic error in the PLL with PID–controller increases the overshoot and control time, and decrease in these parameters of the transition process increases dynamic error.

Thus, the fuzzy controllers provide accuracy fulfills of input influences, and high-speed performance of system PLL much better, then PID–controller.

The system (see fig. 2.12) with a PID-controller it is researched also in the presence of a stationary white noise (Band-Limited White Noise) on an output of discriminator. Implementation of a white noise $v(t)$ is shown at the fig. 2.16,a. A mismatch error on an input of the detector $e(t)$ and an output of a fuzzy controller $m(t)$ thus are casual processes (see fig. 2.16,b and c). Researches of system in the presence of a stationary white noise show that noise of such intensity slightly influences a system output $x(t)$ (see fig. 2.16,d) however error of system increases (we compare fig. 2.15,b and 2.16,c) therefore at small input influences (at small frequency deviations of the generator from set) noise on a frequency detector output will make the considerable impact on a dynamic error of system.

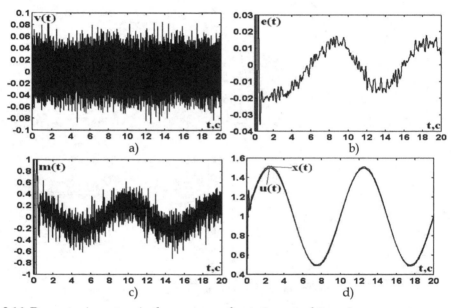

Fig. 2.16. Processes in system in the presence of a stationary white noise

Let's consider the system of the PLL of oscillator with a digital fuzzy controller. One of the main elements of the PLL oscillator is an analog phase detector, the static discrimination characteristic which can be written down in a kind

$$U_{FD} = K_{FD} \cos \varphi \qquad (2.3)$$

where K_{FD} - the constant coefficient equal to the maximum value of voltage on an output of the detector, φ - difference in phase fluctuation (one of which is the reference) of the same frequency, field by to the first and second inputs of the detector (when equality the frequencies of two oscillation, the phase difference of these oscillations is constant).

When you change the frequency of input signal, the phase difference become a function of time:

$$\varphi(t) = \varphi_n + 2\pi \int \Delta f(t) dt \qquad (2.4)$$

where φ_n - starting value of phase difference at the moment $t = 0$, when $\Delta f = f_1 - f_2 = 0$.
Taking into account expressions (2.3) and (2.4) block diagram of a phase detector with variable frequency f_1 and f_2 input signal will have the form shown at the fig.2.17 [7].

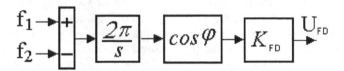

Fig. 2.17. Block diagram of a phase detector

Based on the structural scheme of the phase detector, taking into account the inertia of the filter at the output of the detector and the control element at the input of the oscillator (the filter at the output of the detector and the control element is usually described aperiodic links) can make a mathematical model of system of the PLL frequency control.
The mathematical model system of PLL with a digital fuzzy controller, compiled using the interactive system MATLAB, presented at the fig.2.18. Filter at the output of the digital phase detector and an controlling element of the generator describe the transfer functions:

$$G_1(s) = k / (s + b) = 10 / (s + 12,5), \ G_2(s) = alf / (s + a) = 3 / (s + 20).$$

The digital fuzzy controller (Fuzzy controller at the fig. 2.18) is fulfilled under the block diagram, with the identical triangular membership function erected in degree and consists of the block of the shaper of sizes A (t) and B (t) (block 1 collected by the diagram), the block of comparing of sizes A and B and calculation u_c (block 2 collected by the diagram) and the block of normalization output variable (block 3 collected by the diagram)[2].

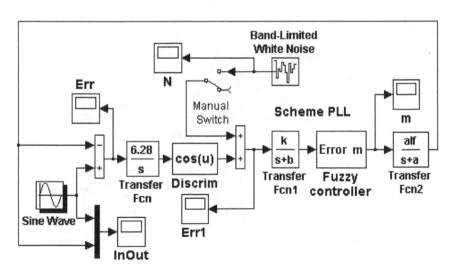

Fig. 2.18. System of the PLL frequency control.

The digitization step is chosen 0,001s. Values of ranges ($Am = \theta_{max} = -\theta_{min}$; $Bm = \dot{\theta}_{max} = -\dot{\theta}_{min}$; $Cm = \ddot{\theta}_{max} = -\ddot{\theta}_{min}$; $Dm = m_{max} = -m_{min}$) at adjustment of a fuzzy controller steal up either manually, or automatically by the decision of the optimization task. At research of the system we will accept, that the difference of frequencies of two fluctuations changes under the sinusoidal law: $\Delta f = 0,2\sin(\pi / 5)$ or $\Delta f = 0,2\sin(\pi / 10)$ (i.e. the maximum deviation of frequency of the generator operated pressure, from the set reaches $\pm 20\%$). System of PLL should compensate a deviation of frequency of the generator, therefore an fuzzy controller it is necessary to adjust on the minimum current error of a mismatch in system. As a result of adjustment it is received following optimum parameters of an fuzzy controller:

$$Am=0,03; Bm=0.5; Cm=10; Dm=20; c=1.$$

Processes in system (see fig.2.18) at setting action $0,2\sin(\pi / 5)$ are presented at the fig.2.19, at setting action $0,2\sin(\pi / 10)$ at the fig. 2.20. In figure $e(t)$ - the error of a mismatch on frequency on an input of the phase detector, $\theta(t)$ – the error of a mismatch on frequency on an output of the phase detector , $m(t)$ - operating pressure on an output of an fuzzy controller, $u(t)$ and $x(t)$ - an input and output of the system accordingly.

Independently of the frequency of input signal the transition process in the system finished for 3 s. Maximum dynamic mismatch error of frequency at the input of the phase detector at the input action $0,2\sin(\pi / 5)$ does not exceed $2,8 \cdot 10^{-3}$ (1,4% of the amplitude of the input action), and for input action $0,2\sin(\pi / 10)$ is approximately $1,4 \cdot 10^{-3}$ (0,7% of the amplitude of the input).

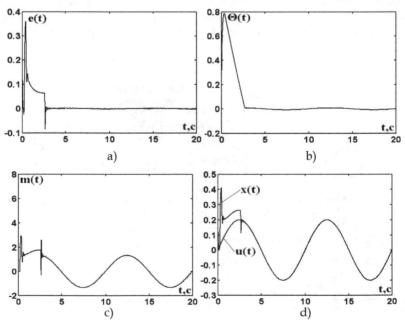

Fig. 2.19. Processes in system at setting action $0,2\sin(\pi / 5)$

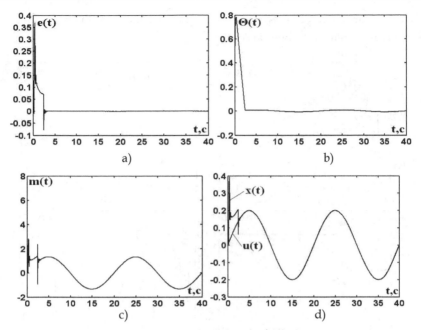

Fig. 2.20. Processes in system at setting action $0,2\sin(\pi / 10)$

As show researches of system (see fig. 2.18), a fuzzy controller allows to increase the accuracy of system PLL practically by two order in comparison with system without a controller.

Research of system PLL, accuracy of tracking which defines a synthesized fuzzy controller, on the basis of a mathematical apparatus of interactive system MATLAB allows to define simply enough one of system key parameters - a strip of dynamic tracking.

The strip of dynamic tracing of system PLL is the greatest offset of frequency of an entry basic signal concerning nominal frequency of oscillations of the voltage-controlled oscillator VCO. In this strip slave devise of synchronization should remain in a mode of tracing irrespective of speed of change of entry frequency in all range of frequencies. In other words, in a strip of dynamic tracing system PLL can track arbitrarily fast changes of the input frequency, including spasmodic changes of frequency at the input of system.

The strip of dynamic tracing of system PLL at research of mathematical model of system PLL in interactive system MATLAB is defined simply enough, namely, submitting step signals on input of system PLL it is necessary to find the value of jump of an input signal at which there is a tracing failure (i.e. at which the system ceases to fulfil jump of an input signal). For researched system transients action (responses to jumps of an input signal) are shown at the fig. 2.21. Disruption of tracking occurs when the amplitude of jump A=0,67. This value also defines a strip of dynamic tracking.

It is necessary to mark that at sinusoidal input action (at the set speed of change of input frequency) tracing failure occurs at certain amplitude of the sinusoidal effect, and the amplitude at which there is a tracing failure in this case will be more than at spasmodic change of an input signal. For researched system processes (responses to input action

$A\sin(\pi/10)$ at various amplitudes A an input signal) are shown at the fig. 2.22. Disruption of tracking occurs when the amplitude A=0,78.

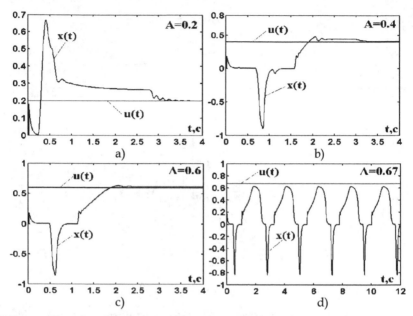

Fig. 2.21. Disruption of tracking occurs when the amplitude of jump A=0,67.

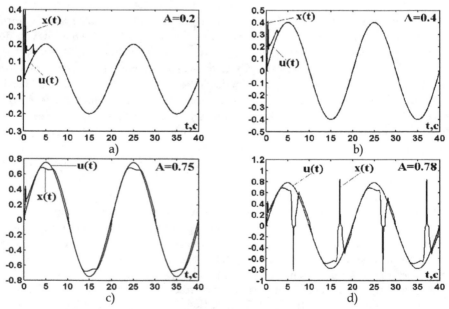

Fig. 2.22. Responses to input action $A\sin(\pi/10)$ at various amplitudes A an input signal.

Disruption of tracking occurs when the amplitude A=0,78.
Consider the fuzzy system PLL generator with a digital phase detector [8]. Version execution a diagram of a phase detector is shown in fig.2.23 a.

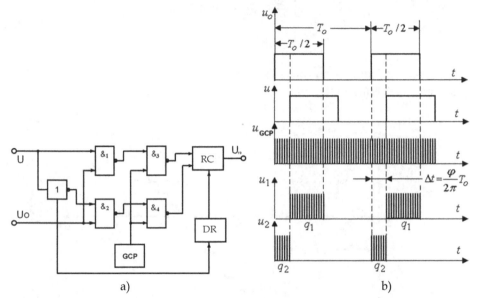

a)   b)

Fig. 2.23. Execution a diagram and principle of operation of a phase detector

The principle of operation of digital phase detector can be explained as follows [7]. At the input of detector come the reference u_o and u input signals, that are previously transformed into meander shape (see. Fig .2.23,b). The positive half-cycle - logical unit, negative - logical zero. We suppose that the periods of both signals are identical and equal T_o, and the phase difference is equal φ. The counting pulses u_{GCP} from the generator counting pulses arrive on an input of 1 reverse counter RC only at coincidence in time of input reference signal and for an input 2 in the presence of reference and absence input signals. At the end of each period, the next number at the output of down reversible counter is equal to the difference between the numbers q_1 and q_2 (see fig.2.23,b) is remembered and the reverse counter is nullified by the device of reset DR.

$K_{FD} = \dfrac{T_o}{2T_c}$ -a constant rate, is equal to the maximum number on the output of the reversible

counter of digital phase detector, T_o- period of reference signal, T_c- period of counting pulses, φ - difference in phase fluctuation (one of which is the reference) of the same frequency, field by to the first and second inputs of the detector (when equality the frequencies of two oscillation, the phase difference of these oscillations is constant).

Sampling interval at phase sample and hold devise is defined as $\delta\varphi = 2\pi\dfrac{T_c}{T_o}$. A phase shift

φ corresponds to a time shift $\Delta t = \dfrac{\varphi}{2\pi}T_o$.

The static discrimination characteristic of the digital phase detector (see fig. 2.24,a) can be represented as the shaper of function, give at on specific intervals

$$Q_{FD}(\varphi) = \begin{cases} \dfrac{2}{\pi}K_{FD}(\dfrac{\pi}{2}-\varphi) & \text{at } 0 \le \varphi \le \pi; \\ \dfrac{2}{\pi}K_{FD}(\varphi-\dfrac{3\pi}{2}) & \text{at } \pi \le \varphi \le 2\pi, \end{cases}$$

(2.5)

And continued periodically on intervals $2k\pi \le \varphi \le 2(k+1)\pi$, $k = 1,2,3...$, and device of sampling-storage DSS (clamp).

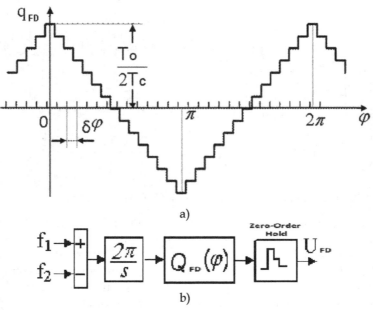

a)

b)

Fig. 2.24. The static discrimination characteristic and block diagram of the digital phase detector

Using the Fourier series expansion is extended periodically at the intervals $2k\pi \le \varphi \le 2(k+1)\pi$, $k = 1,2,3...$, of the functions $Q_{FD}(\varphi)$ we obtain expression in the form

$$Q_{FD}(\varphi) = \frac{8}{\pi^2}K_{FD}[\cos\varphi + \frac{\cos 3\varphi}{9} + \frac{\cos 5\varphi}{25} + \frac{\cos 7\varphi}{49} + ...].$$

(2.6)

As practice shows, for determination of a mathematical model of the static discrimination characteristic of the digital phase detector is sufficient to the first three terms of Fourier series.

When you change the frequencies of input signals, the phase difference becomes a function of time (see the formula (2.4)). Taking into account expressions (2.4), (2.6) and the clamp the block diagram of a digital phase detector under varying frequencies f_1 i f_2 of input signals will have the form, shown at the fig. 2.24,b.

At the output of clamp can be activated a filter for smooth the pulsations, for example, a simple analog filter with a transfer function of an aperiodic link $G_1(s) = k / (s + b)$.

On the basis of the block diagram of the numeral phase detector taking into account inertance of the filter on the output of a detector and a controlling unit on the input of oscillator (a controlling unit is usually also described as an aperiodic link) can be make a mathematical model of system of the PLL frequency control.

The mathematical model of system of PLL with the digital fuzzy controller and digital phase detector, compiled using of interactive system MATLAB, is presented on fig. 2.25.

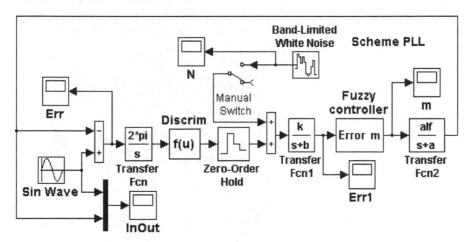

Fig. 2.25. The mathematical model of system of PLL with the digital fuzzy controller and digital phase detector

Filter at the output of the digital phase detector and an controlling element of the generator describe the transfer function:

$$G_1(s) = k / (s + b) = 10 / (s + 12,5), \quad G_2(s) = alf / (s + a) = 3 / (s + 20).$$

The digital fuzzy controller (Fuzzy controller at the fig. 2.25) is fulfilled under the block diagram, with the identical triangular membership function erected in degree and consists of the block of the shaper of sizes A (t) and B (t), the block of comparing of sizes A and B and calculation u_c and the block of normalization output variable[2]. The digitization step is chosen 0,001s. Values of ranges $Am = \theta_{max} = -\theta_{min}$; $Bm = \dot{\theta}_{max} = -\dot{\theta}_{min}$; $Cm = \ddot{\theta}_{max} = -\ddot{\theta}_{min}$; $Dm = m_{max} = -m_{min}$ at adjustment of a fuzzy controller steal up either manually, or automatically by the decision of the optimization task.

At research of the system we will accept, that the difference of frequencies of two fluctuations changes under the sinusoidal law: $\Delta f = 0,2\sin(\pi / 5)$ (i.e. the maximum deviation of frequency of the generator from the set reaches $\pm 20\%$). System of PLL should compensate a deviation of frequency of the generator, therefore a fuzzy controller it is necessary to adjust on the minimum current error of a mismatch in system. As a result of adjustment it is received following optimum parameters of a fuzzy controller, c=1: Am=0,08; Bm=2.5; Cm=50; Dm=100.

Processes in system (see fig.2.25) at setting action $0,2\sin(\pi/5)$ are presented at the fig.2.26.

In the figures $e(t)$ - a mismatch error in frequency at the input of digital phase detector (a) and its steady form in the dynamic mode (b), $\theta(t)$ - error at the output of phase detector–input of fuzzy controller (c) and its steady form in the dynamic mode (d), $m(t)$ - an operating pressure on an output of an fuzzy controller,(e), $u(t)$ and $x(t)$ - an input and output of the system (see fig.2.26) accordingly (f).

Transition process in the system ends in a time not exceeding 0.6sec.The maximum dynamic error of a mismatch on frequency on an input of the phase detector on setting action $0,2\sin(\pi/5)$ does not exceed $4\cdot10^{-3}$. Research shows the system (see fig.2.25), the fuzzy controller can increase the accuracy of the PLL system is almost two orders of magnitude compared to the system without controller.

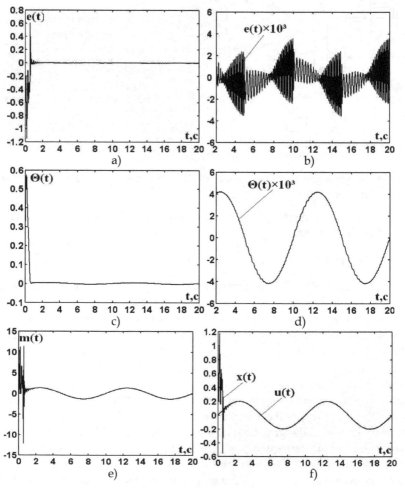

Fig. 2.26. Processes in system at setting action $0,2\sin(\pi/5)$

Application of fuzzy controllers in PLL appropriate. Since the fuzzy controller is a digital correction device, it can be successfully applied in the digital PLL.

2.3 Combined fuzzy-system of PLL
The mathematical model of combined system of PLL with the digital fuzzy controller, made with use of interactive system MATLAB, is presented on fig.2.27.

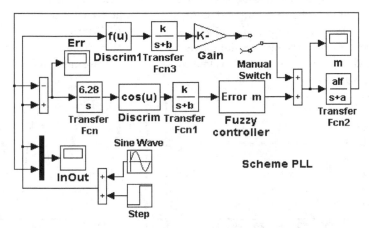

Fig. 2.27. The mathematical model of combined system of PLL with the digital fuzzy controller

Automatic control system name combined (or system with the combined control) when in the law of control except an error, derivatives and integrals from an error, additional communications on setting action or/and on revolting action are entered.

The basic system in detail considered earlier [fig. 2.18], consists of the phase detector which block diagram is resulted on fig. 2.17 and is presented by the comparison device, an integrating link with factor 2π (Transfer Fcn), the discrimination characteristic $\cos\varphi$ (Discrim) and the low-pass filter on an output of the detector with transfer function $G_1(s) = k / (s + b)$ (Transfer Fcn1), an fuzzy controller (Fuzzy controller), the generator operated pressure, with transfer function $G_2(s) = alf / (s + a)$ (Transfer Fcn2), and an individual negative feedback.

Filter at the output of the detector and an operating element of the generator have the transfer functions in a numerical kind: $G_1(s) = k / (s + b) = 10 / (s + 12,5)$; $G_2(s) = alf / (s + a) = 3 / (s + 20)$.

The digital fuzzy controller with the identical triangular membership functions erected in degree (Fuzzy controller at the fig.2.27) is executed under the basic scheme. The fuzzy controller consists of the block of the shaper of sizes A (t)and B (t), the block of comparison of sizes A (t)and B (t) and calculation u_c and the block of normalization output variable[2] The digitization step is chosen 0,001s. Values of ranges ($Am = \theta_{max} = -\theta_{min}$; $Bm = \dot{\theta}_{max} = -\dot{\theta}_{min}$; $Cm = \ddot{\theta}_{max} = -\ddot{\theta}_{min}$; $Dm = m_{max} = -m_{min}$) get out at controller adjustment. Additional coupling on setting action includes following elements: the frequency discriminator with the discrimination characteristic (Discrim1)

$$K(e) = K_d e \exp\{-\frac{e^2}{\Delta^2}\},$$

where $K_d = 1$ and $\Delta = 1$, and the filter of the bottom frequencies with transfer function $G_3(s) = k / (s + b)$ (Transfer Fcn3), and the amplifier (Gain) with changeable factor of strengthening.

From consideration of mathematical model of combined system of PLL with a digital fuzzy controller it is visible, that it is impossible to carry out the transfer function of additional coupling equal to return transfer function of generator $1 / G_2(s) = (s + a) / alf = (s + 20) / 3$, i.e. it is impossible to carry out absolute invariancy of system from setting action, but it is possible to reduce a dynamic error of system by selection of transmission factor of amplifier Gain (to reach ε -invariancy).

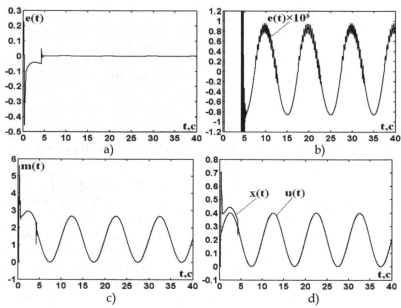

Fig. 2.28. Processes in system at setting action $0,2[1 + \sin(\pi / 5)]$ (at the disconnected coupling on setting action)

At research of the combined system we will accept, that the difference of frequencies of two fluctuations changes under the sinusoidal law: $\Delta f = 0,2[1 + \sin(\pi / 5)]$ (i.e. the maximum deviation of frequency of the generator operated pressure, from the set reaches 40%). System of PLL should compensate a deviation of frequency of the generator, therefore an fuzzy controller it is necessary to adjust on the minimum current error of a mismatch in system. As a result of adjustment it is received following optimum parameters of fuzzy controller:

Am=0,03; Bm=0.5; Cm=10; Dm=20; c=1.

Optimum factor of strengthening of amplifier Gain K=7,3.

Processes in system (see fig.2.27) at setting action $0,2[1 + \sin(\pi / 5)]$ are presented at the fig.2.28 (at the disconnected coupling on setting action) and at the fig. 2.29 (at the included coupling on setting action). In drawings: a) and b) $e(t)$ - a dynamic error of a mismatch on frequency on an input of the phase detector in the transitive and established modes, c) $m(t)$ - operating pressure on an output of an fuzzy controller, d) $u(t)$ and $x(t)$ - an input and output of the system accordingly.

The maximum dynamic error of a mismatch on frequency on an input of the phase detector in system of PLL at the disconnected coupling on setting action $0,2[1 + \sin(\pi / 5)]$ in the established dynamic mode makes size $9,8 \cdot 10^{-4}$, and the maximum dynamic error of a mismatch on frequency on an input of the phase detector in system of PLL at the included coupling on setting action $0,2[1 + \sin(\pi / 5)]$ in the established dynamic mode makes size $3,6 \cdot 10^{-4}$. Transient time (time of capture of an input signal) in system at the disconnected coupling on setting action makes 4,3 seconds, and in system at the included coupling on setting action 2,5 seconds

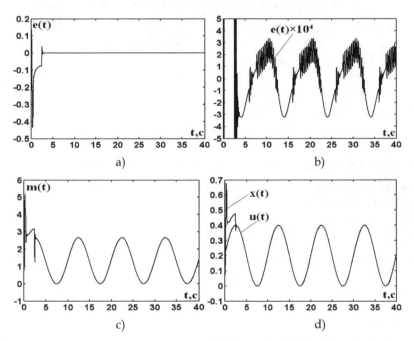

Fig. 2.29. Processes in system at setting action $0,2[1 + \sin(\pi / 5)]$ (at the included coupling on setting action)

Research combined (with additional coupling on setting action) system of PLL with a digital fuzzy controller by method of mathematical modeling has shown, that additional coupling on setting action reduces the established dynamic error in 2,7 times, and time of capture of an input signal in 1,7 times, in comparison with these indicators in system without coupling on setting action.

Ever more reduce the steady dynamic error can be achieved if in additional coupling on setting action to enter ideal forcing link with transfer function $G(Ts+1)$, where $T = 1/a$, and in the factor G should enter k factor and additional adjusting factor K.

The combined system of PLL with the digital fuzzy controller and forcing link shown in Fig.2.30.

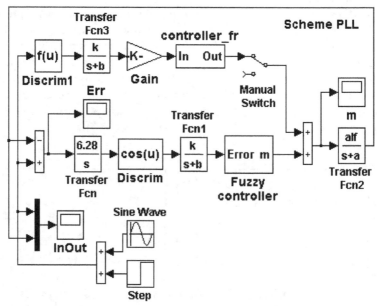

Fig. 2.30. The combined system of PLL with the digital fuzzy controller and forcing link

In this system a digital ideal forcing link (controller _fr) realizes expression (using the first difference from a signal arriving on its input):

$$U_{out}(n) = k\{U_{in}(n) + T[U_{in}(n) - U_{in}(n-1)] / h\} .$$

The scheme of a digital ideal forcing link is resulted on fig. 2.31 (only this link the system on fig. 2.30 differs from the system shown on fig. 2.27). At research of the combined system we will accept, that the difference of frequencies of two fluctuations changes under the sinusoidal law: $\Delta f = 0,2[1 + \sin(\pi / 5)]$ (i.e. the maximum deviation of frequency of the generator, from the set reaches 40%).

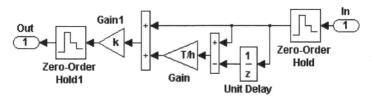

Fig. 2.31. The scheme of a digital ideal forcing link

System of PLL should compensate a deviation of frequency of the generator, therefore a fuzzy controller it is necessary to adjust on the minimum current error of a mismatch in system. As a result of adjustment it is received the same optimum parameters of an fuzzy controller, as in the system shown on fig.2.27: Am=0,03; Bm=0.5; Cm=10; Dm=20; c=1. But the optimum amplification factor of amplifier Gain will be another: K=0,82.

Processes in system (see fig.2.30) at setting action $0,2[1+\sin(\pi/5)]$ are presented on fig.2.32 (at the disconnected coupling on setting action) and on fig. 2.33 (at the included coupling on setting action). In drawings: a) and b) $e(t)$ - a dynamic error of a mismatch on frequency on an input of the phase detector in the transitive and established modes, c) $m(t)$ - operating pressure on an output of an fuzzy controller, d) $u(t)$ and $x(t)$ - an input and output of the system accordingly.

The maximum dynamic error of a mismatch on frequency on an input of the phase detector in system of PLL at the disconnected coupling on setting action $0,2[1+\sin(\pi/5)]$ in the established dynamic mode makes size $9,8\cdot10^{-4}$, and the maximum dynamic error of a mismatch on frequency on an input of the phase detector in system of PLL at the included coupling on setting action $0,2[1+\sin(\pi/5)]$ in the established dynamic mode makes size $2,5\cdot10^{-4}$.

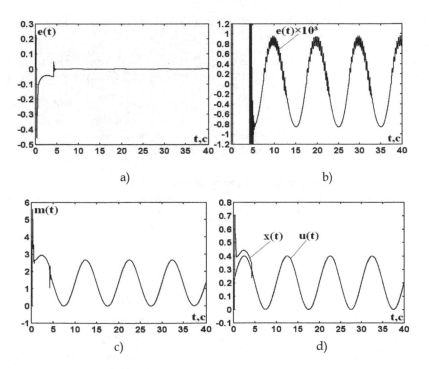

Fig. 2.32. Processes in system at setting action $0,2[1+\sin(\pi/5)]$ (at the disconnected coupling on setting action)

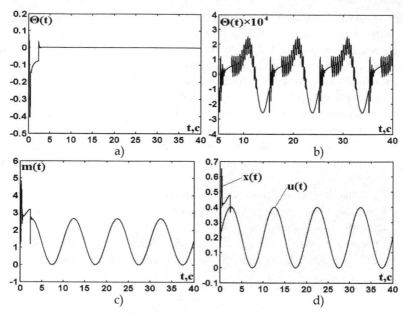

Fig. 2.33. Processes in system at setting action $0,2[1 + \sin(\pi / 5)]$ (at the included coupling on setting action)

Transient time (time of capture of an input signal) in system at the disconnected coupling on setting action makes 4,3 seconds, and in system at the included coupling on setting action 2,4 seconds.

Thus, in system of PLL with the digital fuzzy controller and a digital ideal forcing link additional communication on setting action reduces the established dynamic error in 3,9 times, and time of capture of an input signal in 1,79 times, in comparison with these indicators in system without communication on setting influence.

2.4 System of PLL with the phase-frequency discriminators

The phase-frequency discriminator has the specific characteristic which can be presented a non-linear element of type "saturation" (see fig. 2.34, a,b) that allows to work in broad range of frequencies.

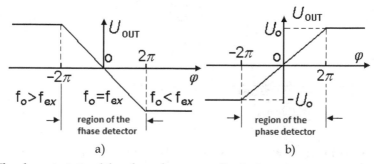

Fig. 2.34. The characteristic of the phase-frequency discriminator

Discrimination characteristic phase-frequency discriminator (see Fig.2.34, a) can be described by

$$K(\varphi) = \begin{cases} 2\pi K_d & \text{at } \varphi < -2\pi, \\ -K_d\varphi & \text{at } -2\pi \le \varphi \le 2\pi, \\ -2\pi K_d & \text{at } \varphi > 2\pi. \end{cases}$$

In interactive system MATLAB the diagram of discriminator with the characteristic presented at the fig. 2.34,a it is possible to present as the connections of three block (see fig. 2.35): the switch (Switch), the inverter (Gain) and the saturation block (Saturation). At the positive signal of an error on a discriminator input (in block Switch parameter Threshold =0.000001) closed a upper contact of switch and the is formed a plot of characteristic $\varphi \ge 0$, at the negative signal of an error on input discriminator is closed bottom contact and formed a plot of characteristic $\varphi \le 0$. Levels of restrictions in a block of saturation (Saturation) are $\pm 2\pi K_d$.

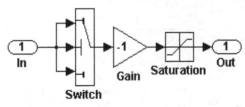

Fig. 2.35. Diagram of discriminator with the characteristic presented at the fig. 2.34,a

Discrimination characteristic phase-frequency discriminator (see fig.2.34, b) can be described by

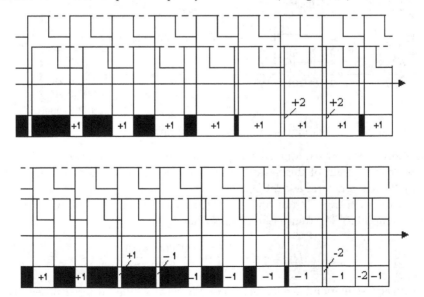

Fig. 2.36. Operating principle of phase-frequency discriminator

$$K(\varphi) = \begin{cases} -U_o & \text{at } \varphi < -2\pi, \\ \dfrac{U_o}{2\pi}\phi & \text{at } -2\pi \le \varphi \le 2\pi, \\ U_o & \text{at } \varphi > 2\pi. \end{cases}$$

In an interactive system MATLAB the diagram of discriminator with the characteristic presented on fig 2.34,b can present only a block saturation (Saturation).

Phase-frequency discriminator with a characteristic shown in fig.2.34, b, is a machine that has five states (-2, -1, 0, +1, +2), and switchable on a leading edge of the reference signal and feedback signal. Reference signal adds to the state machine unit and the feedback signal on the contrary, subtracts. Operating principle of phase-frequency discriminator is shown at the fig.2.36 (darkened color is shown zero state machine).

At fig.2.37 shows the model on which to explore the two systems having the same phase-frequency discriminator (Discrim1), made under the scheme fig.2.35, and the same voltage-controlled oscillator (TransferFcn1), with a transfer function $G(s) = alf / s$. Transfer coefficient VCO $alf = K_G = 104$ rad / ($s \cdot V$).

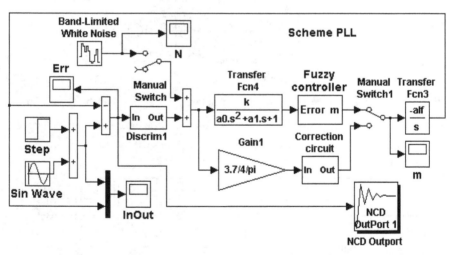

Fig. 2.37. System of PLL with phase-frequency discriminator

With the closure of a switch ManualSwitch1 in the down position simulated the system of PLL. The block diagram of this system, except for blocks Discrim1 and Transfer Fcn1 (is simulating the discriminator and VCO), have two additional blocks: Gain (transfer factor of detector K_{Fd} =3,7/(4π) V/rad) and block Correction circuit (an active filter with an operational amplifier). The transfer function of filter

$$F(s) \cong \frac{\tau_2 s + 1}{\tau_1 s(\tau_3 s + 1)} = \frac{3330(s + 4,55)}{s(s + 100)}.$$

System with active filter on the operational amplifier was studied when exposed to on input of an equivalent harmonic signal $u(t) = 10 + 5\sin 2\pi Ft$ with carrier frequency $F = 0,1 Hz$.

The processes in the system of the PLL frequency control with active filter Correction circuit(see fig.2.37) are shown in fig.2.38 where $u(t)$ – an input action, $x(t)$ –an output system (see fig.2.38,a), $e(t) \equiv$ Err – a mismatch error on the input of the discriminator (see fig.2.38, b). $m(t)$ - a filter output (see fig.2.38,c). At fig.2.38, shows reaction system on step input $u(t) = 10$.

The results show that the system of the PLL frequency control with active filter Correction circuit has a very high exactness working off entrance influence: a dynamic mismatch error for a given harmonic signal is $4,2 \cdot 10^{-4}$ or 0.082% of the amplitude of input sine impact. System performance is also very high. Settling time is approximately equal to 0.06, but the transient process is oscillatory, with overshoot almost 60% .

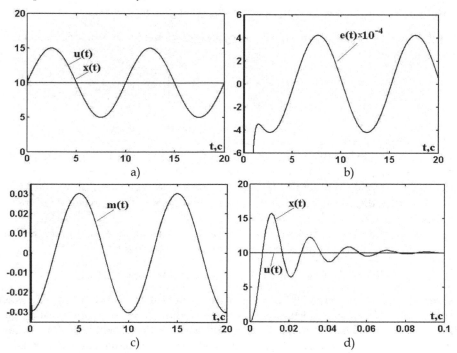

Fig. 2.38. The processes in the system of the PLL frequency control with active filter

With the closure of a switch ManualSwitch1 in the upper position simulated the system of PLL with a low -pass filter LPF pass second and digital fuzzy controller (Fuzzy controller at the fig.2.37) which is executed by the block diagram. The controller consists of the block of the shaper of sizes A (t) and B (t), the block of comparing of sizes A and B and calculation u_c and the block of normalization output variable (block 3 collected by the diagram)[2]. The filter has the transfer function

$$F(s) = \frac{k}{a_0 s^2 + a_1 s + 1} = \frac{0,002}{0,008s^2 + 0,18s + 1},$$

which can also be written as

$$F(s) = \frac{0,25}{s^2 + 22,5s + 125} = \frac{0,25}{(s + 10)(s + 12,5)}.$$

The mismatch error $\theta(t)$ from an output of a low-pass filter arrives on a analog-digital converter (AD converter) (Zero-Order Hold), included at the input of a fuzzy controller. A quantization step of AD converter $h = 0,01s$. On an output of a fuzzy controller is included the digital/analog converter (Zero-OrderHold1).

For simplification of normalization (recalculation of values of signals in values of elements of universal set) ranges of change input and output signals (parameters of a fuzzy controller) we is accepting by symmetric:

$$\theta_{max} = -\theta_{min}; \ \dot{\theta}_{max} = -\dot{\theta}_{min}; \ \ddot{\theta}_{max} = -\ddot{\theta}_{min}; \ m_{max} = -m_{min}.$$

Then recalculation of values of signals in values of elements of universal set perform according to the formulas [2]

$$\left. \begin{aligned} u_1^* &= (\theta^* + A_m) / (2A_m); \\ u_2^* &= (\dot{\theta}^* + B_m) / (2B_m); \\ u_3^* &= (\ddot{\theta}^* + C_m) / (2C_m). \end{aligned} \right\} .$$

Values of ranges ($Am = \theta_{max} = -\theta_{min}$; $Bm = \dot{\theta}_{max} = -\dot{\theta}_{min}$; $Cm = \ddot{\theta}_{max} = -\ddot{\theta}_{min}$; $Dm = m_{max} = -m_{min}$) at adjustment of a fuzzy controller steal up either manually, or automatically by the decision of the optimization task. The system of PLL with a low pass filter LPF and a digital fuzzy controller was investigated when exposed at input an equivalent harmonic signal $u(t) = 10 + 5\sin 2\pi Ft$ with carrier frequency $F = 0,1Hz$.

The adjustment of a fuzzy controller is carried out by criterion of a minimum of a dynamic error. Is received following optimal parameters of fuzzy controller :

$$Am = 0,0174; \ Bm = 0,2458; \ Cm = 4,6607; \ Dm = 249,89.$$

When setting up a fuzzy controller in an interactive system MATLAB we using a block NCD (Nonlinear Control Design), which implements the method of dynamic optimization for the design of control systems. This tool is designed for use with Simulink, automatically adjusts a system parameters (in the system fig.2.37 adjusted parameters of the fuzzy controller, Am, Bm, Cm, Dm,), based on certain constraints on the temporal characteristics (time of regulating and overshoot for reaction to a step action and limits for the dynamic mismatch error).

The processes in the system of the PLL frequency control with low pass filter LPF and the digital fuzzy controller (see fig.2.37) are shown in Fig.2.39 where $u(t)$ - a input action, $x(t)$ – a system output (see fig.2.39, a) $e(t) \equiv$ Err – a mismatch error at the input of the discriminator (see fig.2.39, b), $m(t)$ - an output of fuzzy controller (see fig.2.39, c).

The maximum dynamic error (except for initial burst at the moment of signal capture) does not exceed $4,2 \cdot 10^{-3}$ or $0,82\%$ from amplitude of a sinusoid.

At fig.2.39, d shows the system response to a step action $u(t) = 10$ on the output of system $x(t)$ and the output a fuzzy controller $m(t)$. Transient process have overshoot 3,4%. The system fulfills input action in a time not exceeding 0,16 sec.

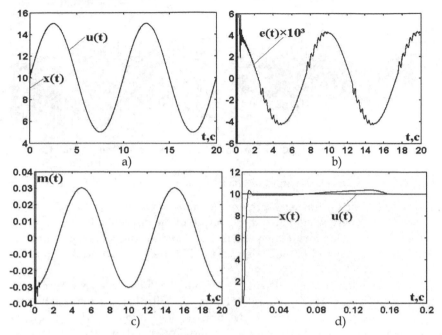

a)

b)

c)

d)

Fig. 2.39. The processes in the system of the PLL frequency control with low pass filter LPF and the fuzzy controller

We remark that the PLL with a low pass filter LPF, but without the digital fuzzy controller, has no stability.

Thus, can conclude that the PLL with a low pass filter LPF and the digital fuzzy controller has a bad quality indicators than the PLL with an active filter on the operational amplifier, but has transient process (overshoot).

Now consider the operation of these systems in the presence of internal noise. In this case, the switch Manual Switch on Fig.2.37 is closed in the upper position, which corresponds to the filing of the noise signal - a stationary white noise (Band-Limited White Noise) on the output phase-frequency detector (Discrim1). Noise signal n (t) represented on Fig.2.40. Amplitude of the noise emissions of approximately 1% of the input signal.

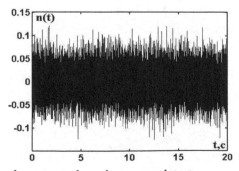

Fig. 2.40. Noise signal on the output phase-frequency detector

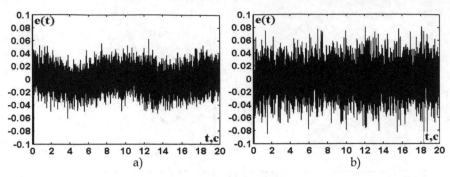

Fig. 2.41. Mismatch errors on the input of phase-frequency discriminator

At fig.2.41 are presented mismatch errors on the input of phase-frequency discriminator at the presence of stationary white noise at the output of the discriminator in the system of a phase-frequency locked loop with low pass filter LPF and the digital fuzzy controller Fuzzy controller (see fig.2.41 a) and in the system of the PLL frequency control with active filter Correction circuit (see Fig.2.41, b).

As seen from the oscillograms the system of system of the PLL frequency control with a low pass filter LPF and a digital fuzzy controller Fuzzy controller has less mismatch error at the input phase-frequency discriminator in the presence of stationary white noise than the system phase-frequency locked loop with active filter Correction circuit.

2.5 Servomechanism of synchronous and in-phase rotation shaft part of drive from the alternating reference voltage

The mathematical model of servomechanism in an interactive system MATLAB is presented in fig.2.42.

The mathematical model of the phase detector is represented serial connection of comparison device, the nonlinearity (Discrim) $K(\varphi) = K_d \sin\varphi$, where K_d - coefficient of conversion of the phase detector, and $\varphi(t) \equiv e(t)$ - a mismatch error on a phase detector input, and the low-pass filter LPF (Transfer Fcn).

Transfer function of a low-pass filter LPF (Transfer Fcn)[2] is

$$G_1(s) = \frac{a}{s+a} = \frac{12,5}{s+12,5}, \quad a = 1/\tau, \quad \tau = RC = 0,08 \text{ s.}$$

Transfer function of the amplifier of power-modulator P-M (Transfer Fcn1)[2]

$$G_2(s) = \frac{K}{s+a_1} = \frac{500}{s+100}, \quad a_1 = 1/T_y, \quad T_y = 0,01 \text{ s.}$$

Transfer function of engine EE (Zero-Pole)[2]

$$G_3(s) = \frac{\alpha}{s(s+b)} = \frac{90}{s(s+10)},$$

where $b = 1/T_{db}$; $T_{db} = 0,1 \ c$; $\alpha = Kdb/T_{db}$; $Kdb = 9 \ rad/(V \cdot s)$

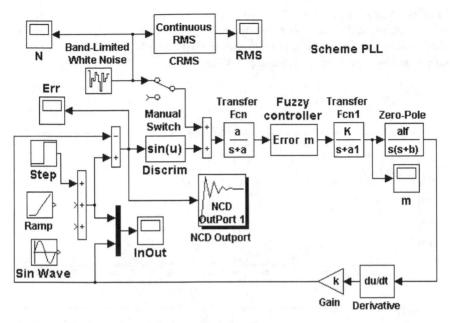

Fig. 2.42. The mathematical model of servomechanism

Transfer function of the tacho-generator (Gane + Derivation)[2]

$$G_4(s) = ks \, , \ k = 0,03 \ V \cdot s \, / \, rad.$$

At adjustment of a fuzzy controller in interactive system MATLAB we use unit NCD (Nonlinear Control Design) which implements a method of dynamic optimization for designing of management systems.

The system is researched at typical influences on an input: input: 1.single jump, 2.the equivalent of a harmonic signal $u(t) = 0,5 \sin 2\pi Ft$ with carrying frequency $F = 0,1Hz$ and 3. a linear signal Ramp $u(t) = t$.

Adjustment of a fuzzy controller is carried out by criterion of a minimum of a dynamic error at the equivalent harmonic signal without influence of noise on a phase detector output (contacts of switch are closed in the lower position). Receive the following optimal parameters of fuzzy controller: Am=0,072; Bm=0,168; Cm=1,579; Dm=61,798.

Processes in servomechanism (fig. 2.42 see) with a fuzzy controller without influence of noise on a phase detector output (contacts of switch Manual Switch are closed in the lower position) are shown on fig. 2.43 at an single jump of an input signal, on fig. 2.44 at influence of the equivalent harmonic signal $u(t) = 0,5 \sin 2\pi F$, with carrying frequency $F = 0,1Hz$ and on fig. 2.45 at of the linear signal $u(t) = t$. In pictures $u(t)$ – input influence, $x(t)$ – a system output, $e(t) \equiv Err$ – a mismatch error on a discriminator input, $m(t)$ - a signal on an engine input.

At an single jump of an input signal transient phenomenon has overshoot of 13 % and ends at time 2,8 (see fig. 2.43). The installed dynamic error is equal to zero. At action of a harmonic signal the maximum dynamic error (except for the release initial at the moment of signal capture) does not exceed 0,5% from amplitude of a sinusoid (see fig. 2.44). At action of the linear signal $u(t) = t$ transient phenomenon comes to an end in time, not exceeding 2c, and the installed dynamic error is close to zero (approximately $2 \cdot 10^{-4}$). Therefore the signal output practically repeats input action (fig. 2.45 see).

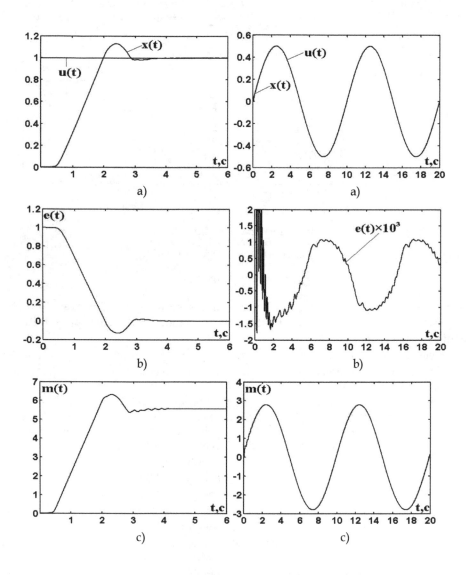

Fig. 2.43. Processes in servomechanis at an single jump

Fig. 2.44. Processes in servomechanism at the equivalent harmonic signal

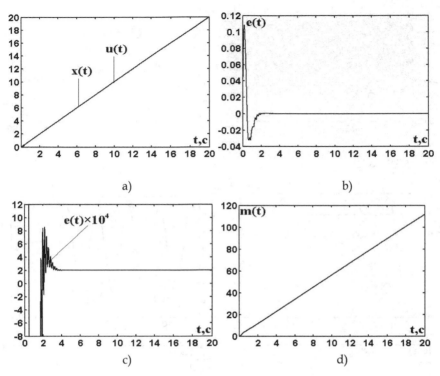

Fig. 2.45. Processes in servomechanism at the linear action

Adjustment of a fuzzy controller by criterion of a minimum of a dynamic error at action of noise on a phase detector output (contacts of switch Manual Switch are closed in the upper position) is enough difficult. The noise signal n (t) - a stationary white noise (Band-Limited White Noise) on a phase detector output (Discrim) is presented on fig. 2.46,a. Current value of a root from root-mean-square of a noise signal (root mean squared value) calculated in unit CRMS is shown at the fig. 2.46b

Instead of fuzzy controller FC (Fuzzy Controller), is executed under the basic scheme, with identical triangular functions of an accessory in the presence of a noise signal on an output of the phase detector for obtaining of a smaller dynamic error in system it is expedient to use fuzzy controller (Fuzzy Controller), fulfilled on the schematic circuit with identical exponential membership functions. For the purpose of an exception (or the considerable decrease) a dynamic error at tracking controlling action, on an output of a fuzzy controller two integrators for giving to a closed circuit of follow-up system astaticism the second order are included.

At system adjustment, except selection of values of ranges Am, Bm, Cm, Dm and parameter c of exponential membership functions in a fuzzy controller, it was required to optimize coefficient k of the tacho-generator of an alternating current. At adjustment of a fuzzy controller in interactive system MATLAB is used unit NCD (Nonlinear Control Design) and received the following optimal parameters of system:

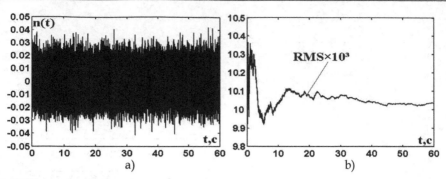

Fig. 2.46. Noise signal

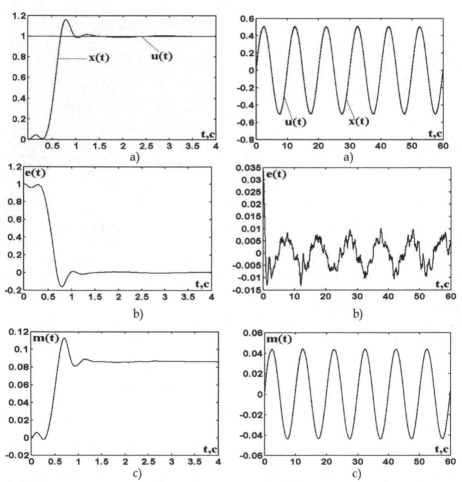

Fig. 2.47. Processes in system at the unit step

Fig. 2.48. Processes in system at the equivalent harmonic signal

$$h=0,01; \ Am=3,9822; \ Bm=8,6779; \ Cm=86,357; \ Dm=116.,64; \ c=0,19476;$$

$$a=12,5; a1=100; K=500; \ alf=90; b=10; k=1,2865.$$

Processes in servomechanism (fig. 2.42 see) with a fuzzy controller at influence of noise on a phase detector output (contacts of switch Manual Switch are closed in the upper position) are shown on fig. 2.47 at an unit step of an input signal, on fig. 2.48 at action of the equivalent harmonic signal $u(t) = 0,5\sin 2\pi F$, with carrying frequency $F = 0,1Hz$ and on fig. 2.49 at action of the linear signal $u(t) = t$. In figure $u(t)$ – an input action, $x(t)$ – a system output, $e(t) \equiv Err$ – a mismatch error on input of a discriminator, $m(t)$ - a signal on an input of engine.

At an single jump of an input signal transient phenomenon has overshoot of 16% and comes to an end during 0,93 s (fig. 2.47 see). The installed dynamic error is equal to zero. At action of a harmonic signal the maximum dynamic error (except for initial burst at the moment of signal capture) does not exceed 1,5% from amplitude of a sinusoid (fig. 2.48 see).

At action of the linear signal $u(t) = t$ transient phenomenon ends at time, not exceeding 1,2 s, and the installed dynamic error does not exceed $8 \cdot 10^{-3}$. The signal output practically repeats input action (fig. 2.49 see).

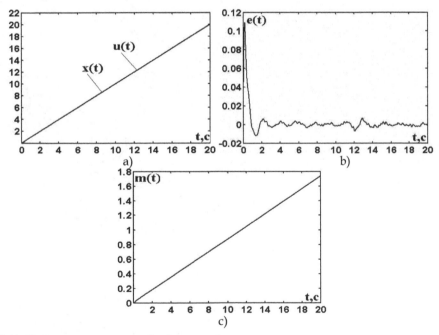

Fig. 2.49. Processes in system at the linear action

3. References

[1] Klepper Dzh., Frenk Dzh. A phase-and frequency-locked frequency. - M.: Energiya, 1977. - 440 s.

[2] Gostev V.I., Skurtov S.N. Fuzzy systems frequency and phase auto-tuning: monograph. - Nezhin: OOO "Vidavnictvo -Aspekt-Poligraf", 2010. 388 p.

[3] Gostev V.I. Fuzzy-system phase-locked loop oscillator // Zviyazok. - 2008. - № 4.

[4] Gostev V.I., Baranov A.A. Storchak K.P. The system clock with a digital fuzzy controller // Zviyazok. - 2007. - № 3 (71). - S.51-54.

[5] Gostev V.I., Kunah N.I., Drobik A.V., Nevol'ko V.A. Investigation of processes in the systems and phase locked loop in the presence of internal noise // Naukovi zapiski Ukrains'kogo naukovo-doslidnogo institutu zvyazku. Naukovo-virobnichii zbirnik. - 2008. - №6(8). p. 51-54

[6] Gostev V.I., Krihoveckii G.Ya., Storchak K.P. The system clock with a digital PID controller with random phase changes of the input // Visnik Derzhavnogo universitetu Informacyino-komunikacyinih tehnologyi. - 2007.- Spec. vip., p. 72-75

[7] Vagapov V.B., Burlyai I.Yu., Ryumshin N.A. Theory of electronic tracking systems. - K.: Tehnika, 2002. - 284 p.

[8] Gostev V.I. Fuzzy-system phase-locked loop oscillator with a digital phase detector // Zviyazok. - 2008. - № 5-6 (81-82). - p. 68-72.

6

Simulation of Rough Surfaces and Analysis of Roughness by MATLAB

F. Gascón[1] and F. Salazar[2]
[1]*Departamento de Física Aplicada II. ETS Arquitectura (US).*
Avda. Reina Mercedes 2, 41012 Sevilla
[2]*Departamento de Física Aplicada. ETSI Minas (UPM).*
C/Ríos Rosas 21, 28003 Madrid
Spain

1. Introduction

The simulation of physical phenomena in science and engineering has become an important tool because it allows studying a wide range of real problems. On the other hand, it allows resolving problems that, because of its difficulty, it would be not possible to solve by analytical methods. Moreover, simulation is fast and versatile since it permits to vary parameters of the problem easily, allowing analyzing the effect of the modification of them in the response of the system examined.

Simulation requires programming, for which there are many different languages. Each of them has a particular internal structure that distinguishes it from others. Therefore, depending on the problem to be study, it may be advisable to use a specific programming language.

In the scientific-technical context MATLAB has been increasingly used by the great advantages that it offers. For example, the instructions are interpreted and not compiled, the user to enter commands interactively. The data processing is flexible. They can be read and stored in two different formats, ASCII and MATLAB format. ASCII has the advantage that the data and results may be used for other programs. However, MATLAB format may be faster. On the other hand, many functions and libraries of MATLAB are written MATLAB language, enabling the user access to the source files. It is possible to execute instructions of the operating system without exiting the program. Moreover, this language is portable in platforms as Windows or Apple, commonly employed by the researcher. From the point of view of numerical calculation, the use of matrices as basic elements makes it efficient and easy to employ, being also possible to perform graphics of curves and surfaces. Finally, the operations can be performed with simple and intuitive expressions similar to those used in science and engineering.

MATLAB has been used for many applications in general physics, mathematics, optics, electronics, chemistry, biology, medicine, and artificial intelligence, among others. Now we want to employ MATLAB to simulate an optical procedure to measure surface roughness. Thus, the aim of this paper is the determination of the roughness of a surface from the analysis of the speckle pattern obtained in the far field, when the object is illuminated with a monochromatic beam perpendicularly to its surface.

The surface analysis of materials is of great importance, since many technological problems require, previously, the study of the surface state. One of the parameters of any material that changes easily with time is the roughness. Indeed, in many sectors, as civil engineering, architecture, mechanical engineering, etc. materials of different forms and properties are commonly employed, which must meet certain requirements to ensure their use. For this reason, the measurement of some surface parameters, as roughness, must be taking into consideration.

There are different methods for determining roughness. One of the most employed is the profilometer (see next section). However, this paper deals with an optical method based on the speckle interferometry which has some advantages. The methodology is fast, accurate, and does not contact the specimen. Above all this we will talk in the next sections

2. Discretization of the problem. Roughness

A classic device for measuring surface roughness is the mechanical profilometer which is formed by a tiny stylus (with a small ball), and a displacement sensor. The typ moves along a straight line parallel to the surface plane and records the displacements in the perpendicular direction, tracing out the outline of the surface. If the ball has a diameter bd it can not be inserted between two grooves whose distance is less than bd, being only possible to detect the topographic level with a distance between grooves greater than bd.

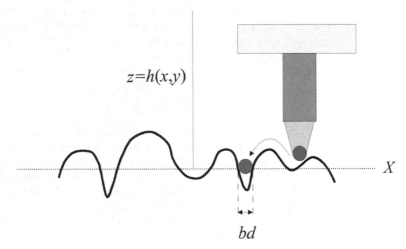

Fig. 1. Classical device for measuring roughness. Observe that when the diameter of the end needle bd is greater than the groove, the transducer can not reproduce the high frequencies of the surface outline.

In this article we are interested in using a speckle technique to measure the roughness of a surface. From a didactic viewpoint, the explained idea of the profilometer may be employed to understand the sampling, when a rough surface is simulated by MATLAB.

To start let us suppose a one-dimensional rough surface, and then we extend the results to the case of two variables.

The height of the rough surface can also be measured by sampling. With this aim let us consider a curve $z=h(x)$ as shown in Fig. (2), aligned on the OX axis. For sampling the function $h(x)$ the X co-ordinate axis is divided into intervals of length u measured with respect the origin O resulting in a system of aligned points of co-ordinates 0, u, 2u, 3u,... The distance u between two neighbor points, i.e. the sample interval, is called the sampling period and its value is chosen depending of the function to be investigated (in our case the form of the surface). The distance u between two points may be likened to the ball diameter bd of the profilometer.

Fig. 2. Rough surface represented by $z=h(x)$. If the sampling period is chosen small, the discrete function $h(xp)$ is very similar to the actual surface.

If N samples are taken, they form a string of N integers for which a value $z_p = h(xp)$ is given. This set of numbers is collecting in a matrix IF of dimension $N \times 1$. The range of variation of the index p is 1, 2, 3,..., N, and it represents the element p of the string. Therefore this index p is related with the sampling period as follows: x = 0, u, 2u, 3u, ..., $(p-1)u$. Two neighboring elements of the IF matrix contain the values of the surface heights of the grooves of two points on the reference plane separated u meters.

As it will see, when studying the phenomenon of diffraction in the far field, the Fourier transformation must be applied. Therefore, we need to study also the sampling in the frequency domain.

When calculating the finite discrete Fourier transform (DFT) of the IF matrix of N elements, a new set of N numbers is obtained which is grouped in another matrix FO of dimension $N \times 1$. Due to the Fourier transform is performed from the discrete values of IF, the result is also discrete. As a result the distance between two points of the transformed numbers in frequency domain is also quantified. Denoting by v (1,2,...N) the index for the matrix FO, the row index represents the harmonic components whose frequencies are α= 0, 1 / (Nu), 2 / (Nu), ..., (v-1) / (Nu). The sampling frequency is defined as $f_s \equiv 1/u$, measured in m^{-1}, and represents the number of measures per unit length. By using this expression, spatial frequency components may also be written in the form α = 0, f_s / N, 2 f_s / N, ..., (v-1) f_s/N. In general, the matrix element v of FO represents the harmonic α_v in the space of frequencies

$$\alpha_v = \frac{(v-1)}{Nu}. \tag{1}$$

Thus there is a correspondence between the index v = 1, 2, 3, ..., N, and the spatial frequency α by means of the factor (f_s/N). Obviously, the sampling process implies that some information about the sampled function is loosed, because no value between two neighboring points is known. However, depending on the physical problem studied, using the Shannon theorem, the sample interval can be modified so that the data be enough for numerical calculus.

Taking into account that the expression obtained for representing a point on the OX-axis has the form $(p-1)u$, it seems to be appropriate to change to non-dimensional variables. To do so we divide x for u resulting $(x/u)=(p-1)$, p being $1,2,...,N$. This new variable represents the distance from the origin O to an arbitrary point on OX (Fig.3), measured in units of the sampling period u, and the elements of the matrix IF the surface heights at each point. The same idea applies to frequency domain.

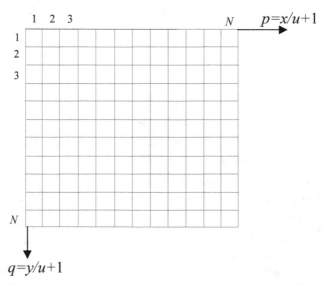

Fig. 3. Reference system without dimensions. The numbers represent the co-ordinates of the matrix elements. At each point (p,q) we assign the corresponding value of the surface height.

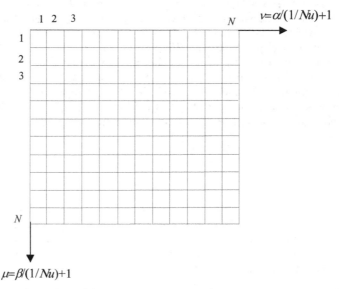

Fig. 4. Space of non-dimensional frequencies. Observe that this grid is initially determined by the matrix IF, then it also has NxN elements

By setting $\alpha(Nu) = \alpha/(1/Nu) = (v-1)$ the spatial frequency α is converted in a dimensionless number representing the basic unities of measurement in this space. Furthermore, $\alpha/(1/Nu)$ is directly the frequency measured in unities of $(1/Nu)$ corresponding to the element v of the matrix FO (Fig.4).

When generating a rough surface the components of IF are real numbers (Fig.3). However, as we will see, the diffraction of a light beam by a surface can introduce phase factors resulting in complex numbers in the elements of matrix IF. In any case the resulting $N \times 1$ string of IF and its fast Fourier transform (FFT), are calculated without difficulty with MATLAB. One advantage of the aforementioned procedure is that the sampling distance u between two points of IF is not directly involved in the numerical calculation, and then it may be considered as a parameter. For this reason the DFT and the FFT of IF, i.e. FO, is universal respect to the parameter u, because the components of FO depend only of the non-dimensional elements of the matrix IF.

Although with the change of variables introduced the components of IF and FO are dimensionless, they have physical meaning. In the present study the p element of IF is a measure of the height of the point at position $x = (p-1)\ u$. FO may be interpreted in the same way. So setting any number to the sampling period u the values obtained for FO show the harmonic amplitudes. For example, giving u the arbitrary value 10^{-4} m, and choosing $N = 64$, we have for the first non-zero frequency components, $\alpha = 156.2, 312.5, 468.8, \ldots$ m^{-1}.

The above is easily applied to a two-dimensional simulation. For this let us consider two coordinates (x,y) of the system OXY (Figs.3,4). For each point of this reference plane is assigned a value which corresponds to the surface height at this point. The data are placed in a two-dimensional array IF. If the sampling is done with the same number of samples, say N, the dimension of the matrix IF is $N \times N$ (Fig. 3). Two points of coordinates (x_i, y_j) and (x_k, y_l) respectively are separated in the matrix IF a distance $((i-j)^2 + (k-l)^2)^{1/2}\ u$, and in dimensionless co-ordinates $((i-j)^2 + (k-l)^2)^{1/2}$. In relation to FO similar expressions may be obtained, but in frequency space. So the spatial frequencies between two points whose coordinates are (α_h, β_k) and (α_l, β_m) is $((h-k)^2 + (l-m)^2)^{1/2}\ (1/Nu)$ in m^{-1}, and without dimensions $((h-k)^2 + (l-m)^2)^{1/2}$.

3. Fraunhofer diffraction with MATLAB

In this section we are interested in the phenomenon of diffraction of light, given the importance to understand the speckle patterns. With this objective let us use the experimental lay-out depicted in Fig.(5). A collimated monochromatic laser beam LB of wavelength λ is directed to a beam splitter BS, which projects the light perpendicularly on a diffracting rough sample S located on the OXY plane. The surface has, in principle, a variable reflectance $R(x,y)$. This means the different scatters that form the surface may have distinct reflection properties. The shape of the radiation beam used determines the geometry and the intensity inside of the illuminated area. If we suppose a beam of homogeneous intensity, its geometry can be expressed easily (in view of the simulation) as an opaque mask M placed on the surface, which has the function to define the illuminated area (Fig. 6). Taking into consideration the most cases studied in optics, we will choose a circular mask of diameter D. An observation screen is placed parallel to the diffracting surface at a distance of z from its plane. The points on the observation plane are specified by means of its x', y' coordinates, with respect to an $O'X'Y'$ coordinate system (on the CCD camera).

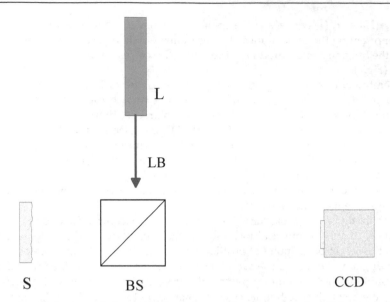

Fig. 5. Experimental set-up. L, laser; LB, laser beam; S, rough sample; BS, beam splitter; CCD camera.

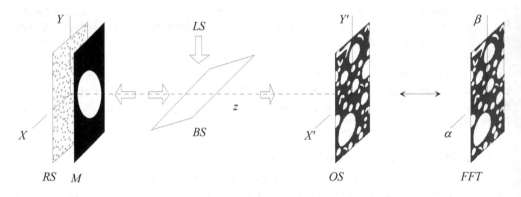

Fig. 6. Steps employed for simulating the rough surface, the aperture, and the speckle pattern. *RS*, rough surface; *M*, mask; *BS*, beam splitter; *FO*, matrix which elements represent the Fourier transform of the reflectance *R*(x,y) on the *OX'Y'* reference system. The intensity $OS = |FO|^2$ can be interpreted also as an angular spectrum (α, β).

Supposing that the scalar diffraction theory applies, the Fresnel-Kirchhoff integral and the theories of Rayleigh-Sommerfeld can be used. However, the calculation of the diffraction pattern through these theories is not always easy to carry out. Sometimes the procedure may be simplified under certain conditions of the problem. So if the linear dimensions of the aperture (mask in our case) is much greater than the wavelength, i.e. D>>λ, and the distance z between the surface and the observation plane is great enough, the paraxial theories apply. In this case, the mathematical expression for the diffracted field depends on the specific dependence between D and z. When expanding the phase term in the Fresnell-Kirchhoff integral is not possible to neglect the quadratic terms that appear we speaks of Fresnel diffraction. On the contrary, if these terms can not be tacked into consideration we have Fraunhofer diffraction. These approximations are the most important cases in the field of the classical optics.

A possible quantitative criterion to be employed in order to use the Fraunhofer approximation, or that of Fresnel, is based on taking a circle of diameter D, which only includes the regions of interest (in the present case the hole of the mask). Let r be the distance from a point on the diffracting surface to the observation point. Let ρ be the distance from the centre of the circle to a point inside its circle. If $2\pi r/\lambda$ varies linearly with ρ, the diffraction is called Fraunhofer diffraction; if the variation has non-linear terms of magnitude comparable with $\pi/2$, the diffraction is said Fresnel diffraction. Therefore, for Fraunhofer diffraction we obtain $z \gg D^2/(4\lambda)$. In short, the diffracting area must be greater than λ and the observation of the intensity pattern must be carried out from a large distance with respect to the scatter surface. In other circumstances, i.e. if the distance z does not fulfil the conditions needed, non-paraxial terms of the phase must be included in the integrand of the Fresnell-Kirchhoff integral (higher expansion coefficients).

Fraunhofer diffraction is related with the Fourier transform which takes an angular spectrum of the reflectance (or transmittance) to be considered. From a physical point of view it is equivalent to observe the phenomenon in the far field (another possibility is to employ a lens and locate the observation plane on its back focal plane). This angular spectrum means that the Fraunhofer diffraction gives the behaviour of the field amplitude for the directions in space. If we use two variables, the amplitude of the diffracted field done through the Fourier transform depends on α and β, which are related with the directions (θ_x, θ_y) through the following expressions

$$\alpha = \frac{\cos\theta_x}{\lambda}, \beta = \frac{\cos\theta_y}{\lambda}. \tag{2}$$

As we will see in the following section, the proposed method for measuring roughness is developed under the supposition that the conditions of the Fraunhofer diffraction apply. Therefore, this case must be translated to the context of MATLAB.

With this aim, the basic results of the preceding section should used. The elements fo_{ij} of the matrix FO belonging to a row or column represent the complex amplitude of two harmonics separated $1/(Nu)$. Therefore the first angular direction is $\theta_x = \cos^{-1}\left((v-1)(\lambda f_s/N)\right)_{v=1} = \frac{\pi}{2}$, which corresponds to the frequency $\alpha = 0$ and the direction for the least coefficient of FO is $\theta_x = \cos^{-1}[(N-1)\lambda f_s/N]$ corresponding to the higher frequency $\alpha = (N-1) f_s/N$. In the case of non-dimensional variables we can use for the two axes $Nu \cos \theta_x/\lambda$, and $Nu \cos\theta_y/\lambda$, respectively. If the diffraction pattern is observed on a plane screen a distance z from the diffusing surface, the spatial frequencies may be related with points on that plane. For small angles θ it can be written:

$$\alpha = \frac{\cos\theta_x}{\lambda} \approx \frac{x'}{\lambda z}, \tag{3}$$

and

$$\beta = \frac{\cos\theta_y}{\lambda} \approx \frac{y'}{\lambda z}.$$

Due to the properties of the Fourier transform, the FFT of the reflectance will contain $N/2$ of positive frequencies, and $N/2$ negative, whose zero spatial frequency occurs at $v = 1$. In the FFT, the independent variable is the frequency, and in the representation with positive and negative frequencies its maximum value will be $f_s/2$. Based on a reflectance matrix of NxN elements located at the XOY axes associated, practically centred in the middle, we calculate FO by means of the FFT, obtaining another matrix from the centre of which the amplitude of the null frequency harmonic component is indicated.

The intensity registered over a direction (α,β) is found by computing the square modulus of the Fourier transform (FT) of the scattering surface delimited by the mask M, after centring the FFT by means of the command $C(i,j)=(-1)^{(i+j)}$.

4. Speckle pattern generation

When a laser beam illuminates a rough surface at scale of the wavelength, the diffraction pattern consists of a random distribution of intensity called speckle. The apparition of speckle may be understood by the fact that the coherent waves falling on the rough surface travel a different optical path from the diffusing surface to the observation point. When the object is rough, the reflectance is a random function on the aperture, and then the corresponding optical paths for the different scatters vary rapidly. As a result, the intensity on the observation screen (or space) also varies very quickly from one point to another of its surroundings, giving brilliant and dark spots irregular in shape.

A model of diffusing and non-absorbent surface is proposed, in which the height of the scatters with respect to a reference plane are supposed as a random variable, and with a gaussian probability density function. A surface of these characteristics is, for example, a metal which is not well polished. We suppose that the rough surface is illuminated by a collimated light beam perpendicularly to its plane resulting in a speckle pattern which is calculated by means of the FFT (Fig. 7).

Due to that optical path δ followed by the different points of the wavefront is not the same, consequently, neither is the phase $2\pi\delta/\lambda$. As we have to count the return path, the path length and height $h(x,y)$ of the surface referred to the plane $z=0$ are related by the expression $4\pi h(x,y)/\lambda$. Thus, the reflectance will be proportional to the exponential of this phase factor, adopting the form

$$R(x,y) = R_0(x,y)\exp\left(\frac{4\pi i}{\lambda}h(x,y)\right), \tag{4}$$

where $R_0(x,y)$ is the reflection coefficient of the surface, and $(4\pi i h(x,y)/\lambda)$ is the phase. In the simulation presented in this paper we choose $R_0(x,y)=1$.

By measuring the random height $h(x,y)$ of the sampled points (Fig.8), it would be possible to construct the reflectance matrix of $N \times N$ elements. Following the nomenclature of the

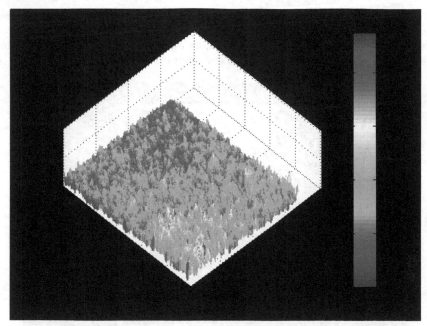

Fig. 7. Three dimensional representation of the intensity of a speckle pattern captured by a CCD camera in the laboratory. The values of the intensity over the OZ axis are in the interval [0,255].

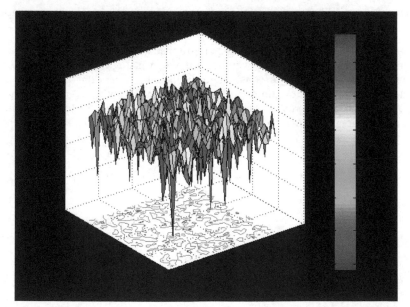

Fig. 8. Rough surface generated by MATLAB. The plane of the figure (OXY) depicts a plot of the surface contour.

preceding section we call this array the *IF* matrix (Fig.9). The elements of *IF* contain the complex reflectance $R(x,y)$ corresponding to each point of the surface, which are separated from their neighbors a distance equal to the sampling period u. The area of the delimiting mask will be represented by points outside a circle with zero reflectance.

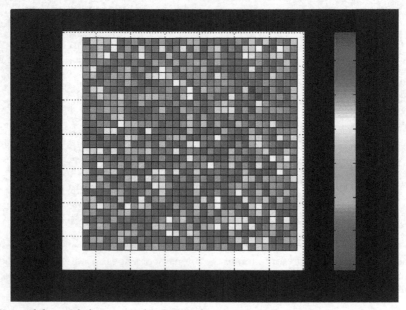

Fig. 9. View of the grid chosen on the *OXY* reference plane for *N*=64. The colours represent the surface heights at each point (pixel).

Following the same way as in preceding paragraphs, we employ the ratio h/λ as a non-dimensional variable, which will be very useful when changing the wavelength. In the model this variable is equal to a constant multiplied by a random number, which will provide information on the roughness in the simulation. We will call in the program this constant *RU* and it represents a roughness modulating factor. Random numbers with Gaussian distribution are generated in MATLAB by the command *randn*. The mathematical expression for reflectance is

$$R(x,y) = R_0(x,y)\exp\left(\frac{4\pi i}{\lambda} RU(rndn(N))\right),\tag{5}$$

where

$$\frac{h}{\lambda} = RU \times randn(N),\tag{6}$$

and the phase

$$\frac{\delta}{\lambda} = 4\pi \times RU \times randn(N).\tag{7}$$

Thus, an element of *RUrandn* is a number equal to an optical path measured in wavelengths. For example, an *RU*=1 and a *randn*=2 give rise max(*RUrandn*)=2, which indicates a maximum path difference of 2λ, that is to say, a groove on the reflecting surface with depth equal to λ. However with the same *randn*, but with the modulating factor equal to 0.1, the roughness would be a tenth part. Hence the *RU* factor represents the roughness measured in wavelengths.

To account the transversal geometry of the incident laser beam on the surface, the rough surface is delimited by means of a round mask of diameter D (geometry could be different; see section 7.2). The diameter D must be greater than the wavelength and the sampling period u. On the other hand it is supposed that the number of sampled points inside the diameter D is large enough, in order be sure that the statistics applies.

Once that the characteristics of the surface and beam are defined, the diffraction pattern is obtained by means of the FFT of the reflectance matrix *IF*. The registered intensity of the diffracted light by the rough surface is proportional to the square modulus of the diffracted amplitude, e.g. $|FO|^2$.

5. Definitions of roughness

In this section we try to adapt some definitions of roughness to our specific problem. We start the quantitative definition of the average roughness R_a from the mean surface level, as the average absolute value of the height, for all the points along a straight line (remember the profilometer). Then in a circular matrix of diameter D inside the *IF*, corresponds $\pi BD^2/4$ elements. Therefore, the roughness of the sample may be expressed by the following formulae

$$R_a = \frac{4\sum_{BD}|h(x,y)|}{\pi BD}, \tag{8}$$

where the sum is extended to the sampled points within the circle of diameter *BD*. As previously, if we transform this Eq.(8) to non-dimensional variables, we get

$$\frac{R_a}{\lambda} = \frac{4\sum_{BD}\left|\frac{h(x,y)}{\lambda}\right|}{\pi BD} = \frac{4\cdot RU}{\pi BD}\sum_{BD}|randn(N)|. \tag{9}$$

The number of elements G within the beam of diameter D (BD) is less than the $N\times N$ elements of *IF*. Say L the length of the square side where the surface is defined. In any case $BD = \chi L$, χ being a constant $(\chi \le 1)$, then it holds

$$G = \frac{1}{4}\pi\chi^2(N\times N), \tag{10}$$

whose maximum value is 0.8, approximately $(\chi = 1)$. If N and BD are large enough, and surface heights are randomly distributed, the G values are representative and R_a can be calculated using G elements.

Similarly, the roughness R_q (root mean square) could be expressed as function of BD. In fact, considering the usual definition of this parameter, the following formulae may be written

$$R_q = 2. \sqrt{\frac{\sum_{BD} |h(x,y)|^2}{\pi BD}},$$
(11)

and its non-dimensional value

$$\frac{R_q}{\lambda} = \sqrt{\frac{4\sum_{BD} \left|\frac{h(x,y)}{\lambda}\right|^2}{\pi BD}} = 2 \cdot RU \sqrt{\frac{\sum_{BD} |randn(N)|^2}{\pi BD}}.$$
(12)

6. Programming using MATLAB

We will see that the simulated specklegram corresponding to the diffraction of a monochromatic radiation by a rough surface is altered by the roughness of the object within a certain range, which depends on the wavelength of the beam used. Therefore, by analyzing some characteristics of the intensity pattern it would be possible to measure roughness.

To understand the idea let us suppose a flat surface, well polished, delimited by an aperture (mask). If a beam strikes on the surface, the delimiting aperture diffracts it resulting in an intensity pattern that depends on the geometry of the obstacle. Now if the surface is scratched, the intensity registered changes, although the aperture maintains its geometry. In both cases the autoconvolution of the intensity is different, which means that the roughness produced on the surface is the cause of the change. Therefore, the convolution of the diffraction pattern could be indicative of the degree of surface polish.

To test the hypothesis, first we constructed a computer model of a rough surface, and second we simulate the diffraction of a collimated monochromatic beam by this surface. The resulting random intensity, that is, the speckle, is stored in a matrix (FO) and its autoconvolution (CO) is performed. Once all data of CO are obtained, the functional relationship of the maximum value of the autoconvolution and its relation with the roughness is analyzed.

The program consists of the following steps:
1. Begin by setting the number of samples N along each axis.
2. The matrix IF is constructed by using the command RAN = $randn$ (N).
3. The diameter of the laser beam BD is specified, measured in number of array elements.
4. A value to the RU is assigned.
5. The BS array is constructed. The mask is 0 outside the circle and 1 inside.
6. The matrix RURAN = RU * RAN is introduced, representing the surface heights for each pixel on the area NxN.
7. The matrix hs is defined as hs = RURAN.*BS. It represents the height of the points inside the circle (mask M).
8. The reflectance matrix is obtained. Its expression is ts = exp (4πi RURAN).
9. The array FO is calculated, which is the FFT of ts.
10. The intensity of the diffraction pattern is determined , $FIDI = |FO|^2$.

11. The autoconvolution CO of FIDI, and its maximum COV is computed.
12. In order to manipulate the data more easily, the logarithm of COV is given ($\log(COV)$).
The detailed program may be found in appendix A

7. Computer results

7.1 Circular beam

Figures 10 shows the results of numerical calculations performed with a PC. In order to the numerical calculations are easy to obtain the data were $N = 64$, $BD = 6$, $RU = 0$, 0.1, 0.2, 0.3 0.4 0.5. The successive rows of the figure refer to these values of roughness, respectively. The first column of the figure corresponds to the surface height along the diameter of the illuminated area. The second column represents the intensity of the diffraction pattern, FIDI, and the third one shows the autoconvolution, CO.

For beginning a surface without roughness was chosen. The first row shows the area under study for a perfect mirror, illuminated by a circular beam of diameter $BD = 6$. The calculated diffraction pattern shows the classical Airy disc corresponding to diffraction by a hole. With the proposed values $N = 64$ and $BD = 6$ is $N/BD = 64/6$, and as $D = BDu$, gives $Nu = 64D/6$. The analysis of Figure 4 shows that the first minimum of the Airy disc in the frequency space is 24, approximately. From Fig 1 it follows

$$\alpha_v = \frac{\cos\theta}{\lambda} = \frac{(v-1)}{Nu} \approx \frac{(12-1)}{64u} = \frac{11}{64u} = 0.17\frac{1}{u}.$$

On the other hand, the first minimum given in the theory of diffraction by a circular hole is

$$\alpha_v = \frac{\cos\theta}{\lambda} \approx 1.22\frac{1}{Du} = 1.22\frac{1}{6u} = 0.20\frac{1}{u}.$$

Both results agree and differ in a small amount. The difference can be attributed to the small number of values chosen.

The second row refers to the same mirror, but not completely polished, and with a coefficient $RU = 0.1$. The profile shows small heights and valleys. The Airy disk is a little blurred, and not as clear as in the previous case. In the third row $RU = 0.2$ the central disk appears deformed and a speckleled. In the fourth and fifth rows the figure is quit different with respect to the first one, and the speckles are on all the pattern. In the last row only speckle may be seen, and no traces of the Airy disk are present. When the roughness is $RU = 0.5$ (bottom row) yields a rough surface with high grooves. The intensity is formed by irregular random spots being unknown directly the form of the mask, e.g. the symmetrical intensity circle of the Airy function. In summary, diffraction by a specular surface delimited by an aperture produces an intensity pattern concentrated around the direction of the reflected beam, but if the roughness is increasing, the light is diffracted producing speckle which structure is random.

The third figure of each row (third column) corresponds to autoconvolución (CO), which has a maximum at the center (COV). In effect, the values for the logarithm of COV are, respectively: $\log COV(RU=0.0) = 7.78$, $\log COV(RU=0.1) = 7.10$, $\log COV(RU=0.2) = 6.86$, $\log COV(RU=0.3)=6.90$, $\log COV(RU=0.4)= 6.88$, and $\log COV(RU=0.5)=6.91$. In this calculus the logarithm of the autoconvolution hass been used because the maximum value of CO is very large. Employing $\log(COV)$, the data are easier to manipulate.

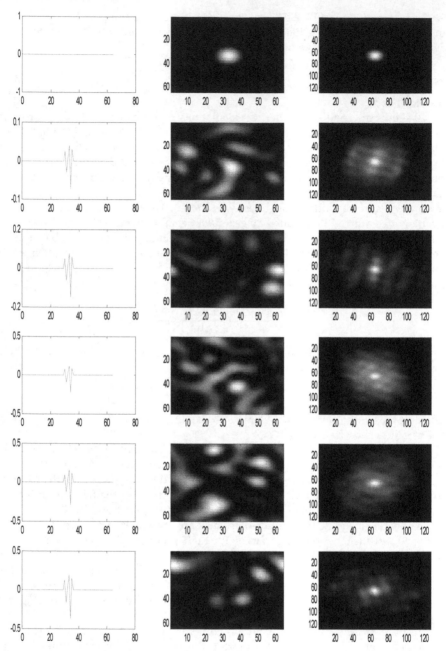

Fig. 10. Computer results for $N = 64$, $BD = 6$, $RU = 0, 0.1, 0.2, 0.3 \ 0.4 \ 0.5$. The first column shows the roughness along the illuminated area. The second represents the intensity of the diffraction pattern, $FIDI$, and the third column is the autoconvolution, CO. The rows correspond to the different values of RU.

These results show that the values of their maxima are not the same. On the contrary, the maximum value for each one depends on the surface roughness. For this reason it seems suitable to employ the maximum value of the autoconvolution of the speckle pattern, as a possible procedure for measuring the roughness of a surface, if the roughness is smaller than the wavelength of light used in the experiment.

At the same time, COV depends on the diameter of the beam used (BD) also. To see the effect in the autoconvolution when the wide of the laser is changed, we computed $\log COV$ with N and D for two different number of data and diameters. For example if N= 64, and BD = 32, it yields

$$\log COV = 12.0, 11.7, 10.7, 9.8, 9.7, 9.7,$$

whereas with $N = 128$ and $BD = 32$

$$\log COV = 12.6, 12.3, 11.3, 10.4, 10.3, 10.3 \ .$$

Therefore the maximum reached by the autoconvolution depends on the number of samples N and the beam diameter BD.

This result is reasonable if we bear in mind the definition of autoconvolution. In fact, convolution may be regarded as the overlapping area between two functions (in this case the same function) when one is reversed and moves on the other. The result depends on the wide and height of the functions involved. Therefore, if the diameter of the beam changes the autoconvolution modifies its value too.

With the aim to apply this result to laboratory experiments, it seems necessary to have more values of the autoconvolution in other circumstances. In he same way as explained, the following table provide useful data of the $\log COV$, for N=512 when the diameter D ranges from 2^3 to 2^{3+m} (m=1,2,...5). The detailed results for this calculation can be seen in the appendix B.

D\RU	0.0	0.1	0.2	0.3	0.4	0.5
8	10.233	9.231	9.148	9.185	9.078	9.128
18	12.036	10.867	10.35	10.351	10.348	10.368
32	13.810	12.558	11.536	11.546	11.548	11.542
64	15.607	14.294	12.734	12.736	12.740	12.742
128	17.412	16.037	13.945	13.938	13.941	13.937
256	19.216	17.838	15.149	15.141	15.145	15.142
512	21.257	19.881	16.428	16.347	16.347	16.349

Table 1. Values of the autoconvolution $\log(COV)$ for different diameters and roughness parameters. The results in yellow do not give information since they are very similar.

From these results may be inferred that if the area of the illuminated surface is known, measuring experimentally the autoconvolution of the speckle pattern, it would be possible measuring the roughness of this surface. To conduct laboratory experiments would be necessary to build larger tables with more values, for different incident beam intensities.

By examining the calculations it also follows that for values of RU close to zero, the difference between $\log COV$, corresponding to a BD, and a diameter corresponding to half value, is approximately constant and equal to 2, i.e.

$$logCOV'-logCOV=2 \qquad\qquad => COV'/COV=10^2,$$

and, in general,

$$\frac{COV(N')}{COV(N)}=10^{\left(\frac{N'}{N}\right)}. \qquad\qquad (13)$$

This property will be important for ulterior calculations.

7.2 Square mask

In the preceding developing calculations, a circular geometry for the beam was supposed. However, other possibilities may occur. For instance, when a laser ray is directed onto a sample under an angle of incidence θ, the effective area intersected by the beam has a quasi-elliptical form. Although an elliptical mask is easy to simulate with MATLAB, this paragraph deals with the study of the effect of employing a square aperture. This approximation simplifies the program, since there is no need the beam diameter datum. Moreover, from the point of view of the results, it has little influence in the final values when comparing these values with those obtained for an elliptical mask.

The simulation gives the results of $\log(COV)$ for RU = 0.0, 0.1, ... 0.5, and N = 16, 32, 64, 128, 256, 512, that appear in the following table:

N\RU	0.0	0.1	0.2	0.3	0.4	0.5
16	9.63	9.24	8.08	7.52	7.59	7.57
32	12.04	11.72	10.73	9.49	9.33	9.34
64	14.45	14.10	13.05	11.47	11.14	11.14
128	16.86	16.51	15.48	13.81	12.95	12.95
256	19.27	18.92	17.89	16.19	14.80	14.75
512	21.67	21.33	20.30	18.57	16.68	16.56

Table 2. Values of the autoconvolution $\log(COV)$ for different data and roughness parameter RU. The results in green do not give information.

Figure 11 represents the values of the attached table II. These curves show the dependence of $\log(COV)$ with the roughness for different values of N, provide that the roughness is less than 0.4. Therefore, the trend is maintained even if the aperture is different. From the figure it follows that, except for values marked in green on the table, the dependence of $\log COV$ with roughness is approximately parabolic, and can be approximated by the equation

$$\log COV = a + b \times RU^2. \qquad\qquad (14)$$

As in section 7.1., the difference of the $\log(COV)$ for consecutive values of RU, follows certain regularity. In fact, if the values of $\log(COV)$ for $RU=0$ are examined (see figure 11), we observe that for adjacent values of this variable, the differences between two consecutive points (corresponding to double N) are: 2.41, 2.41, 2.41, 2.41, 2.40. Taking into consideration these differences, the following mathematical relationship is verified:

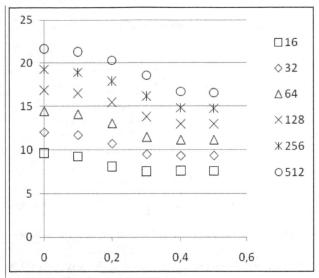

Fig. 11. Values of log(COV) for roughness RU = 0.0, 0.1, ... 0.5.

$$\log COV' - \log COV = 2.41 \quad \Rightarrow \quad \frac{COV'}{COV} = 10^{2.41} = 257 \approx 2^8 \quad \forall N'/N \approx 2 \cdot \qquad (15)$$

Table 3 below relates the difference of logarithms with the ratio N'/N.

N'/N	1	2	4	8	.....	2^n
logCOV'-logCOV	0	2.41	2×2.41	3×2.41	.....	n×2.41

Table 3. Logarithmic difference for RU=0

From these values it yields,

$$\frac{N'}{N} = 2^n \quad \Rightarrow \quad n = \frac{\log(N'/N)}{\log 2}, \qquad (16)$$

therefore,

$$\log COV' - \log COV = 2.41 \frac{\log(N'/N)}{\log 2} \quad \Rightarrow \quad \log \frac{COV'}{COV} =$$

$$\log(N'/N)^{2.41/\log 2} = \log(N'/N)^{7.999} \approx \log(N'/N)^8$$

$$\Rightarrow \quad \frac{COV'}{COV} = (N'/N)^{2.41/\log 2} \quad \Rightarrow \quad \frac{COV'}{N'^{2.41/\log 2}} = \frac{COV}{N^{2.41/\log 2}} \equiv k \quad \Rightarrow \quad COV = kN^{2.41/\log 2} \approx kN^8,$$

where k is a constant. From the definition of k it follows that

$$\log k = \log COV - \frac{2.41}{\log 2} \log N \cdot \qquad (17)$$

Applying this formula for N = 64 we have

$$\log k = 14.45 - \frac{2.41}{\log 2}\log 64 = -0.01000 \quad \Rightarrow \quad k = 0.9772, \tag{18}$$

therefore,

$$\log COV = -0.01 + \frac{2.41}{\log 2}\log N = -0.01 + 8.006\log N. \tag{19}$$

Using this result to the values of N: 32, 64, 256, 512 (RU=0), we btain for log(COV): 12.04, 14.45, 16.86, 19.27, and 21.68, respectively. These results agree with those of the table II.
A more general fit for log(COV) considering and RU can be found, provided that $RU \leq 0.4$:

$$\log COV = -0.01000 + 8.006\log N + b \times RU^2. \tag{20}$$

To determine the value of b, we choose, for example, N=128 and RU=0.2, which yields

$$15.48 = -0.01000 + 8.006\log 128 + b \times 0.2^2 \quad \Rightarrow \quad b = -34.50 \tag{21}$$

$$\Rightarrow \quad \log COV = -0.01000 + 8.006\log N - 34.50 RU^2 \approx 8.006\log N - 34.50 RU^2.$$

Solving the unknown in Eq. (20) we have

$$RU = \sqrt{\frac{1}{34.5}\log\left(\frac{N^8}{COV}\right)}. \tag{22}$$

The advantage of this formula is that it allows calculating the value of the roughness for each N and D.
To verify the accuracy of these results, we introduce some values of roughness and number of samples in Eq.(20).
For RU=0.1, N=32:

$$\log COV = 8.006\log 32 - 34.50 \times 0.1^2 = 11.70.$$

For RU =0.1, N =512:

$$\log COV = 8.006\log 512 - 34.50 \times 0.1^2 = 21.35.$$

For RU =0.3, N =32:

$$\log COV = 8.006\log 32 - 34.50 \times 0.3^2 = 8.95.$$

For RU =0.3, N =512:

$$\log COV = 8.006\log 512 - 34.50 \times 0.3^2 = 18.59.$$

It may be seen that the differences between these values calculated with the formula (20) and those displayed in table II are equal to or less than 0.02, except for the case N = 32, RU = 0.3, which is 0.15. But as in this case the value of the table does not correspond to the difference of logarithms (marked in green), it follows that the equation obtained is suitable for the specified intervals.

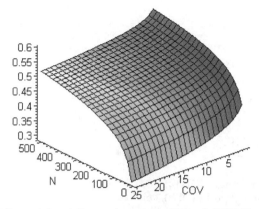

Fig. 12. Values of RU (from 0.0 to 0.5) as a function of N and COV (Eq.(22)).

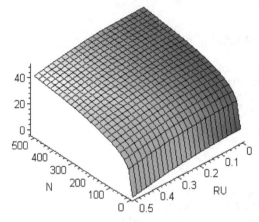

Fig. 13. Thissurface represents the function log(COV) for differerent values of N and RU (Eq.(21)).

8. Apendix A

L=.......?
BD=.....?

RAN=randn(L);
colormap(gray)

RU1=0
RU2=0.1
RU3=0.2
RU4=0.3
RU5=0.4
RU6=0.5

for i=1:L
 for j=1:L
  if (BD/2)^2<=((i-.5-L/2)^2+(j-.5-L/2)^2)

```
  BS(i,j)=0;
  else
  BS(i,j)=(-1)^(i+j);
  end
  end
end

RURAN1=RU1*RAN;
 h1=RURAN1.*BS;
 C1=h1(L/2,:);
 ts1=BS.*exp(4i*pi*RURAN1);
 FO1=fft2(ts1);
 FIDI1=(abs(FO1)).*(abs(FO1));
 CO1=conv2(FIDI1,fliplr(flipud(FIDI1)));
 COV1=conv2(FIDI1,fliplr(flipud(FIDI1)),'valid')
LCOV1=log10(COV1)
 RURAN2=RU2*RAN;
 h2=RURAN2.*BS;
 C2=h2(L/2,:);
 ts2=BS.*exp(4i*pi*RURAN2);
 FO2=fft2(ts2);
 FIDI2=(abs(FO2)).*(abs(FO2));
 CO2=conv2(FIDI2,fliplr(flipud(FIDI2)));
 COV2=conv2(FIDI2,fliplr(flipud(FIDI2)),'valid')
LCOV2=log10(COV2)
 RURAN3=RU3*RAN;
 h3=RURAN3.*BS;
 C3=h3(L/2,:);
 ts3=BS.*exp(4i*pi*RURAN3);
 FO3=fft2(ts3);
 FIDI3=(abs(FO3)).*(abs(FO3));
 CO3=conv2(FIDI3,fliplr(flipud(FIDI3)));
 COV3=conv2(FIDI3,fliplr(flipud(FIDI3)),'valid')
LCOV3=log10(COV3)
 RURAN4=RU4*RAN;
 h4=RURAN4.*BS;
 C4=h4(L/2,:);
 ts4=BS.*exp(4i*pi*RURAN4);
 FO4=fft2(ts4);
 FIDI4=(abs(FO4)).*(abs(FO4));
 CO4=conv2(FIDI4,fliplr(flipud(FIDI4)));
 COV4=conv2(FIDI4,fliplr(flipud(FIDI4)),'valid')
LCOV4=log10(COV4)

RURAN5=RU5*RAN;
 h5=RURAN5.*BS;
 C5=h5(L/2,:);
 ts5=BS.*exp(4i*pi*RURAN5);
 FO5=fft2(ts5);
 FIDI5=(abs(FO5)).*(abs(FO5));
 CO5=conv2(FIDI5,fliplr(flipud(FIDI5)));
```

```
  COV5=conv2(FIDI5,fliplr(flipud(FIDI5)),'valid')
LCOV5=log10(COV5)

RURAN6=RU6*RAN;
 h6=RURAN6.*BS;
 C6=h6(L/2,:);
 ts6=BS.*exp(4i*pi*RURAN6);
 FO6=fft2(ts6);
 FIDI6=(abs(FO6)).*(abs(FO6));
 CO6=conv2(FIDI6,fliplr(flipud(FIDI6)));
  COV6=conv2(FIDI6,fliplr(flipud(FIDI6)),'valid')
LCOV6=log10(COV6)

subplot(6,3,1)
plot(C1)
subplot(6,3,2)
imagesc(FIDI1)
subplot(6,3,3)
imagesc(CO1)
subplot(6,3,4)
plot(C2)
subplot(6,3,5)
imagesc(FIDI2)
subplot(6,3,6)
imagesc(CO2)
subplot(6,3,7)
plot(C3)
subplot(6,3,8)
imagesc(FIDI3)
subplot(6,3,9)
imagesc(CO3)
subplot(6,3,10)
plot(C4)
subplot(6,3,11)
imagesc(FIDI4)
subplot(6,3,12)
imagesc(CO4)

subplot(6,3,13)
plot(C5)
subplot(6,3,14)
imagesc(FIDI5)
subplot(6,3,15)
imagesc(CO5)

subplot(6,3,16)
plot(C6)
subplot(6,3,17)
imagesc(FIDI6)
subplot(6,3,18)
imagesc(CO6)

return
```

9. Apendix B

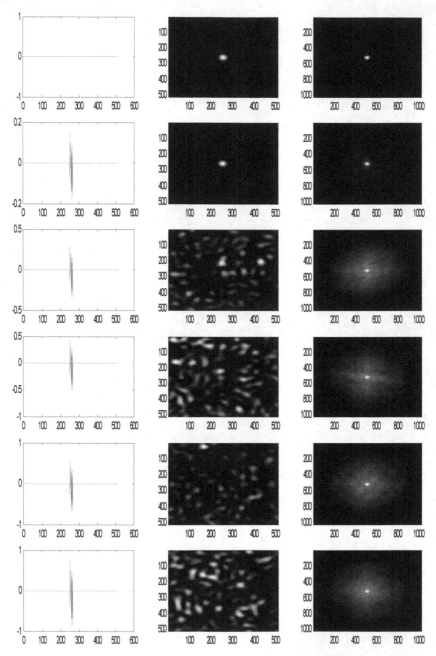

Fig. 14. $N=500$; $D=8$; $RU=$ 0.0, 0.1, 0.2, 0.3, 0.4, 0.5. (a) Surface height along the diameter. (b) Diffraction pattern. (c) Autoconvolution.

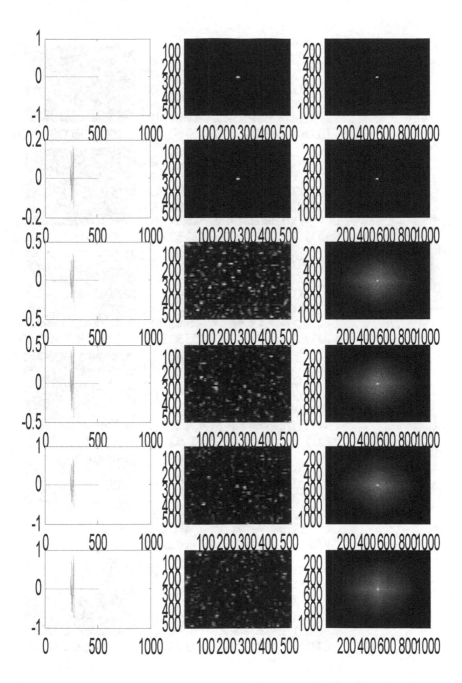

Fig. 15. $N=500$; $D=16$; $RU=$ 0.0, 0.1, 0.2, 0.3, 0.4, 0.5. (a) Surface height along the diameter. (b) Speckle pattern. (c) Autoconvolution.

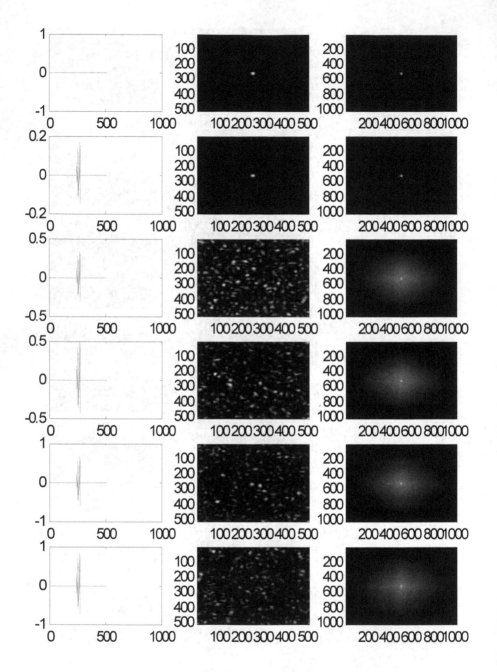

Fig. 16. N=500; D=32; RU= 0.0, 0.1, 0.2, 0.3, 0.4, 0.5. (a) Surface height along the diameter. (b) Speckle pattern. (c) Autoconvolution.

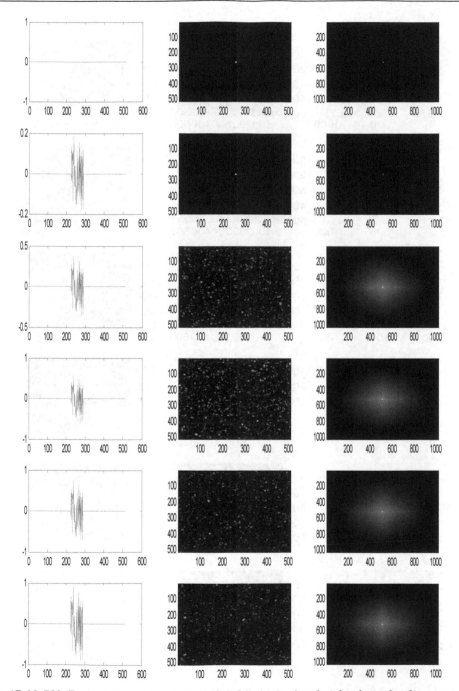

Fig. 17. N=500; D=64; RU= 0.0, 0.1, 0.2, 0.3, 0.4, 0.5. (a) Surface height along the diameter. (b) Speckle pattern. (c) Autoconvolution.

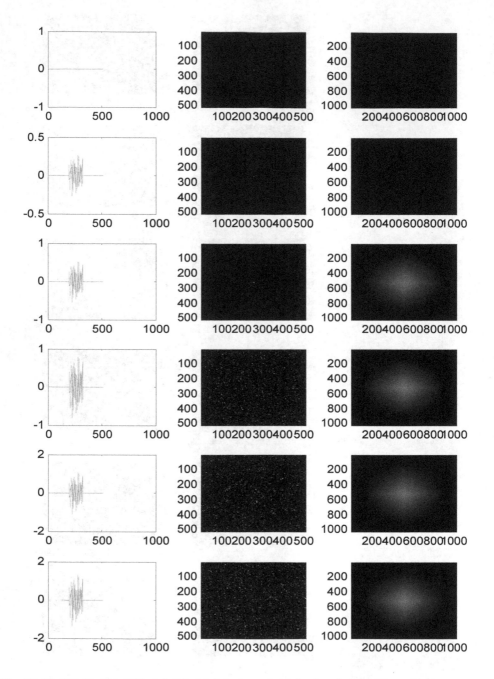

Fig. 18. N=500; D=128; RU= 0.0, 0.1, 0.2, 0.3, 0.4, 0.5. (a) Surface height along the diameter. (b) Speckle pattern. (c) Autoconvolution.

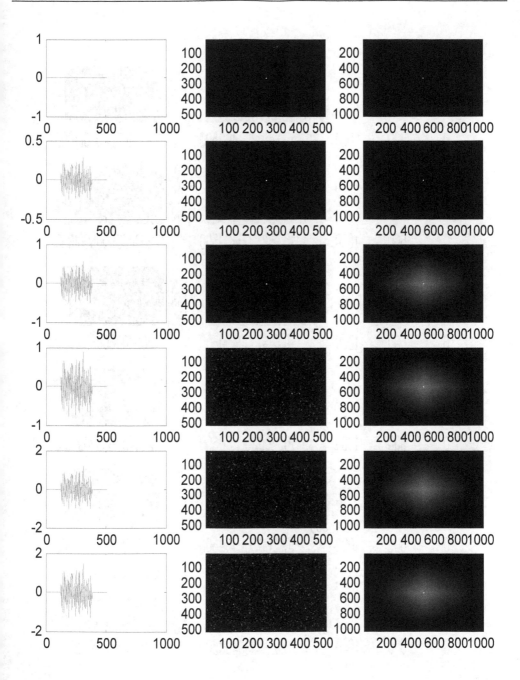

Fig. 19. N=500; D=256; RU= 0.0, 0.1, 0.2, 0.3, 0.4, 0.5. (a) Surface height along the diameter. (b) Speckle pattern. (c) Autoconvolution.

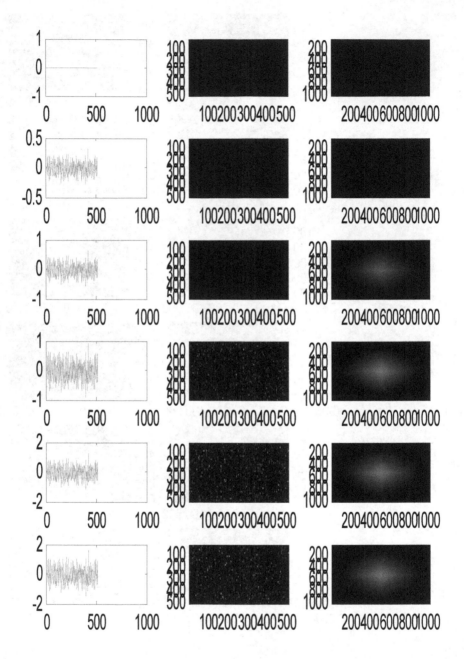

Fig. 20. N=500; D=500; RU= 0.0, 0.1, 0.2, 0.3, 0.4, 0.5. (a) Surface height along the diameter. (b) Speckle pattern. (c) Autoconvolution.

10. References

Born, M; Wolf, E; (1999) Principles Optics, Cambridge University Press. pp. 412-484.

Etter, D.M.; (1997) Engineering problem solving with MATLAB. Prentice-Hall.

Gascón, F.; Salazar, F.; (2006) A simple method to simulate diffraction and speckle patterns with a PC, *Optik*, Vol. 117, pp. 49-57.

Gascón, F.; Salazar, F.; (2008) Numerical computation of in-plane displacements and their detection in the near field by double-exposure objective speckle photography, *Opt. Commun.*, Vol. 281, pp- 6097-6106.

Glio, M.; Musazzi, S.; Perini, U.; Surface measurement by means of speckle wavelength decorrelation", *Opt. Commun.* Vol. 28, 1979, pp. 166-170.

Goodman, J.W.; (1975) Dependence of image speckle contrast on surface roughness. *Opt. Commun*, Vol. 14, pp. 324-327.

Huntley, J.M.; (1989) Speckle photography fringe analysis: assessment of current algorithms, *Appl. Opt.* Vol. 28, pp. 4316-4322. (See references therein).

Kreis, T.; (2005) Handbook of Holographic Interferometry. Wiley-VCH, Weinheim, Ch.1, 2.

Lehmann, P.; Patzelt, S.; Schöne, A.; (1997) Surface roughness measurement by means of polychromatic speckle elongation. *Appl. Opt.* Vol. 36, pp. 2188-2197.

Leonhardt, K.; Tiziani, H.J.; (1982) Removing ambiguities in surface roughness measurement. *Optica Acta*, Vol. 29, pp. 493-499

Lipson, S.G.; Lipson, H.; (1995) Tannhauser: Optical Physics. Cambridge University Press, Cambridge, p.162.

Patzelt, S.; Horn, F; Goch, (2006) G; Fast integral optical roughness measurement of specular reflecting surfaces in the nanometer range. *XVIII Imeko World Congress*, Rio de Janeiro, Brazil.

Persson, U.; (2006) Surface roughness measurement on machined surfaces using angular speckle correlation. J. Mater. *Process. Tech.*, Vol. 180, pp. 233-238.

Pearson, U.; (1993) Measurement of surface roughness on rough machined surfaces using spectral speckle correlation and image analysis. *Wear*, Vol. 160, pp. 221-225.

Pérez Quintián, F., Rebollo, M.A; Nogert, E.N.; Landau M. R.; Gaggioli, N.G.; (1996) Relationship between speckle correlation and refraction index variations: applications for roughness measurements", *Opt. Eng.* Vol 35, , pp. 1175-1178.

Ruffing, B.; (1986) Application of speckle-correlation methods to surface-roughness measurement: a theoretical study, *J. Opt. Soc. Am. A*, vol. 3, pp. 1297-1304.

Ruffing, B.; (1987) Non-contacting roughness measurement of technical surfaces by speckle-correlation method. Doctoral Thesis. University of Karlsruhe. (In german)

Spagnolo, G.S.; Paoletti, D.; (1996) Digital speckle correlation for on-line real-time measurement. *Opt. Commun.* Vol. 132, pp. 24-28.

Stratton, J.A.: (1961) Théorie de l'électromagnétisme, Dunod, Paris. p. 531

Tay, C. J.; Toh, S. L.; Shang, H. M.; Zhang, J.; (1995) Whole-field determination of surface roughness by speckle correlation. *Appl. Opt*, vol. 34, pp. 2324-2335.

Xiaomei, Xu.; (2009) Non-contact Surface Roughness Measurement Based on Laser Technology and Neural Network. *Proc. IEEE*, International Conference on Mechatronics and Automation. Changchun, China.

Yamaguchi, I.; Kobayashi, K.; Yaroslavsky, L.; (2004) Measurement of surface roughness by speckle correlation. *Opt. Eng.*, Vol. 43, pp. 2753-2761.

Yoshimura, T.; Kato, K.; Nakagawa, K.; (1990) Surface-roughness dependence of the intensity correlation function under speckle-pattern illumination, *J. Opt. Soc. Am. A,* Vol. 7, pp. 2254-2259.

Zhao, Gao; Xuezeng, Zhao; (2008) On-Line Surface Roughness Measurement Based on Specular Intensity Component of Speckle Patterns. *Proc. IEEE* 2008, International Conference on Information and Automation. Zhangjiajie, China.

7

Non Linear Algorithm for Automatic Image Processing Applications in FPGAs

Emerson Carlos Pedrino[1], Valentin Obac Roda[2] and Jose Hiroki Saito[1,3]
[1]*Federal University of Sao Carlos, Department of Computer Science*
[2]*Federal University of Rio Grande do Norte, Department of Electrical Engineering*
[3]*Faculty of Campo Limpo Paulista*
Brazil

1. Introduction

Mathematical morphology supplies powerful tools for low-level image analysis. The design of morphological operators for a given application is not a trivial one. For some problems in low level image processing the best result is achieved applying to the image an ordered sequence of morphological operators, that can be done manually, but is not easy and not always leads to the best solution. Genetic programming (GP) is a branch of evolutionary computing, and it is consolidating as a promising method for applications of digital image processing. The main objective of genetic programming is to discover how computers can learn to solve problems without being programmed for that. In the search for a practical automatic solution for low level image processing using mathematical morphology and genetic programming we present in this chapter a Matlab algorithm used for this purpose. Two sample images feed the Matlab application, the first one the original image with all defects, the second one the goal image where the defects of the original image were corrected. If we want to find the mathematical morphology operators that implement a certain filter that removes specific noise from the image, we supply a noisy image and an image were the noise was removed. The second image can be obtained from the noisy image applying an image manipulation program. After the parameters are supplied to the Matlab algorithm, the developed program starts to search for the sequence of morphological operators that leads to the best solution. The program works iteratively, and at each iteration compares the result of the morphological operations applied to the image set with the previous ones. To quantify how good is the solution at each iteration the resulting image is compared with the reference image using the mean absolute error (MAE) of the pixels. The best solution of the process is the image from a certain set whose error is less than a reference error indicated to the function. Using this methodology it was possible to solve a number of low level image processing problems, including edge detection, noise removal, separation of text from figures, with an error less than 0.5%, most of the time. Examples are presented along the text to clarify the use of the proposed algorithm. In addition, the sequence of operators obtained by the Matlab procedure was used to reconfigure an hardware architecture implemented in FPGAs to process images with the generated instructions in real time.

2. Theoretical background

In this section it will be presented a brief review of the theoretical background needed to understand the concepts used in the development of the current work. Firstly, it will be presented the theoretical basis of mathematical morphology followed by the fundamentals ideas of the genetic programming approach.

2.1 Mathematical morphology

Morphological image processing is a nonlinear branch in image processing developed by Matheron and Serra in the 1960´s, based on geometry, and on the mathematical theory of order (Dougherty, 1992; Serra, 1982; Weeks, 1996; Soille, 1999; Sonka et al., 1993; Facon, 1996). Morphological image processing has proved to be a powerful tool for binary and grayscale image computer vision processing tasks, such as edge detection, noise suppression, skeletonization, segmentation, pattern recognition, and enhancement. Initial applications of morphological processing were biomedical and geological image analysis problems. In the 1980´s, extensions of classical mathematical morphology and connections to other fields were developed by several research groups worldwide along various directions, including: computer vision problems, multi scale image processing, statistical analysis, and optimal design of morphological filters, to name just a few (Pedrino et al., 2010). The basic operations in mathematical morphology are the dilation and the erosion, and these operations can be described by logical and arithmetic operators. Dilation and erosion morphological operators can be represented respectively by the sum and subtraction of Minkowski sets (Dougherty, 1992):

$$A \oplus B = \cup \{B + a \mid a \in A\} \tag{1}$$

$$A \ominus -B = \cap \{A + b \mid b \in B\} \tag{2}$$

In Equation (1), A is the original binary image, B is the structuring element of the morphological operation, and B+a is the B displacement by a. Therefore, the dilation operation is obtained by the union of all B displacements in relation to the valid A elements. In Equation (2), -B is the 180º rotation of B in relation to its origin. Therefore, the erosion operation corresponds to intersection of the A displacements by the valid points of -B. According to Equation (1), the dilation operation will expand an image, and the erosion operation will shrink it. These operations are fundamental to morphological processing, and many of the existing morphological algorithms are based on these two primitives operations. These ideas can be extended to gray level image processing using maximum and minimum operators, too (Gonzalez & Woods, 2008). Many applications examples can be found in that text. In addition, color is known to play a significant role in human visual perception. The application of mathematical morphology to color images is difficult due to the vector nature of the color data. Mathematical Morphology is based on the application of lattice theory to spatial structures (Angulo & Serra, 2005). The definition of morphological operators needs a totally ordered complete lattice structure. A lattice is a partially ordered set in which any two elements have at least an upper bound (supremum) and a greatest lower bound (infimum). The supremum and the infimum are represented by the symbols ∨ and ∧, respectively. Thus, a lattice is complete if every subset of the lattice has a single supremum and a single infimum. The application of mathematical morphology to color images is difficult due to the vector nature of the color data. The extension of concepts from grayscale morphology to color morphology must first choose an appropriate color ordering, a color space that determines the way in which colors are represented, and an infimum, and a supremum operator in the selected color space should also be defined. There are several techniques for ordering vectors. The two main approaches are marginal ordering and vector ordering. In the marginal ordering, each component P of a pixel is ordered independently, and the operations are applied to each channel; unfortunately, this procedure has some drawbacks, e.g., producing new colors that are not contained in the original image and may be unacceptable in applications that use color for object recognition. The vector ordering method for morphological processing is more advisable. Only one processing over the three dimensional data is performed using this method. There are several ways of establishing the order, e.g., ordering by one component, canonical ordering, ordering by distance and lexicographical ordering (Chanussot & Lambert, 1998). Once these orders are defined, then the morphological operators are defined in the classical way (Pedrino, 2010).

2.2 Genetic programming

Genetic programming (GP) is a technique for automatic programming nowadays and may provide a better context for the automatic generation of morphological procedures. GP is a branch of evolutionary computation and artificial intelligence, based on concepts of genetics and Darwin's principle of natural selection to genetically breed and evolve computer programs to solve problems (Koza, 1992). Genetic Programming is the extension of the genetic algorithms (Holland, 1975) into the space of programs. That is, the objects that constitute the population are not fixed-length character strings that encode possible solutions to a certain problem. They are programs (expressed as parse trees) that are the candidate solutions to the problem. There are few applications of GP for the automatic construction of morphological operators. According to Koza, in GP, populations of many computer programs are genetically bred by means of the Darwinian principle of survival and reproduction of the fittest individual in a population. In this approach, GP starts with an initial population of computer programs generated randomly, in which each program is represented by functions and terminals (operands) appropriate to a certain problem domain. Each chromosome (computer program) in the population is measured in terms of its fitness measure. This measure indicates how well a particular individual performs in a particular problem environment. The nature of the fitness depends on the problem at hand. A new offspring population of chromosomes is generated based on the current population using the Darwinian principle of reproduction and survival of the fittest, as seen before. In addition, the genetic crossover operator is used, too. The reproduction operator can copy, in proportion to a fitness, a chromosome (computer program) from current population into the new population. The crossover operator can produce new offspring computer programs from two parental chromosomes based on their fitness. Typically, the programs are of different sizes and shapes. After these process, a new population of individuals is generated and the old one is deleted. This process is repeated for many generations until a desired result can be obtained.

3. Developed system

The developed system for automatic construction of morphological operators uses a genetic programming algorithm that operates with two images from a certain image set, an input image, and an image containing only features of interest which should be extracted from the input image. The genetic procedure looks in the space of mathematical morphology operators for sequences that allow extracting the features of interest from the original image. The operators are predefined procedures from a database that work with any kind of structuring elements having different shapes and sizes. It is also possible to include new operators in the database when necessary. The program output is a tree based structure containing the best individual of the final population. The genetic algorithm parameters are supplied by the user using a text user interface. The main parameters are: tree depth, number of chromosomes, number of generations, crossover rate, mutation rate, and certain kinds of operators suited to a particular problem. The mean absolute error (MAE) was used as a fitness measure. The cost function using the MAE was calculated as follows:

$$d(a,b) = \sum_i \sum_j |(a(i,j)-b(i,j)|/XY \tag{3}$$

In Equation (3), 'a' is the resulting image evaluated by a particular chromosome (program), and 'b' is the goal image with the same size as 'a', and '(i,j)' is the pixel coordinate. The programs are encoded as tree structure chromosome. The main steps of the proposed algorithm are illustrated in Figure 1. In the Figure, the index 'i' refers to an individual in the population. The reproduction rate is 'pr', the crossover rate is 'pc', and the mutation rate is 'pm'. The goal image can be created using an editor program. As Figure 1 shows, initially the genetic parameters are selected by the user, along with a couple of sample images that represent the problem to be solved. Then, the genetic procedure generates a random population of computer programs (chromosomes), according to the user specifications. A fitness value is assigned to each program, after the operations of reproduction, crossover and mutation, a new population of individuals is generated. The described evolutionary process is repeated by many generations and can be stopped according to a stop condition. The mutation operator, that was not previously discussed, simply generates an individual belonging to the space of solutions of the problem and connects it to a random point of a particular randomly chosen chromosome. Such operation is performed with a given probability.

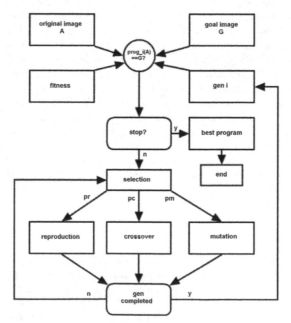

Fig. 1. Flowchart of developed system

The process of evaluating a given depth four chromosome of the population of individuals is shown in Figure 2. 'Img_in' corresponds to the input image, 'ero' and 'dil' instructions corresponds to the erosion and dilation operations respectively. The argument 'end_n' matches an address of a table containing all combinations of structuring element for a given problem. Both the instructions, and the arguments are found in an intelligent manner when a pair of input images are presented to the genetic procedure. It can be seen in Figure 2 that initially the input image is eroded, followed by two dilations and the resulting image is eroded again. All the morphological operators in the example use the same structuring element pointed by 'end_n'.

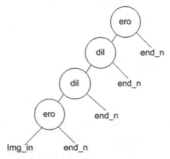

Fig. 2. Example of a chromosome representing a morphological filter and its arguments

The tournament selection method was the one chosen to be used in this work (Koza, 1992). The training set, used to extract the pair of images used in the presented method, was obtained using samples of synthetic images of various resolutions. For each resolution the maximum depth size for each chromosome tree and the error calculation functions were changed. The training will be further detailed in Section 3.1. As follows, the Matlab developed algorithm is presented along with some examples. In all the examples binary images were used, however, the method can be extended to handle any type of image.

3.1 Matlab algorithm
The Matlab algorithm for binary images mathematical morphology automatic processing developed in this work is presented as follows.

```
%  - Developed Algorithm
%  - pop: Initial Population
%  - nc: number of chromosomes
%  - cr: randomly generated chromosome
%  - cr_col: columns of cr
%  - num_instr: number of instructions
%  - profd: maximum tree depth
%  - arg: pointer to the table of arguments
pop=pop_init(nc,cr,cr_col,num_instr,profd,arg);
%  - ger: generations
%  - ng: number of generations
%  - ct_aux: auxiliary cost
ger=0;
ct_aux=inf;
while (ger<=ng)
```

```
% - ct_gn: costs from generation 'n'
% - img_org: input image
% - img_obj: goal image
% - instr: instruction table
ct_gn=cost(nc,pop,img_org,img_obj,instr,profd);
% - elt: best program of generation 'n'
% - ct_min: cost of best program
[elt,ct_min]=elit_indv(pop,ct_gn);
% - Elitism
% - sol: best program found
if (ct_min < ct_aux)
   ct_aux=ct_min;
   sol=elt;
end
% err: tolerated error
if (ct_aux<=err)
   break;
end
% - Crossover
% - pop_g: new population
% - tx_cs: crossover rate
tx_cs_conv=(-10*tx_cs/100)+10;

pop_g=crossover(tx_cs_conv,pop,nc,img_org,img_obj,instr
,profd,sol);
   % - Mutation
   tx_mt_conv=(-10*tx_mt/100)+10;
   pop=mutation(pop_g,num_instr,profd,nc,tx_mt_conv,arg);
   ger=ger+1;
end
```

According to the previous code, the function *pop_init* is responsible for generating randomly, using user provided parameters, the initial population of individuals. The parameters are described as follows.
- nc: number of chromosomes (programs);
- cr: initial chromosome user created;
- cr_col: number of columns of cr;
- num_instr: instruction number;
- profd: maximum depth tree tolerated;
- arg: pointers vector for the arguments table;

The implementation of the algorithm *pop_init* function is shown as follows. This function uses another function called *ger_cr* to generate chromosomes randomly.

```
function p_i=pop_init(nc,cr,cr_col,num_instr,profd,arg)
% Initial Population of Individuals
pop(1,1:cr_col)=cr;
for i=2:nc
        cr=gera_cr(num_instr,profd,arg);
        pop(i,:)=cr;
end
p_i=pop;
```

```
function cr=ger_cr(num_instr,profd,arg)
cr=zeros(1,profd*4);
[~,num_arg]=size(arg);
for i=1:4:profd*4
    aleat=round(rand*(num_instr-1));
    cr(i)=aleat;
    aleat=round(rand*(num_arg-1))+1;
    cr(i+1)=aleat;
    aleat=round(rand*(num_arg-1))+1;
    cr(i+2)=aleat;
    aleat=round(rand*(num_arg-1))+1;
    cr(i+3)=aleat;
end
```

The cost function is responsible for calculating the cost of each chromosome in current population of individuals. Internally, it uses two other functions, *build_op* and *comp*, the first one is responsible for building the program, according to the tree structure shown previously, and the second is responsible for calculating the fitness of chromosomes. Below, the code part related to the *cost* and *build_op* functions is presented. Following, the function *comp* is presented, too. The main parameters used for each function are the following.

- nc: number of chromosomes;
- pop: current population;
- img_org: input image;
- img_obj: goal image;
- instr: instructions vector;
- profd: maximum depth allowed to each chromosome.

The *build_op* function is responsible for the construction of each individual, using functions and arguments provided by the user through the instructions vector and by the table of arguments. The input image is applied to each program generated automatically and the *comp* function tests whether the object pixels and the image background pixels correspond to the pixels of the object and background of the goal image, thereby creating a vector containing all the costs associated to each program obtained in the present generation.

```
function c=cost(nc,pop,img_org,img_obj,instr,profd)
% - It Evaluates the Cost of Each Individual from the Current
Population
c=ones(1,nc);
for i=1:nc
    sample=build_op(instr,pop(i,:),profd,img_org);
    c(i)=comp(amostra_c,img_obj);
end


function op = build_op(instr,cr,profd,img)
% - It Builds a Program
%    to be Applied to the
%    Input Image
op=eval([char(instr(cr(1)+1)),'(','img',',',num2str(cr(2)),',
',num2str(cr(3)),',',num2str(cr(4)),')']);
```

```
aux_op=op;
% - Building
for i=5:4:profd*4
        op=eval([char(instr(cr(i)+1)),'(','aux_op',',',num2str(
cr(i+1)),',' ,num2str(cr(i+2)),',',num2str(cr(i+3)),')']);
        aux_op=op;
end


function comp_ab = comp(a,b)
% - It Compares two images (a and b)
TP=0.005;
FN=0.005;
TN=0.005;
FP=0.005;
[lin,col]=size(a);
for i=1:lin
    for j=1:col
        if b(i,j) && a(i,j)
            TP=TP+1;
        else
            if b(i,j) && ~a(i,j)
                FP=FP+1;
            else if ~b(i,j) && ~a(i,j)
                    TN=TN+1;
                else
                    if ~b(i,j) && a(i,j)
                        FN=FN+1;
                    end
                end
            end
        end
    end
end
SV=TP/(TP+FN);
SP=TN/(TN+FP);
comp_ab=1-(sqrt((1-SP)^2+(1-SV)^2))/sqrt(2);
comp_ab=1-comp_ab;
```

The *elit_indv* function returns the best current generation chromosome, the elite, and their associated cost; its parameters are the following.
-    pop: current population;
-    ct_gn: vector cost for the current population;
The implementation of the *elit_indv* function is shown as follows.

```
function [elt,ct_min]=elite_indv(pop,ct)
% Best Individual
[ct_min,ind]= min(ct);
elt=pop(ind,:);
```

The next function implemented was the genetic crossing (crossover), which can be seen below. Its main parameters are:

- tx_cs: crossing rate, between 0 and 1 (0 - 100%);
- pop: current population;
- nc: number of chromosomes;
- img_org: input image;
- img_obj: goal image;
- instr: instructions vector;
- profd: maximum depth allowed for each chromosome;
- sol: best chromosome (program) found so far.

The crossing is performed between two trees in the population of individuals, selected according to a given probability, user specified. The crossing method used is similar to the one implemented by Koza (Koza, 1992).

```
function
pop_g=crossover(tx_cs,pop,nc,img_org,img_obj,instr,profd,sol)
% - Crossover.
pop_g=pop;
pop_g(1,:)=sol;
pop_indv_at=2;
while (pop_indv_at<=nc)
    rd_c=round(rand*nc+.5);
    p1=pop(rd_c,:);
    rd_c=round(rand*nc+.5);
    p2=pop(rd_c,:);
    rd_c=round(rand*nc+.5);
    p3=pop(rd_c,:);
    px=[p1;p2;p3];
    % - Tournament selection.
    ct_gn=custo(3,px,img_org,img_obj,instr,profd);
    [elt,~]=elite_indv(px,ct_gn);
    % father
    p=elt;
    [~,ind_p2]=sort(ct_gn);
    % mother
    m=px(ind_p2(2),:);
    rd_num=rand*10;
    if (rd_num>tx_cs)
        ind_imp=1:4:profd*4;
        [~,c_ind_imp]=size(ind_imp);
        ind_p=ind_imp(round(rand*(c_ind_imp)+0.5));
        ind_m=ind_imp(round(rand*(c_ind_imp)+0.5));
        gen_p=p(ind_p);
        gen_m=m(ind_m);
        p(ind_p)=gen_m;
        m(ind_m)=gen_p;
        aux=round(rand*(3)+0.5);
        crt_p=ind_p+aux;
        crt_m=ind_m+aux;
        gen_p=p(crt_p:ind_p+3);
        gen_m=m(crt_m:ind_m+3);
        p(crt_p:ind_p+3)=gen_m;
```

```
                    m(crt_m:ind_m+3)=gen_p;
                    pop_g(pop_indv_at,:)=p;
                    pop_indv_at=pop_indv_at+1;
                    if (~rem(nc,2))
                        pop_g(pop_indv_at,:)=m;
                        pop_indv_at=pop_indv_at+1;
                    end
              else
                    pop_g(pop_indv_at,:)=p;
                    pop_indv_at=pop_indv_at+1;
                    if (~rem(nc,2))
                        pop_g(pop_indv_at,:)=m;
                        pop_indv_at=pop_indv_at+1;
                    end
              end
        end
```

- The mutation function swaps parts of the selected programs, according to a given probability, with parts of programs belonging to the space of solutions of a given problem; its parameters are shown as follows.
- pop: current population;
- num_instr: number of instructions;
- profd: maximum depth allowed for each chromosome;
- nc: number of chromosomes;
- tx_mt: mutation rate, between 0 and 1 (0 - 100%);
- arg: pointers vector for the argument table.

```
      function pop_g=mutation(pop,num_instr,profd,nc,tx_mt,arg)
      % Mutation.
      [~,num_arg]=size(arg);
      pop_g=pop;
      for i=1:nc
          for j=1:4:profd*4
              rd_num=rand*10;
              if (rd_num>tx_mt)
                  rd=round(rand*(num_instr-1));
                  pop_g(i,j)=rd;
              end
              rd_num=rand*10;
              if (rd_num>tx_mt)
                  rd=round(rand*(num_arg-1))+1;
                  pop_g(i,j+1)=rd;
              end
              rd_num=rand*10;
              if (rd_num>tx_mt)
                  rd=round(rand*(num_arg-1))+1;
                  pop_g(i,j+2)=rd;
              end
              rd_num=rand*10;
              if (rd_num>tx_mt)
                  rd=round(rand*(num_arg-1))+1;
```

```
                    pop_g(i,j+3)=rd;
               end
          end
     end
```

3.2 Application examples

In this subsection some application examples, using the algorithm described in the previous subsection, are presented. All examples are for binary images and use equations 1 and 2 shown in subsection 2.1. A synthetic image containing four objects with different shapes was generated for implementation of the examples. The training set consisted of three samples with different resolutions for each picture object. In addition, they were used three different maximum allowed sizes for each tree size, representing the chromosomes. Also, in each case the algorithm was run three times. In the first example, it was tried to find a combination of morphological filters and logical operators to recognize the star present in the input image (Figure 3). In this figure it is possible to see the desired image and the training process. The error found for this example was zero. Other training pairs were used through the training set also resulting in errors very close to zero. For this example the following genetic parameters and arguments were used.

$ng=50$,

$nc=500$,

$tx\_cs=90\%$,

$tx\_mt=10\%$,

arg=[1 2 3 4 5 6 7 8],

tb_arg=[0 0 0;0 0 1;0 1 0;0 1 1;1 0 0;1 0 1;1 1 0; 1 1 1].

The 'arg' vector pointers to 'tb_arg' that corresponds to the table of structuring elements used in the morphological operations. The instructions vector used in this example was the following:

instr={'nop' 'dil' 'ero' 'or1' 'and1' 'sto1' 'cpl'},

were:

nop means no operation;

dil corresponds to a dilation through the structuring elements contained in *tb_arg*;

ero corresponds to an erosion through the structuring elements contained in *tb_arg*;

or1 is equivalent to a logical OR operation;

and1 is equivalent to a logical AND operation;

sto1 corresponds to a storage operator of the current results in a temporary memory variable;

cpl is equivalent to a logical NOT operation.

"5	4	2	4	2	7	5	2	3	5	3	6	3	2	2	8	4	4	5	6	6	6	7
2	1	2	4	5	2	4	4	4	6	6	3	7	4	6	3	6	2	7	5	7	4	4	7
7	3	7	3	2	4	6	7	3	5	2	4	5	2	2	3	6	4	5	7	2	4	7	5
1	3	2	7	3	5	5	5	7	6	6	6	1	1	2	8	8	2	5	7	6	6	5	5
8	0	6	6	5	1	6	5	2	6	1	2	2	6	4	3	3	1	5	2	7	2	7	2
4	6	6	2	3	4	5	1	2"														

Figure 4 shows the algorithm generated to recognize the star presented in the input image. The arguments are pointers to the arguments table containing the structuring elements for the morphological operators. The generated machine code, in decimal, for the given example considering the architecture cited in this work can be seen as follows.

The above code is transferred to a FPGA dedicated processor architecture. The FPGA processor processes in real time the images from a video camera with the objective of determining the shapes intended, according to the training algorithm. The addresses for the arguments table containing the structuring elements are shown in bold characters, thus the three arguments will point to three rows of the table forming a structuring element of size 3x3, equivalent to the size used in implementing each stage of the above architecture. Using this approach it is possible to build 512 different shapes structuring elements. The numbers representing the functions are pointers to the instruction vector 'instr', whose index starts at zero, and are not represented in bold characters. Thus, for example, code 1 **6 5 2** corresponds to the instruction dil (img, [1 0 1, 1 0 0, 0 0 1]), which is a dilation of 'img' by the structuring element shown as argument. The image 'img' is obtained from the result of the previous instruction by a pipeline process, and so on.

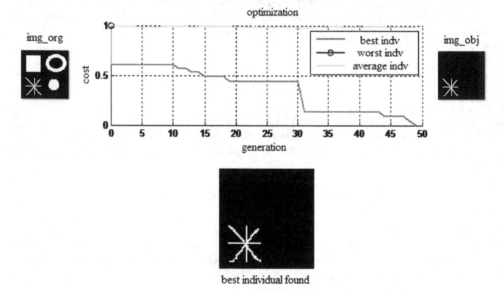

best individual found

Fig. 3. Example of an automatic filter construction for recognizing the star present in the input image

Another application example obtained by the developed system, was the decomposition of an any shape structuring element in smaller size 3x3 structuring elements. For this example we used the same parameters of the previous example. The training process for the evolutionary system of the given problem is illustrated in Figure 5. A binary 17x17 size object, not decomposed by the algorithm proposed by Park and Chin (Park & Chin, 1995), could be decomposed by the proposed methodology. The process converged after iteration 300, and the error obtained was zero. The following opcode was generated for the addressed problem.

"0   7   2   5   0   1   2   4   0   5   1   2",

where the zeros correspond to successive dilations of the input image by the following structuring elements.

[1 1 0;0 0 1;1 0 0], [0 0 0;0 0 1;0 1 1], e [1 0 0;0 0 0;0 0 1]

After successive dilations of a central point by the above structuring elements, it was possible to find the object shown in Figure 5.

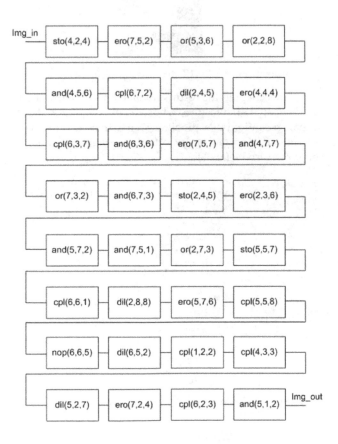

Fig. 4. Algorithm generated for the automatic pattern recognition filter construction problem shown in Figure 3

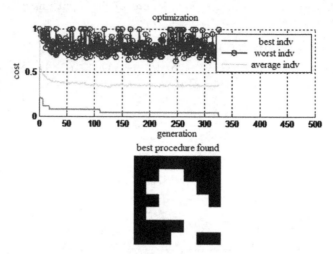

Fig. 5. Example of decomposition of a 17x17 structuring element

As mentioned earlier in this chapter, the results obtained by the aforesaid system were used to set up a FPGA implemented architecture, whose block diagram is shown in Figure 6. The architecture has several reconfigurable pipeline stages that can deal with 3x3 structuring elements. The concatenation of several stages allows operations with larger size structuring elements, whose shape can also be flexible.

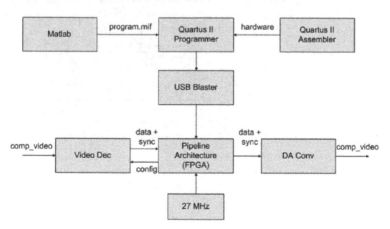

Fig. 6. Architecture used to process the programs generated by the proposed system (Pedrino et al., 2010)

4. Conclusion

The construction of a Matlab algorithm using a methodology for automatic construction of morphological and logical operators by the use of genetic programming was presented in this chapter. When presenting pairs of images to the system from a training set, a set of instructions and arguments for a given problem and appropriate genetic parameters, an evolutionary process builds a sequence of nonlinear image operators that given an input image produces an output image as close as possible to the goal image provided. The algorithm generated in this work was also used to configure a pipeline processing architecture in FPGA, capable of processing images in real time, with the images provided by a CCD video camera. Examples were shown in the text in order to demonstrate the feasibility of the developed methodology for automatic construction of image processing algorithms. The task of designing an imaging processing sequence of operators is not so trivial, so the proposed methodology might be very helpful as an aid for the expert in this situation.

5. Acknowledgments

Emerson C. Pedrino is grateful to the "Fundação de Amparo a Pesquisa do Estado de São Paulo" for the financial support of this work, thoughout the project, proc. 2009/17736-4. The authors are also grateful to the Departament of Computer Science/University Federal de São Carlos, Faculty of Campo Limpo Paulista, and to the Department of Electrical Engineering/UFRN.

6. References

Dougherty, E. R. (1992). *An Introduction to Morphological Image Processing*, SPIE, Bellingham, Wash, USA

Serra, J. (1982). *Image Analysis and Mathematical Morphology*, Academic Press, San Diego, Calif, USA

Weeks Jr., A. R. (1996). *Fundamentals of Electronic Image Processing*, SPIE, Bellingham, Wash, USA

Soille, P. (1999). *Morphological Image Analysis, Principles and Applications*, Springer, Berlin, Germany

Sonka, M., Hlavac, V. & Boyle, R. (1993). *Image Processing, Analysis and Machine Vision*, Chapman & Hall, Boca Raton, Fla, USA

Facon, J. (1996). *Morfologia Matemática: Teoria e Exemplos*, Editora Universitária da Pontifícia Universidade Católica do Paraná, Prado Velho, Brazil (In portuguese)

Pedrino, E. C., Roda, V. O. & Saito, J. H. (2010). A Genetic Programming Approach to Reconfigure a Morphological Image Processing Architecture. *International Journal of Reconfigurable Computing*, Vol.2011, pp. 712494-712503

Gonzalez, R. C. & Woods, R. E. (2008). *Digital Image Processing*. Prentice Hall, Upper Saddle River, NJ

Angulo, J. & Serra, J. (2005). Morphological Coding of Color Images by Vector Connected Filters, In: *Centre de Morphologie Mathématique*, Ecole des Mines de Paris, Paris, France

Chanussot, J. & Lambert, P. (1998). Total ordering based on space filling curves for multivalued morphology, In: *Proceedings of the 4th International Symposium on Mathematical Morphology and Its Applications*, 51–58

Koza, J. (1992). *Genetic Programming*, MIT Press, Cambridge, Mass, USA

Holland, J. (1975). *Adaptation in Natural and Artificial Systems*, MIT Press, Cambridge, Mass, USA

Park, H. & Chin, R. T. Decomposition of arbitrarily shaped morphological structuring elements, *IEEE Trans. Pattern Anal. Mach. Intell.*, Vol.17, No1, pp. 2-15

Part 2

Image Processing

8

MATLAB as a Tool in Nuclear Medicine Image Processing

Maria Lyra, Agapi Ploussi and Antonios Georgantzoglou
Radiation Physics Unit, A' Radiology Department, University of Athens
Greece

1. Introduction

Advanced techniques of image processing and analysis find widespread use in medicine. In medical applications, image data are used to gather details regarding the process of patient imaging whether it is a disease process or a physiological process. Information provided by medical images has become a vital part of today's patient care.

The images generated in medical applications are complex and vary notably from application to application. Nuclear medicine images show characteristic information about the physiological properties of the structures-organs. In order to have high quality medical images for reliable diagnosis, the processing of image is necessary. The scope of image processing and analysis applied to medical applications is to improve the quality of the acquired image and extract quantitative information from medical image data in an efficient and accurate way.

MatLab (**Mat**rix **Lab**oratory) is a high performance interactive software package for scientific and engineering computation developed by MathWorks (Mathworks Inc., 2009). MatLab allows matrix computation, implementation of algorithms, simulation, plotting of functions and data, signal and image processing by the Image Processing Toolbox. It enables quantitative analysis and visualisation of nuclear medical images of several modalities, such as Single Photon Emission Computed Tomography (SPECT), Positron Emission Tomography (PET) or a hybrid system (SPECT/CT) where a Computed Tomography system (CT) is incorporated to the SPECT system. The Image Processing Toolbox (Mathworks Inc., 2009) is a comprehensive set of reference-standard algorithms and graphical tools for image processing, analysis, visualisation and algorithm development. It offers the possibility to restore noisy or degraded images, enhance images for improved intelligibility, extract features, analyse shapes and textures, and register two images. Thus, it includes all the functions that MatLab utilises in order to perform any sophisticated analysis needed after the acquisition of an image. Most toolbox functions are written in open MatLab language offering the opportunity to the user to inspect the algorithms, to modify the source code and create custom functions (Wilson et al., 2003, Perutka, 2010).

This chapter emphasises on the utility of MatLab in nuclear medicine images' processing. It includes theoretical background as well as examples. After an introduction to the imaging techniques in nuclear medicine and the quality of nuclear medicine images, this chapter proceeds to a study about image processing in nuclear medicine through MatLab. Image processing techniques presented in this chapter include organ contouring, interpolation, filtering, segmentation, background activity removal, registration and volume quantification. A section about DICOM image data processing using MatLab is also presented as this type of image is widely used in nuclear medicine.

2. Nuclear medicine imaging

Nuclear Medicine is the section of science that utilises the properties of radiopharmaceuticals in order to derive clinical information of the human physiology and biochemistry. According to the examination needed for each patient, a radionuclide is attached to a pharmaceutical (tracer) and the whole complex is then delivered to the patient intravenously or by swallowing or even by inhalation. The radiopharmaceutical follows its physiological pathway and it is concentrated on specific organs and tissues for short periods of time. Then, the patient is positioned under a nuclear medicine equipment which can detect the radiation emitted by the human body resulting in images of the biodistribution of the radiopharmaceutical.

In Nuclear Medicine, there are two main methods of patient imaging, the imaging with Planar Imaging, Dynamic Imaging or SPECT and the PET. During the last decade, hybrid systems have been developed integrating the CT technique with either SPECT or PET resulting in SPECT/CT and PET/CT respectively. This chapter will concentrate on the implementation of MatLab code in gamma camera planar imaging, SPECT and SPECT/CT methods.

The gamma camera is composed of a collimator, a scintillator crystal usually made of NaI (or CsI), the photomultiplier tubes, the electronic circuits and a computer equipped with the suitable software to depict the nuclear medicine examinations. In planar imaging, the patient, having being delivered with the suitable radiopharmaceutical, is sited under the gamma camera head. The gamma camera head remains stable at a fixed position over the patient for a certain period of time, acquiring counts (disintegrations). These will constitute the radiopharmaceutical distribution image. The counts measured in a specific planar projection originate from the whole thickness of patient (Wernick & Aarsvold, 2004).

In SPECT, the gamma camera head rotates around the patient remaining at well defined angles and acquiring counts for specific periods of time per angle. What makes SPECT a valuable tool in nuclear medicine is the fact that information in the three dimensions of the patient can be collected in a number of slices with a finite known volume (in voxels). Thus, SPECT technique is used to display the radiopharmaceutical distribution in a single slice removing the contribution from the overlying and underlying tissues.

In order to obtain the most accurate quantitative data from SPECT images, two issues that have to be resolved are the attenuation correction and the Compton scattering that the photons are undergone until reach and interact with the slice of interest tissues. As an examining organ has certain dimensions, each slice along the axis of the gamma camera has different distance from the detector. Thus, each photon experiences different attenuation. These two phenomena usually lead to distortion of the measured activity concentration (Wernick & Aarsvold, 2004). The acquired data are processed in order to correct and compensate the undesired effect of these physical phenomena. The projection data of each slice constitute the sinogram. As a result, a series of sinograms is the files acquired. However, this kind of files needs reconstruction in order to get an image with diagnostic value. The most known reconstruction methods are the Filtered Back-Projection (FBP) and the Iterative methods.

Attenuation correction is resolved by using the constant linear attenuation coefficient (μ) method or using the transmission source method. In the first one, the distance that each photon has travelled is calculated based on the patient geometry and the exponential reduction of their intensity. Then, considering the human body as a uniform object, an attenuation map is implemented in the reconstructed image. The latter method utilises a transmission source which scans the patient. This depicts each pixel or voxel of the patient with a specific μ producing an attenuation coefficient map. Finally, the attenuation map is implemented on the image resulting in a more accurate diagnosis.

The second issue of scatter correction can be resolved by the electronics of the gamma camera and the filtering process during reconstruction. When a photon undergoes scattering, its energy reduces. So, a well defined function can accept for imaging photons with energy at a certain narrow energy window around the central photopeak of the γ-emission.

A hybrid SPECT/CT scanner is capable of implementing both a CT scan and a SPECT scan or it can be used for each of these scans separately. Using the CT scan, the anatomy of a specific patient area can be imaged while the SPECT scan can depict the physiology of this area. Then, the registration of the two images drives at an image of advanced diagnostic value. Moreover, the CT data is used for the implementation of attenuation correction. (Delbeke et al., 2006)

The range of nuclear medicine examinations is fairly wide. It includes, among others, patients' studies, as myocardium perfusion by ^{99m}Tc-Tetrofosmin or ^{99m}Tc-Sestamibi, striatum imaging in brain by ^{123}I-Ioflupane (DaTSCAN), renal parenchyma imaging by ^{99m}Tc-De-Methylo-Sulfo-Acid (DMSA) and ^{99m}Tc-Methylo-Di-Phosphonate (MDP) for bone scintigraphy. Fundamental image analysis methods of myocardium, brain, kidneys, thyroid, lungs and oncological (e.g. neuroblastoma) nuclear medicine studies include regions' properties, boundary analysis, curvature analysis or line and circle detection.

Image processing serves in reconstruction of images acquired using SPECT techniques, in improvement of the quality of images for viewing and in preparation of images for quantitative results.

Data of the mentioned examinations are used in the following applications of MatLab algorithms to make the image processing and analysis in nuclear medicine clear and show the MatLab utility for these studies.

2.1 Image quality in nuclear medicine

Image quality plays an important role in nuclear medicine imaging as the goal is a reliable image of the projected organ to be provided, for accurate diagnosis or therapy. The physical characteristics that are used to describe image quality are (1) contrast, (2) spatial resolution and (3) noise.

Image contrast is the difference in intensity corresponding to different concentration of activity in the patient. For high diagnostic accuracy, nuclear medicine images must be of high contrast. The image contrast is principally affected by the radiopharmaceutical that is used for imaging and the scattered radiation. In general, it is desirable to use a radiopharmaceutical which has a high uptake within the target organ.

Spatial resolution is defined as the ability of the imaging modality to reproduce the details of a nonuniform radioactive distribution. The spatial resolution is separated into intrinsic resolution (scintillator, photomultiplier tubes and electronic circuit) and system resolution (collimator, scintillator, photomultiplier tubes and electronic circuit). The intrinsic resolution depends on the thickness of scintillation crystal while the system resolution depends mainly on the distance from the emitting source to collimator. The resolution of a gamma camera is limited by several factors. Some of these are the patient motion, the statistical fluctuation in the distribution of visible photons detected and the collimators geometry (Wernick & Aarsvold, 2004).

Noise refers to any unwanted information that prevents the accurate imaging of an object. Noise is the major factor in the degradation of image quality. Image noise may be divided into random and structured noise. Random noise (also referred as statistical noise) is the result of statistical variations in the counts being detected. The image noise is proportional to $N^{1/2}$ where N is the number of detected photons per pixel. Therefore, as the number of counts increases the noise level reduces. Image noise is usually analysed in terms of signal-to-noise-ratio (SNR). SNR is equal to $N/ N^{1/2}$. If the SNR is high, the diagnostic information of an image is appreciated regardless of the noise level. Structured noise is derived from non-uniformities in the scintillation camera and overlying structures in patient body.

2.2 Complex topics

In the previous section, several issues arising from the need of achieving the best image quality have to be resolved. Sometimes, the whole procedure becomes really hard to be completed. Some concepts in image processing and analysis are theory-intensive and may be difficult for medical professionals to comprehend.

Apart from that, each manufacturer uses different software environment for the application of reconstruction and presentation of the images. This drives at a lack of a standard pattern based on which a physician can compare or parallel two images acquired and reconstructed by nuclear imaging systems of different vendors. This is a node on which MatLab can meet a wide acceptance and utilisation.

These complex topics can be analysed and resolved using MatLab algorithms to turn up the most effective techniques to emerge information through medical imaging.

3. Image analysis and processing in nuclear medicine

In the last several decades, medical imaging systems have advanced in a dynamic progress. There have been substantial improvements in characteristics such as sensitivity, resolution, and acquisition speed. New techniques have been introduced and, more specifically, analogue images have been substituted by digital ones. As a result, issues related to the digital images' quality have emerged.

The quality of acquired images is degraded by both physical factors, such as Compton scattering and photon attenuation, and system parameters, such as intrinsic and extrinsic spatial resolution of the gamma camera system. These factors result in blurred and noisy images. Most times, the blurred images present artefacts that may lead to a fault diagnosis. In order the images to gain a diagnostic value for the physician, it is compulsory to follow a specific series of processing.

Image processing is a set of techniques in which the data from an image are analysed and processed using algorithms and tools to enhance certain image information that is more useful to human interpretation (Nailon, 2010). The processing of an image permits the extraction of useful parameters and increases the possibility of detection of small lesions more accurately.

Image processing in nuclear medicine serves three major purposes: a) the reconstruction of the images acquired with tomographic (SPECT) techniques, b) the quality improvement of the image for viewing in terms of contrast, uniformity and spatial resolution and, c) the preparation of the image in order to extract useful diagnostic qualitative and quantitative information.

3.1 Digital images

In all modern nuclear medicine imaging systems, the images are displayed as an array of discrete picture elements (pixels) in two dimensions (2D) and are referred as digital images. Each pixel in a digital image has an intensity value and a location address (Fig. 1). In a nuclear medicine image the pixel value shows the number of counts recorded in it. The benefit of a digital image compared to the analogue one is that data from a digital image are available for further computer processing.

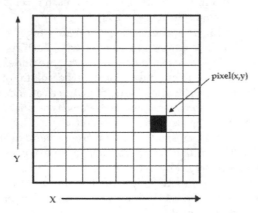

Fig. 1. A digital image is a 2D array of pixels. Each pixel is characterised by its (x, y) coordinates and its value.

Digital images are characterised by matrix size, pixel depth and resolution. The matrix size is determined from the number of the columns (m) and the number of rows (n) of the image matrix (m×n). The size of a matrix is selected by the operator. Generally, as the matrix dimension increases the resolution is getting better (Gonzalez et al., 2009). Nuclear medicine images matrices are, nowadays, ranged from 64×64 to 1024×1024 pixels.

Pixel or bit depth refers to the number of bits per pixel that represent the colour levels of each pixel in an image. Each pixel can take 2^k different values, where k is the bit depth of the image. This means that for an 8-bit image, each pixel can have from 1 to 2^8 (=256) different colour levels (grey-scale levels). Nuclear medicine images are frequently represented as 8- or 16- bit images.

The term resolution of the image refers to the number of pixels per unit length of the image. In digital images the spatial resolution depends on pixel size. The pixel size is calculated by the Field of View (FoV) divided by the number of pixels across the matrix. For a standard FoV, an increase of the matrix size decreases the pixel size and the ability to see details is improved.

3.2 Types of digital images – MatLab

MatLab offers simple functions that can read images of many file formats and supports a number of colour maps. Depending on file type and colour space, the returned matrix is either a 2D matrix of intensity values (greyscale images) or a 3D matrix of RGB values. Nuclear medicine images are grey scale or true colour images (RGB that is Red, Green and Blue).

The image types supported from the Image Processing Toolbox are listed below:

- Binary Images. In these, pixels can only take 0 or 1 value, black or white.
- Greyscale or intensity images. The image data in a greyscale image represent intensity or brightness. The integers' value is within the range of $[0... 2^{k-1}]$, where k is the bit depth of the image. For a typical greyscale image each pixel can represented by 8 bits and intensity values are in the range of $[0...255]$, where 0 corresponds to black and 255 to white.
- True color or RGB. In these, an image can be displayed using three matrices, each one corresponding to each of red-green-blue colour. If in an RGB image each component uses 8 bits, then the total number of bits required for each pixel is $3\times8=24$ and the range of each individual colour component is $[0...255]$.
- Indexed images. Indexed images consist of a 2D matrix together with an m×3 colour map (m= the number of the columns in image matrix). Each row of map specifies the red, green, and blue components of a single colour. An indexed image uses direct mapping of pixel values to colour map values. The colour of each image pixel is determined by using the corresponding value of matrix as an index into map.

The greyscale image is the most convenient and preferable type utilised in nuclear medicine image processing. When colouring depiction is needed, the RGB one should be used and processed. The indexed type images should be converted to any of the two other types in order to be processed. The functions used for image type conversion are: `rgb2gray`, `ind2rgb`, `ind2gray` and reversely. Any image can be also transformed to binary one using the command: `im2bw`. Moreover, in any image, the function `impixelinfo` can be used in order to detect any pixel value. The user can move the mouse cursor inside the image and the down left corner appears the pixel identity (x, y) as well as the (RGB) values. The pixel range of the image can be displayed by the command `imdisplayrange`.

3.3 MatLab image tool

The Image Tool is a simple and user-friendly toolkit which can contribute to a quick image processing and analysis without writing a code and use MatLab language. These properties makes it a very useful tool when deep analysis is not the ultimate goal but quick processing for better view is desirable.

The Image Tool opens by simply writing the command `imtool` in the main function window. Then a new window opens and the next step is loading an image. In the menu, there are many functions already installed in order to use it as simple image processing software. The tools include image information appearance, image zooming in and out, panning, adjustment of the window level and width, adjustment of contrast, cropping, distance measurement, conversion of the image to a pixel matrix and colour map choices (grey scale, bone colour, hot regions among others). These are the most common functions likely to be performed in the initial processing approach. Moreover, the user can make some further manipulations such as 3D rotation to respective 3D images and plotting of pixel data.

3.4 Image processing techniques - MatLab

Image processing techniques include all the possible tools used to change or analyse an image according to individuals' needs. This subchapter presents the most widely performed image processing techniques that are applicable to nuclear medicine images. The examples used are mostly come from nuclear medicine renal studies, as kidneys' planar images and SPECT slices are simple objects to show the application of image processing MatLab tools.

3.4.1 Contrast enhancement

One of the very first image processing issues is the contrast enhancement. The acquired image does not usually present the desired object contrast. The improvement of contrast is absolutely needed as the organ shape, boundaries and internal functionality can be better depicted. In addition, organ delineation can be achieved in many cases without removing the background activity.

The command that implements contrast processing is the imadjust. Using this, the contrast in an image can be enhanced or degraded if needed. Moreover, a very useful result can be the inversion of colours, especially in greyscale images, where an object of interest can be efficiently outlined. The general function that implements contrast enhancement is the following:

```
J = imadjust(I,[low_in high_in],[low_out high_out],gamma);
```

while the function for colour inversion is the following:

```
J = imadjust(I,[0 1],[1 0],gamma); or J = imcomplement(I);
```

suppose that J, is the new image, I, is the initial image and gamma factor depicts the shape of the curve that describes the relationship between the values of I and J. If the gamma factor is omitted, it is considered to be 1.

3.4.2 Organ contour

In many nuclear medicine images, the organs' boundaries are presented unclear due to low resolution or presence of high percentage of noise.

In order to draw the contour of an organ in a nuclear medicine image, the command imcontour is used. In addition, a variable n defines the number of equally spaced contours required. This variable is strongly related with the intensity of counts. For higher n values, the lines are drawn with smaller spaces in between and depict different streaks of intensity. The type of line contouring can be specified as well. For example, when a contour of 5 level contours, drawn with solid line, is the desirable outcome, the whole function is:

Example 1I = imread('kindeys.jpg');

```
figure, imshow(I)
```

```
J = imcontour(I,5,'-');
```

```
Figure, imshow(J)
```

where J and I stands for the final and the initial image respectively and the symbol (' – ') stands for the solid line drawing. An example of the initial image, the contour with n=15 and n=5 respectively, follows.

Fig. 2. (a) Original image depicting kidneys, (b) organs contoured with n = 15, (c) organs contoured with n = 5.

3.4.3 Image interpolation

Interpolation is a topic that has been widely used in image processing. It constitutes of the most common procedure in order to resample an image, to generate a new image based on the pattern of an existing one. Moreover, re-sampling is usually required in medical image processing in order to enhance the image quality or to retrieve lost information after compression of an image (Lehmann et al., 1999).

Interpreting the interpolation process, the user is provided with several options. These options include the resizing of an image according to a defined scaling factor, the choice of the interpolation type and the choice of low-pass filter.

The general command that performs image resizing is imresize. However, the way that the whole function has to be written depends heavily on the characteristics of the new image. The size of the image can be defined as a scaling factor of the existing image or by exact number of pixels in rows and columns. Concerning the interpolation types usually used in nuclear medicine, these are the following: a) nearest-neighbour interpolation ('nearest'), where the output pixel obtains the value of the pixel that the point falls within, without considering other pixels, b) bilinear interpolation ('bilinear'), where the output pixel obtains a weighted average value of the nearest 2x2 pixels, c) cubic interpolation ('bicubic'), where the output pixel obtains a weighted average value of the nearest 4x4 pixels (Lehmann et al., 1999).

When an image has to resize in a new one, with specified scaling factor and method, then the function Implementing that, is the following:

```
NewImage = imresize(Image, scale, method);
```

For example, for a given image I, the new image J shrunk twice of the initial one, using the bilinear interpolation method, the function will be:

```
J = imresize(I, 0.5, 'bilinear');
```

This way of image resizing contributes to the conversion of image information during any such process, a fact that is valuable in the precision of a measurement. Bilinear interpolation is often used to zoom into a 2D image or for rendering, for display purposes. Apart from the previous methods, the cubic convolution method can be applied to 3D images.

3.4.4 Image filtering

The factors that degrade the quality of nuclear medicine images result in blurred and noisy images with poor resolution. One of the most important factors that greatly affect the quality of clinical nuclear medicine images is image filtering. Image filtering is a mathematical processing for noise removal and resolution recovery. The goal of the filtering is to compensate for loss of detail in an image while reducing noise. Filters suppressed noise as well as deblurred and sharpened the image. In this way, filters can greatly improve the image resolution and limit the degradation of the image.

An image can be filtered either in the frequency or in the spatial domain. In the first case the initial data is Fourier transformed, multiplied with the appropriate filter and then taking the inverse Fourier transform, re-transformed into the spatial domain. The basics steps of filtering in the frequency domain are illustrated in Fig. 3.

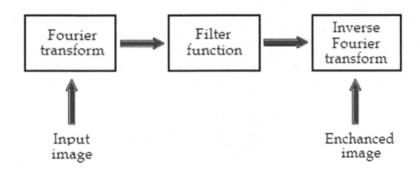

Fig. 3. Basics steps of frequency domain filtering.

The filtering in the spatial domain demands a filter mask (it is also referred as kernel or convolution filter). The filter mask is a matrix of odd usually size which is applied directly on the original data of the image. The mask is centred on each pixel of the initial image. For each position of the mask the pixel values of the image is multiplied by the corresponding values of the mask. The products of these multiplications are then added and the value of the central pixel of the original image is replaced by the sum. This must be repeated for every pixel in the image. The procedure is described schematically in Fig. 4.

If the filter, by which the new pixel value was calculated, is a linear function of the entire pixel values in the filter mask (e.g. the sum of products), then the filter is called linear. If the output pixel is not a linear weighted combination of the input pixel of the image then the filtered is called non-linear.

According to the range of frequencies they allow to pass through filters can be classified as low pass or high pass. Low pass filters allow the low frequencies to be retained unaltered and block the high frequencies. Low pass filtering removes noise and smooth the image but at the same time blur the image as it does not preserve the edges. High pass filters sharpness the edges of the image (areas in an image where the signal changes rapidly) and enhance object edge information. A severe disadvantage of high pass filtering is the amplification of statistical noise present in the measured counts.

The next section is referred to three of the most common filters used by MatLab: the mean, median and Gaussian filter.

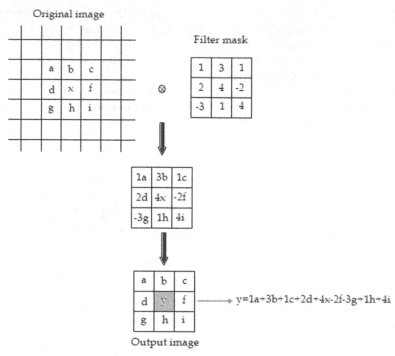

Fig. 4. Illustration of filtering process in spatial domain.

3.4.4.1 Mean filter

Mean filter is the simplest low pass linear filter. It is implemented by replacing each pixel value with the average value of its neighbourhood. Mean filter can be considered as a convolution filter. The smoothing effect depends on the kernel size. As the kernel size increases, the smoothing effect increases too. Usually a 3×3 (or larger) kernel filter is used. An example of a single 3×3 kernel is shown in the Fig. 5.

$$\begin{array}{|c|c|c|} \hline a & b & c \\ \hline d & e & f \\ \hline g & h & i \\ \hline \end{array} \longrightarrow \frac{1}{9}(a + b + c + d + e + f + g + h + i)$$

Fig. 5. Filtering approach of mean filter.

The Fig.5 depicts that by using the mean filter, the central pixel value would be changed from "e" to " (a+b+c+d+e+f+g+h+i) 1/9".

3.4.4.2 Median filter

Median filter is a non linear filter. Median filtering is done by replacing the central pixel with the median of all the pixels value in the current neighbourhood.

A median filter is a useful tool for impulse noise reduction (Toprak & Göller, 2006). The impulse noise (it is also known as salt and paper noise) appears as black or (/and) white pixels randomly distributed all over the image. In other words, impulse noise corresponds to pixels with extremely high or low values. Median filters have the advantage to preserve edges without blurring the image in contrast to smoothing filters.

Fig. 6. Filtering approach of Median Filter.

3.4.4.3 Gaussian filter

Gaussian filter is a linear low pass filter. A Gaussian filter mask has the form of a bell-shaped curve with a high point in the centre and symmetrically tapering sections to either side (Fig.7). Application of the Gaussian filter produces, for each pixel in the image, a weighted average such that central pixel contributes more significantly to the result than pixels at the mask edges (O'Gorman et al., 2008). The weights are computed according to the Gaussian function (Eq.1):

$$f(x) = \frac{1}{\sigma\sqrt{2\pi}} e^{-(x-\mu)^2 / (2\sigma^2)} \tag{1}$$

where μ, is the mean and σ, the standard deviation.

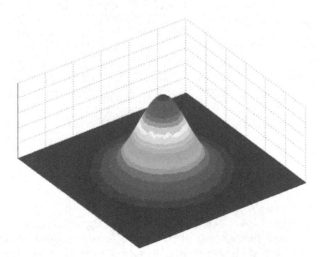

Fig. 7. A 2D Gaussian function.

The degree of smoothing depends on the standard deviation. The larger the standard deviation, the smoother the image is depicted. The Gaussian filter is very effective in the reduction of impulse and Gaussian noise. Gaussian noise is caused by random variations in the intensity and has a distribution that follows the Gaussian curve.

3.5 Filtering in MatLab

In MatLab, using Image Processing Toolbox we can design and implemented filters for image data. For linear filtering, MatLab provides the `fspecial` command to generate some predefined common 2D filters.

```
h=fspecial(filtername, parameters)
```

The `filtername` is one of the average, disk, gaussian, laplacian, log, motion, prewitt, sobel and unsharp filters; that is the `parameters` related to the specific filters that are used each time. Filters are applied to 2D images using the function `filter2` with the syntax:

```
Y = filter2(h,X)
```

The function `filter2` filters the data in matrix X with the filter h. For multidimensional images the function `imfilter` is used.

```
B = imfilter(A,h)
```

This function filters the multidimensional array A with the multidimensional filter h. `imfilter` function is more general than `filter2` function. For nonlinear filtering in MatLab the function `nlfilter` is applied, requiring three arguments: the input image, the size of the filter and the function to be used.

```
B = nlfilter(A, [m n], fun)
```

Example 2

The following example describes the commands' package that can be used for the application of the mean (average) filter in a SPECT slice for different convolution kernel sizes (for 3×3, 9×9, 25×25 average filter).

```
h=fspecial('average', [3 3]);
b=imfilter(a,h);
figure, imshow(b);
i=fspecial('average', [9 9]);
c=imfilter(b,h);
figure, imshow(c);
j=fspecial('average', [25 25]);
d=imfilter(c,h);
figure, imshow(d);
```

Figure 8 presents different implementations of the mean filter on a kidneys image with filters 3x3, 9x9, 15x15, 20x20 and 25x25.

As it can be easily noticed, the mean filter balances and smoothes the image, flattening the differences. The filtered images do not present edges at the same extent as in the original one. For larger kernel size, the blurring of the image is more intense. Image smoothening can be used in several areas of nuclear medicine and can serve in different points of view of the examined organ.

Example 3

In this example we will try to remove impulse noise from a SPECT slice, for example in a renal study. For this reason we mix the image with impulse noise (salt and pepper). The image has a 512×512 matrix size and grey levels between 0 and 255. The most suitable filter

for removing impulse noise is the median filter. Because it is a nonlinear filter, the command
nlfilter is now used.

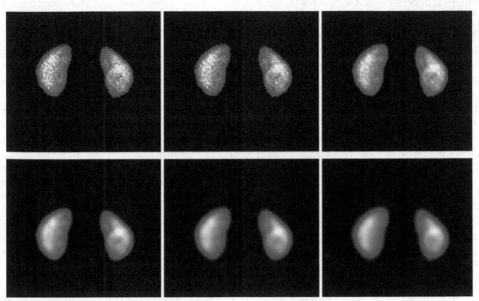

Fig. 8. Mean filter applied on kidneys image (a) Original image, (b) average filter 3x3, (c)
average filter 9x9, (d) average filter 15x15, (e) average filter 20x20 and, (f) average filter
25x25 [(a) to (f) from left to right].

```
I = imread('kidneys.tif');
figure, imshow(I);
J = imnoise(I,'salt & pepper',0.05);
figure, imshow(J);
fun = @(x) median(x(:));
K = nlfilter(J,[3 3],fun);
figure, imshow(K);
```

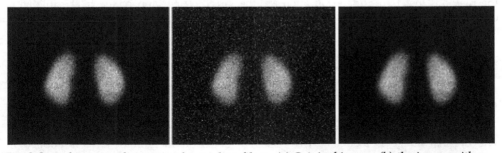

Fig. 9. Impulse noise elimination by median filter. (a) Original image (b) the image with
impulse noise (c) the image on which the noise is suppressed with the median filter. [(a) to
(c) from left to right]

Example 3 can be very useful in the nuclear medicine examinations of parenchymatous organs (liver, lungs, thyroid or kidneys) as it consists of a simple enough method for the reduction of noise which interferes in the image due to the construction of electronic circuits.

3.6 Image segmentation

The image segmentation describes the process through which an image is divided into constituent parts, regions or objects in order to isolate and study separately areas of special interest. This process assists in detecting critical parts of a nuclear medicine image that are not easily displayed in the original image.

The process of segmentation has been developed based on lots of intentions such as delineating an object in a gradient image, defining the region of interest or separating convex components in distance-transformed images. Attention should be spent in order to avoid 'over-segmentation' or 'under-segmentation'. In nuclear medicine, segmentation techniques are used to detect the extent of a tissue, an organ, a tumour inside an image, the boundaries of structures in cases that these are ambiguous and the areas that radiopharmaceutical concentrate in a greater extent. Thus, the segmentation process serves in assisting the implementation of other procedures; in other words, it constitutes the fundamental step of some basic medical image processing (Behnaz et al., 2010).

There are two ways of image segmentation: a) based on the discontinuities and, b) based on the similarities of structures inside an image. In nuclear medicine images, the discontinuity segmentation type finds more applications. This type depends on the detection of discontinuities or else, edges, inside the image using a threshold. The implementation of threshold helps in two main issues: i) the removal of unnecessary information from the image (background activity) and, ii) the appearance of details not easily detected.

The edge detection uses the command edge. In addition, a threshold is applied in order to detect edges above defined grey-scale intensity. Also, different methods of edge detection can be applied according to the filter each of them utilises. The most useful methods in nuclear medicine are the 'Sobel', 'Prewitt', 'Roberts', 'Canny' as well as 'Laplacian of Gaussian'. It is noted that the image is immediately transformed into a binary image and edges are detected. The general function used for the edge detection is the following:

```
[BW] = edge (image, 'method', threshold)
```

Where [BW] is the new binary image produced, image is the initial one; 'method' refers to the method of edge detection and 'threshold' to the threshold applied. In nuclear medicine, the methods that find wide application are the *sorbel*, *prewitt* and *canny*. In the following example, the *canny* method is applied in order to detect edges in an image.

Example 4

```
I = imread('kidneys.jpg');
figure, imshow(I)
J = edge(I,'canny', 0.048);
figure, imshow(J)
```

Another application of segmentation in nuclear medicine is the use of gradient magnitude. The original image is loaded. Then, the edge detection method of *sobel* is applied in accordance with a gradient magnitude which gives higher regions with higher grey-scale intensity. Finally, the foreground details are highlighted and segmented image of the kidneys is produced. The whole code for that procedure is described below.

Fig. 10. Edge detection (a) Original kidneys image, (b) edge detection with *canny* method and threshold 0.2667, (c) edge detection with *prewitt* method and threshold 0.038. *[(a) to (c) from left to right]*

Example 5

```
I = imread('kidneys.jpg');
Figure, imshow(I)
hy = fspecial('sobel');
hx = hy';
Iy = imfilter(double(I), hy, 'replicate');
Ix = imfilter(double(I), hx, 'replicate');
gradmag = sqrt(Ix.^2 + Iy.^2);
figure, imshow(gradmag,[])
se = strel('disk', 20);
K = imopen(I, se);
figure, imshow(K)
```

Fig. 11. Gradient Magnitude process: (a) Original image, (b) image after implementation of filter and gradient magnitude, (c) image after masking of foreground objects *[(a) to (c) from left to right]*

In the final image, the outline of the organs is depicted. The area inside the kidney has been separated into larger parts with grey-scale intensity weighted and decided from the closest 20 pixels in a circular region. In the areas of kidney that have higher activity concentrated, more than one layer of circular regions have been added presenting a final lighter region.

3.7 Background activity removal

One of the first steps to be completed in the medical image processing is removing the background activity. This procedure is based on image segmentation as in order to achieve the background activity removal, the organs' boundaries are first defined. The steps in this procedure are the following: i) the image is read, ii) the image is appeared, iii) a grey level threshold is decided by MatLab, iv) the image is transformed into binary image in order to isolate the two kidneys, v) the binary image is multiplied by the initial one, vi) the final image is appeared, vii) the colour can change (or not) according to individuals' needs. The following example of kidneys image describes the process.

Example 6

```
I = imread('kidneys.jpg');
figure, imshow(I)                                               (fig.12a)
graythresh(I) and the value of the threshold is calculated:  ans = 0.2667
I2 = im2bw(I, 0.2667)                                           (fig.12b)
I3 = immultiply(I2, I)
imshow(I3)                                                      (fig.12c)
colormap(hot)                                                   (fig.12d)
```

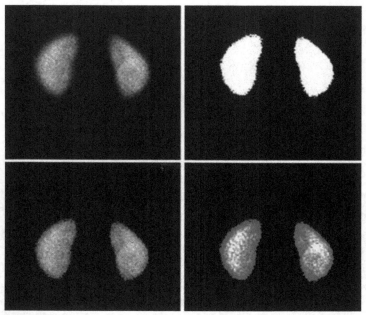

Fig. 12. Background subtraction: (a) Original image, (b) segmented binary image after thresholding depicting only sharp organ boundaries, (c) image after background removal, (d) change of colour to nuclear medicine pattern. [*(a) to (d) from left to right*]

3.8 Image registration

Image registration is used for aligning two images of the same object into a common coordinate system presenting the fused image. The one image is usually referred as reference and the other as sensed (or referred). Image registration is a spatial transform. The images can be acquired from different angles, at different times, by different or same modalities. A typical example of the use of image registration from different modalities in nuclear medicine is the combination of SPECT and CT images (SPECT/CT) or PET and CT (PET/CT). Image registration is used mainly for two reasons: i) to obtain enhanced information and details from the image for more accurate diagnosis or therapy (Li & Miller, 2010) and, ii) to compare patient's data (Zitova & Flusser, 2003). MatLab can be used in order to perform such a process. The whole procedure shall follow a specific order.

The first step of the procedure includes the image acquisition. After that, each image is reconstructed separately. Any filters needed are applied as well as enhancements in brightness and contrast. The process of filter application has been described in a previous section. The next step includes the foundation of a spatial transformation between the two images, the one of SPECT and the other of CT. The key figure in this step concerns about the alignment of the two images. A spatial transformation modifies the spatial relationship between the pixels of an image relocating them to new positions in a new image. There are several types of spatial transformation including the affine, the projective the box and the composite (Delbeke et al., 2006). The final step in image registration is the overlapping of the two images allowing a suitable level of transparency. A new image is created containing information from both pictures from which, the first has been produced. The whole procedure can be described with a set of commands which is user customised as different registration function packages can be constructed for different uses.

3.9 Intensity volume and 3-D visualisation

Volume visualisation in nuclear medicine consists of a method for extracting information from volumetric data utilising and processing a nuclear medicine image (Lyra et al., 2010b). In MatLab, this can be achieved by constructing a 3D surface plot which uses the pixel identities for (x, y) axes and the pixel value is transformed into surface plot height and, consequently, colour. Apart from that, 3D voxel images can be constructed; SPECT projections are acquired, iso-contours are depicted on them including a number of voxels and, finally all of them can be added in order to create the desirable volume image. (Lyra et al., 2010a).

Volume rendering - very often used in 3D SPECT images - is an example of efficient coding in MatLab. Inputs to the function are the original 3D array, the position angle, zoom or focus of the acquired projections. The volume rendering used in 3D myocardium, kidneys, thyroid, lungs and liver studies, took zoom and angles of 5.6 degrees, a focal length in pixels depending of the organs' size. The size of the re-projection is the same as the main size of input image (e.g. 128x128 for the 128x128x256 input image). The volume rendering by MatLab is slow enough but similar to other codes' volume rendering. An example image of myocardial 3-D voxel visualisation follows (Fig. 13):

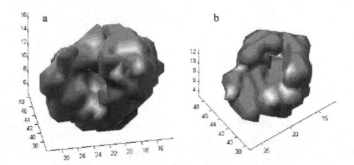

Fig. 13. 3D myocardial voxel visualisation; the image does not depicts the real volume but the voxelised one (Lyra et al 2010a).

4. MatLab mesh plot

MatLab is unique in data analysis in neurological imaging. We used MatLab and the functions of Image Processing Toolbox, to extract 3D basal ganglia activity measurements in dopamine transporters DaTSCAN scintigraphy. It can be easily run in an ordinary computer with Windows software, provides reproducible - user independent - results allowing better follow-up control comparing to the semi-quantitative evaluation of tracer uptake in basal ganglia.

The surface plot or the mesh plot can be used in order to extract information about the consistency of an organ or the loss of functionality. In order to construct a surface plot from a striatum image, the series of images that include the highest level of information was selected (Lyra et al 2010b) (Fig. 14):

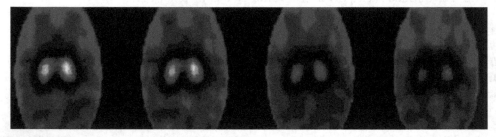

Fig. 14. A Series of central 123I-DaTSCAN SPECT imaging slices of I-123/Ioflupane; uptake is highest in middle 4 slices, and these were summarized for region of interest analysis (Lyra et al 2010b).

After the selection, ROI analysis was performed in order to concentrate on the area of interest which is the middle site of the image. The area of interest was selected and a package of functions was implemented.

Example 7

```
I = imread('striatum.jpg');
figure, imshow(I)
[x,y] = size(I);
X = 1:x;
Y = 1:y;
[xx,yy] = meshgrid(Y,x);
J = im2double(I);
figure, surf(xx,yy,J);
shading interp
view(-40,60)
```

The whole procedure was, finally, resulted in the surface plot that is presented in the Fig. 15.

A point of interest could be that although the images that were used to construct the surface plot were small and blurred, the final plot is clear and gives a lot of information regarding the activity concentration in these two lobes. The angle of view can be defined by the user giving the opportunity to inspect the whole plot from any point of view.

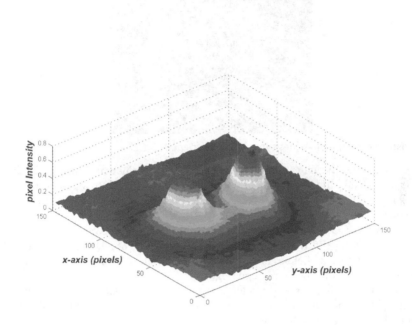

Fig. 15. Surface Plot of pixel intensity; x and y axes represent the pixels identities while the z axis represents the pixel intensity.

5. DICOM image processing using MatLab

The digital medical image processing started with the development of a standard for transferring digital images in order to enable users to retrieve images and related information from different modalities with a standardised way that is identical for all imaging modalities. In 1993, a new image format was established by National Electrical Manufacturers Association (NEMA). The Digital Imaging and Communication in Medicine (DICOM) standard allows the communication between equipment from different modalities and vendors facilitating the management of digital images. The DICOM standard defines a set of common rules for the exchange, storage and transmission of digital medical images with their accompanying information (Bidgood & Horii, 1992).

A DICOM file consists of the data header (so called metadata) and the DICOM image data set. The header includes image related information such as image type, study, modality, matrix dimensions, number of stored bits, patient's name. The image data follow the header and contains 3D information of the geometry (Bankman, 2000). The DICOM files have a .dcm extension.

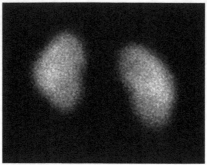

Fig. 16. Posterior image of kidneys in a DICOM format.

In nuclear medicine, the most common and supported format for storing 3D data using DICOM is to partition the volume (as myocardium or kidneys) into slices and to save each slice as a simple DICOM image. The slices can be distinguished either by a number coding in the file name or by specific DICOM tags.

MatLab supports DICOM files and is a very useful tool in the processing of DICOM images. An example of reading and writing metadata and image data of a DICOM file using MatLab is given in the next section. Let us consider a planar projection from a kidneys scan study for a 10-month-old boy as the DICOM image (Fig. 16).

The specific DICOM image is a greyscale image. Assuming "kidneys" is the name of the DICOM image we want to read, in order to read the image data from the DICOM file use the command dicomread in the following function.

```
I = dicomread('kidneys.dcm');
```

To read metadata from a DICOM file, use the dicominfo command. The latter returns the information in a MatLab structure where every field contains a specific piece of DICOM metadata. For the same DICOM image as previously,

```
info = dicominfo('kidneys.dcm')
```

A package of information appears in the command window including all the details that accompany a DICOM image. This is a great advantage of this image format in comparison to jpeg or tiff formats as the images retain all the information whereas the jpeg or tiff ones lose a great majority of it. For the specific image, the following information appears:

```
info =
Filename: 'kidneys.dcm'
FileModDate: '17-Feb-2011 14:04:18'
FileSize: 128000
Format: 'DICOM'
FormatVersion: 3
Width: 256
Height: 256
BitDepth: 16
```

```
ColorType: 'grayscale'
FileMetaInformationGroupLength: 212
FileMetaInformationVersion: [2x1 uint8]
MediaStorageSOPClassUID: '1.2.840.10008.5.1.4.1.1.7'
MediaStorageSOPInstanceUID: [1x57 char]
TransferSyntaxUID: '1.2.840.10008.1.2.1'
ImplementationClassUID: '1.2.840.113619.6.184'
ImplementationVersionName: 'Xeleris 2.1220'
SourceApplicationEntityTitle: 'XELERIS-6400'.
```

The rest of the information has been omitted as there is a huge amount of details. To view the image data imported from a DICOM file, use one of the toolbox image display functions imshow or imtool.

```
imshow(I,'DisplayRange',[]);
```

Similarly, an anterior planar image of thyroid gland can be imported and displayed in a DICOM format by using the toolbox image display function

```
imshow(K,'DisplayRange',[]);
```

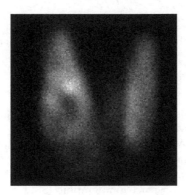

Fig. 17. Anterior planar image of thyroid gland in a DICOM format.

The image loaded can be now modified and processed in any desirable way. Many times, words or letters that describe the slice or projection appear within the image. These can be deleted and a new image without letters is created. To modify or write image data or metadata to a file in DICOM format, use the dicomwrite function. The following commands write the images I or K to the DICOM file kidneys_file.dcm and the DICOM file thyroid_file.dcm

```
dicomwrite(I, .dcm'), dicomwrite(K, .dcm')
```

On a DICOM format image any filtering, segmentation and background removing can be applied to get the final image and extract the most possible information useful in Diagnosis. In Fig.18 a DICOM format planar image of thyroid gland is imported and displayed (a) and further processed (b) by Gaussian filter and background removing.

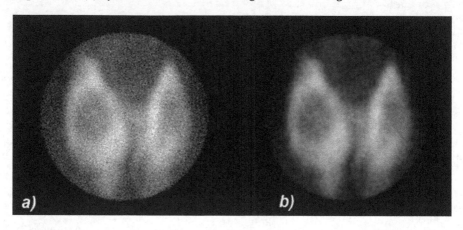

Fig. 18. (a) Thyroid gland DICOM image and (b) Gaussian filter and background removing are applied on the same image

The `dicomwrite` function is very useful too, in the case that we have to partition a volume into slices and to storage each slice as a simple DICOM image for further processing and analysis.

6. Conclusion

Image processing and analysis applied to nuclear medicine images for diagnosis, improve the acquired image qualitatively as well as offer quantitative information data useful in patient's therapy and care. Advanced techniques of image processing and analysis find widespread use in nuclear medicine. MatLab and Image Processing Toolbox enable both quantitative analysis and visualization of Nuclear Medicine images acquired as planar or angle projected images to reconstruct tomographic (SPECT, PET) slices and 3D volume surface rendering images.

7. Acknowledgment

The authors would like to acknowledge Ms Maria Gavrilelli, Medical Physicist, MSc from "Medical Imaging" Athens Paediatric Nuclear Medicine Center, Athens, Greece, for her medical images contribution.

8. References

Bankman, I. (2000). *Handbook of Medical Imaging*, Academic Press, ISSN 0-12-077790-8, United States of America

Bidgood, D. & Horii, S. (1992). Introduction to the ACR-NEMA DICOM standard. *RadioGraphics*, Vol. 12, (May 1992), pp. (345-355)

Delbeke, D.; Coleman, R.E.; Guiberteau M.J.; Brown, M.L.; Royal, H.D.; Siegel, B.A.; Townsend, D.W.; Berland, L.L.; Parker, J.A.; Zubal, G. & Cronin, V. (2006). Procedure Guideline for SPECT/CT Imaging 1.0. *The Journal of Nuclear Medicine*, Vol. 47, No. 7, (July 2006), pp. (1227-1234).

Gonzalez, R.; Woods, R., & Eddins, S. (2009) *Digital Image Processing using MATLAB*, (second edition), Gatesmark Publishing, ISBN 9780982085400, United States of America

Lehmann, T.M.; Gönner, C. & Spitzer, K. (1999). Survey: Interpolation Methods in Medical Image Processing. *IEEE Transactions on Medical Imaging*, Vol.18, No.11, (November 1999), pp. (1049-1075), ISSN S0278-0062(99)10280-5

Lyra, M.; Sotiropoulos, M.; Lagopati, N. & Gavrilleli, M. (2010a). Quantification of Myocardial Perfusion in 3D SPECT images – Stress/Rest volume differences, Imaging Systems and Techniques (IST), 2010 IEEE International Conference on 1-2 July 2010, pp 31 – 35, Thessaloniki, DOI: 10.1109/IST.2010.5548486

Lyra, M.; Striligas, J.; Gavrilleli, M. & Lagopati, N. (2010b). Volume Quantification of I-123 DaTSCAN Imaging by MatLab for the Differentiation and Grading of Parkinsonism and Essential Tremor, *International Conference on Science and Social Research*, Kuala Lumpur, Malaysia, December 5-7, 2010. http://edas.info/p8295

Li, G. & Miller, R.W. (2010). Volumetric Image Registration of Multi-modality Images of CT, MRI and PET, Biomedical Imaging, Youxin Mao (Ed.), ISBN: 978-953-307-071-1, InTech, Available from:
http://www.intechopen.com/articles/show/title/volumetric-image-registration-of-multi-modality-images-of-ct-mri-and-pet

O' Gorman, L.; Sammon, M. & Seul M. (2008). *Practicals Algorithms for image analysis*, (second edition), Cambridge University Press, 978-0-521-88411-2, United States of America

Nailon, W.H. (2010). Texture Analysis Methods for Medical Image Characterisation, Biomedical Imaging, Youxin Mao (Ed.), ISBN: 978-953-307-071-1, InTech, Available from:
http://www.intechopen.com/articles/show/title/texture-analysis-methods-for-medical-image-characterisation

MathWorks Inc. (2009) *MATLAB User's Guide*. The MathWorks Inc., United States of America

Perutka K. (2010). Tips and Tricks for Programming in Matlab, Matlab - Modelling, Programming and Simulations, Emilson Pereira Leite (Ed.), ISBN: 978-953-307-125-1, InTech, Available from: http://www.intechopen.com/articles/show/title/tips-and-tricks-for-programming-in-matlab

Toprak, A. & Guler, I. (2006). Suppression of Impulse Noise in Medical Images with the Use of Fuzzy Adaptive Median Filter. *Journal of Medical Systems*, Vol. 30, (November 2006), pp. (465-471)

Wernick, M. & Aarsvold, J. (2004). *Emission Tomography: The Fundamentals of PET and SPECT*, Elsevier Academic Press, ISBN 0-12-744482-3, China

Wilson, H.B.; Turcotte, L.H. & Halpern, D. (2003). *Advanced Mathematics and Mechanics Applications Using MATLAB* (third edition), Chapman & Hall/CRC, ISBN 1-58488-262-X, United States of America

Zitova, B. & Flusser J. (2003). Image Registration methods: a survey. *Image and Vision Computing*. Vol 21, (June 2003), pp. (977-1000)

9

Image Processing for Optical Metrology

Miguel Mora-González, Jesús Muñoz-Maciel, Francisco J. Casillas,
Francisco G. Peña-Lecona, Roger Chiu-Zarate
and Héctor Pérez Ladrón de Guevara
Universidad de Guadalajara, Centro Universitario de los Lagos
México

1. Introduction

Optical measurements offer the desirable characteristics of being noninvasive and nondestructive techniques that are able to analyze in real time objects and phenomena in a remote sense. Science areas that involve optical characterization include physics, biology, chemistry and varied fields of engineering. The use of digital cameras to record objects or a specific phenomenon permits the exploitation of the potential of that the associated images can be processed to determine one or several parameter or characteristics of what is being recorded. These images need to be processed and securely there will be a model associated with the optical metrology that will provide an insight or a comprehensive understanding of the image being analyzed. Matlab® is the suitable platform to implement image processing algorithms due to its ability to perform the whole processing techniques and procedures to analyze and image. At the same time it provides a flexible and a fast programming language for user constructing algorithms. In the present chapter we provide some fundamentals about image acquisition, filtering and processing, and some applications. Some applications are well-know techniques while others offer the state of the art in the field under study. All authors agree that Matlab® is a powerful tool for image processing and optical metrology.

All algorithms and/or sentences used in this chapter are made in such manner so that they work in the Matlab® R2007b platform or superior. Matlab® is a trade mark of Mathworks Inc., from here on we will refer it as Matlab only. Also the Matlab functions and parameters used along the chapter are typed in italics and in apostrophes, respectively.

Algorithms in present chapter are presented in two formats depending on the algorithm extension: 1) Image titles and/or figure captions for low algorithms extension; 2) Subsection ends for larger algorithms.

2. Image processing and acquisition

In the present section, image and processing acquisition principles in Matlab are established.

2.1 Image acquisition

Image acquisition is the initial stage in every vision system for human or artificial image data interpretation. Image acquisition is the recording process of a real object, this implies that the vision process totally depends on quality acquisition; this could be an analogical or digital. The analogical acquisition process is a representation of the object with several techniques like designing, painting, photography, and video. In a similar way, digital imaging acquisition is able to represent a real object, however object properties are presented in a discrete form. Every object characteristics are mapped from a real plane to a digital plane where a group of discrete values (i.e 1, 2, 3, ...,) represent position, form, color and texture.

2.1.1 Acquisition and digital image representation

Image acquisition process in Matlab can be done by the use of either *imread* or *getsnapshot* functions for stored images or video, respectively. Each function stores the object representation in a discrete *lxmxn* array, where *l* can be related to color data; *m* and *n* indexes represent the image spatial coordinates.

An example of a real image is shown in Figure 1a, and in Figure 1b, the representation in a matrix array of the selected area from the image. Digital images are described as a bi-dimensional $f(x,y)$ function, where x and y represent the spatial coordinates. The f value at the (x,y) position point is proportional to the intensity or gray scale of the image.

In Matlab, a digital image satisfies following conditions: first, spatial and gray scale values must be discrete; and second, intensities are sampling at 8 bits (255 values).

$$im_{color} = imread('lagos.jpg','jpg')$$

a)   b)

Fig. 1. a) real color image, and b) matrix of the green color component of the selected area.

2.1.2 Image discretization

Image discretization is the process of converting an analogical image to a digital image; this process depends on the sampling and quantization stages.

Correspondence between analogical and digital images is given by the number of pixels used. If the number of pixels is enough to satisfy the Nyquist criteria (Oppenheim et al., 1997), the acquired image is a satisfactory representation of the real object observed. Quantization is the process of assigning a color or gray discrete level to each sample.

Therefore, image discretization quality depends on frequency sampling as in quantization levels used. It must be noted that Matlab only reads digital images. Acquisition process can be done with scanners, CCD cameras, etc.

2.2 Thresholding and high contrast image

Frequently, acquired images under real conditions present a background problem. When relevant foreground elements are mixed with low interest background ones. Another problem that hides the desired information is a low contrast image. Therefore, the use of algorithms that deals with can be implemented in order to enhance the images. Equalization, binarization and thresholding algorithm are alternatives that have proved to be successful.

In the following subsection, a method for the conversion of color images into gray levels is presented. Next, by using histogram equalization, a high contrast image from the gray scale levels is obtained. Finally, binarization process by establishing a thresholding is described in order to get a two color image (black (0) and white (255)) from a gray level scale (Poon & Banerjee, 2001).

2.2.1 Histogram

Histogram is the graphical representation of pixels gray values distribution. Images can be classified according to its histogram as high, medium or low contrast images. A low contrast image has a histogram with a low fraction of all possible gray values, around less than 40% of the whole scale. A high contrast image has more than 90% of the gray values.

Color images can also be classified in accordance with its histogram by considering human ocular sensitivity to primary colors. This is given by the first component of the YIQ matrix:

$$Y = 0.299R + 0.587G + 0.114B, \qquad (1)$$

Where Y and RGB are the lumma components used in color television systems NTSC (that represents a gray scale in the YIQ space) and the primary components, red, green and blue, respectively. The histogram transformation for a color image is given by the following pixel to pixel operation:

$$T_{gsl}(r_k) = s_k, \qquad (2)$$

where r_k and s_k are the original pixel intensities in color and gray scale levels (gsl) respectively. In figure 2 is shown the image obtained by the use of equation (2) and its corresponding histogram, these operations can be done by using the Matlab functions *rgb2gray* and *imhist*.

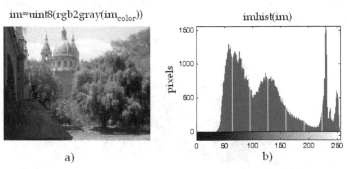

Fig. 2. a) gsl photography, b) histogram.

2.2.2 Histogram equalization

Histogram equalization is the transformation of the intensity values of an image that is typically applied to enhance the contrast of the image. As an example, the contrast of the image of the figure 2a, can be handled by applying histogram equalization and it is shown in figure 3 with its respective histogram, this operation can be done by using the Matlab function *histeq*.

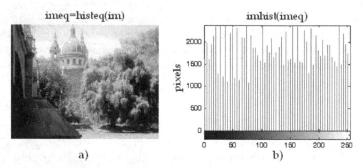

Fig. 3. a) Photography equalization, b) histogram.

In order to get the discrete values in a gsl, the following equation is used

$$T_{eq}(s_k) = \sum_{j=0}^{k} \frac{n_j}{n}(L-1),\tag{3}$$

where $k = 0,1,2,...,$ (L-1), L represents the gray level numbers into an image (255 as an example), n_j is the frequency of appearance of an specific j-th gray level and n is the total number of pixels of the image.

2.2.3 Thresholding by histogram

Thresholding is a non-linear operation for image segmentation that consists in the conversion of a gsl image into a binary image according to a threshold value. This operation is used to separate some regions of the foreground of an image from its background. Thresholding operation can be done by using the Matlab function *graythresh*. Binarization may be considered as an especial case of thresholding as shown in figure 4. The Matlab function that binaries an image is *im2bw*.

Fig. 4. Image binarization by thresholding.

2.3 Spatial filtering

In order to reduce noise or enhance some specific characteristics of an image some filters like high-pass, low-pass, band-pass or band-stop are used. These filters can be applied in the frequency domain (section 2.4) or in the spatial domain. Spatial domain filtering is described in this section. Filtering operations are directly applied to the image (pixel to pixel). The mathematical functions applied in the spatial domain are well known as convolution, and are described by (Mora-González et al., 2008)

$$f(x,y) * g(x,y) = \sum_{m=-\frac{M+1}{2}}^{\frac{M+1}{2}} \sum_{n=-\frac{N+1}{2}}^{\frac{N+1}{2}} f(m,n)g(x-m,y-n), \qquad (4)$$

where f, g,(x,y), (m,n) and $M{\times}N$ are the original image, the convolution mask or matrix, the original image coordinates, the coordinates where the convolution is performed, and the size of convolution mask, respectively. Equation (4) is applied by doing a homogeneous scanning with the convolution mask versus the whole image to be convolved. These filters are also known as Finite Impulse Response (FIR) filters because they are applied to a finite section of the spatial domain (In this case the finite section is the image). Equation (4) can be implemented in Matlab by using nested *for* loops, also *conv2*, *fspecial* or *imfilter* functions can be used too. These kinds of filters are dependent of the convolution mask form as is explained in the following two subsections.

2.3.1 Low-pass filters
Low-pass filters applied to images have the purpose of image smoothing, by blurring the edges into the image and lowering the contrast. The main characteristic of a low-pass convolution mask is that all of its elements have positive values. Some commonly used low-pass filters are: averaging, gaussian, quadratic, triangular and trigonometric. These mask are presented in a matrix form like

$$g(m,n) = \frac{1}{\sum_{m=1}^{M}\sum_{n=1}^{N} w_{m,n}} \begin{bmatrix} w_{1,1} & w_{1,2} & \cdots & w_{1,N} \\ w_{2,1} & w_{2,2} & \cdots & w_{2,N} \\ \vdots & \vdots & \ddots & \vdots \\ w_{M,1} & w_{M,2} & \cdots & w_{M,N} \end{bmatrix}, \qquad (5)$$

with

$$w = \begin{cases} A\exp\left(-B\left[\left(m-\frac{M+1}{2}\right)^2 + \left(n-\frac{N+1}{2}\right)^2\right]\right), & gaussian \\ A\left[1 - B\left(m-\frac{M+1}{2}\right)^2 - B\left(n-\frac{N+1}{2}\right)^2\right], & cuadratic \\ \frac{A}{2}+\frac{A}{4}\cos\left[B\left(m-\frac{M+1}{2}\right)\right]+\frac{A}{4}\cos\left[B\left(n-\frac{N+1}{2}\right)\right], & trigonometric \\ A, & average \end{cases}, \qquad (6)$$

where A, B and w are the amplitude, the width function factor and the weight function of the spatial filter, respectively. In order to determine the effectiveness of the masks of the equations (5) and (6), Magnitude Spectra (MS) are obtained to analyze the low frequencies allowed to pass by the filter and high frequencies attenuation. This is expressed as

$$MS(\omega) = 20\log\left|\Im\{g(m,n)\}\right|, \qquad (7)$$

where ω and $\mathfrak{I}$ are the MS frequency component and the Fourier transform operator, respectively.

In figure 5, the MS of the convolution mask from equations (5) and (6) are shown. Spatial gaussian filter behavior is more stable because allows low frequencies to pass and also attenuate middle and high frequencies faster than other filters, as can be observed. The mask for nine elements is shown in table 1. It must be mentioned that the processing time slow down conforming the convolution mask increases. Spatial filtering also has a problem in the image edges, because they cannot be convolved and there are $(M-1)/2$ and $(N-1)/2$ lost information elements in x and y axes, respectively. By using the *fspecial* function, low-pass masks can be generated by applying the *'gaussian'* or *'average'* Matlab parameters.

Another mask types designed for signal processing can be implemented on image processing by a two dimensional extension. In figure 6 it is shown three different low-pass filters applied in the test image.

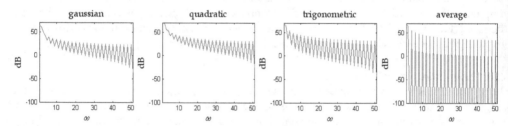

Fig. 5. MS of equations (5) and (6) masks, with $A=1$, $B=1$ and $w=1$. Matlab code representation of equation (7) is: $MS=20*log10(abs(fft(g)))$.

Gaussian	Quadratic	Trigonometric	Average
$\begin{pmatrix} .0449 & .1221 & .0449 \\ .1221 & .3319 & .1221 \\ .0449 & .1221 & .0449 \end{pmatrix}$	$\begin{pmatrix} 0 & .1667 & 0 \\ .1667 & .3333 & .1667 \\ 0 & .1667 & 0 \end{pmatrix}$	$\begin{pmatrix} .1011 & .1161 & .1011 \\ .1161 & .1312 & .1161 \\ .1011 & .1161 & .1011 \end{pmatrix}$	$\frac{1}{9}\begin{pmatrix} 1 & 1 & 1 \\ 1 & 1 & 1 \\ 1 & 1 & 1 \end{pmatrix}$

Table 1. 3x3 convolution masks g for low-pass filters of equations (5) and (6), with $A=1$, $B=1$ and $w=1$.

imfilter(im,fspecial('average'))   imfilter(im,fspecial('gaussian'))   imfilter(im,fspecial('disk'))

a)   b)   c)

Fig. 6. Low-pass 3x3 filters examples applied to figure 1a. Matlab parameters used: a) average, b) gaussian and c) disk.

2.3.2 High-pass filters

High frequency components are mostly located in image borders, like fast tone changes and marked details. The main purpose of a high-pass filter is to highlight the image details for skeletonizing, geometrical orientation, contrast enhancement, and revealing hidden characteristics, among many others. One of the most common high-pass spatial filters is the high-boost that consists in an interactive subtraction process between the original image and low-pass filters. The weighting function for a 3x3 matrix is obtained by

$$w = \begin{cases} 9C - \frac{1}{9}, & m = 2, n = 2 \\ -\frac{1}{9}, & m \neq 2, n \neq 2 \end{cases}.$$

(8)

The differential filters are another kind of high-pass filters that get its weighting function based on the partial derivates applied to the image. The most usual differential filters are the gradient and laplacian, based on the following equations

$$|\nabla(f(x,y))| = \sqrt{\left(\frac{\partial f}{\partial x}\right)^2 + \left(\frac{\partial f}{\partial y}\right)^2} \approx \left|\frac{\partial f}{\partial x}\right| + \left|\frac{\partial f}{\partial y}\right|, \quad gradient\ magnitude,$$

(9)

and

$$\nabla^2(f(x,y)) = \frac{\partial^2 f}{\partial x^2} + \frac{\partial^2 f}{\partial y^2}, \quad laplacian,$$

(10)

if the magnitude of the partial derivatives work with a 3x3 mask, then

$$\left|\frac{\partial f}{\partial x}\right| = \frac{1}{\kappa + 2}\left[(w_{1,3} + \kappa \cdot w_{2,3} + w_{3,3}) - (w_{1,1} + \kappa \cdot w_{2,1} + w_{3,1})\right]$$

(11)

and

$$\left|\frac{\partial f}{\partial y}\right| = \frac{1}{\kappa + 2}\left[(w_{1,1} + \kappa \cdot w_{1,2} + w_{1,3}) - (w_{3,1} + \kappa \cdot w_{3,2} + w_{3,3})\right].$$

(12)

Other used filters based on gradients are the Sobel, Prewitt and Canny. The Sobel spatial filter uses the central weight constant $k=2$ (Pratt, 2001). Meanwhile the Pewwit space filter uses $k=1$. The Canny space filter uses two different thresholds for weak and strong edges detection (Canny, 1986). Table 2 shows the nine elements masks of the most utilized high-pass filters. Figure 7 shows six examples of the application of these functions as high-pass filters to figure 1a. It is observed that the Canny filter is the most powerful edge detector filter.

2.4 Mathematical discrete transforms

Discrete transform analysis has played an important role in digital image processing. Several transform types are applicable to digital image processing, but due to their optical metrology potential applications, Fourier and Radon transforms are presented in this chapter section.

2.4.1 Fourier transform

Discrete Fourier Transform (DFT) represents the change from spatial to frequency domain. In convergent optical systems this transform represents the propagated optical perturbation from exit pupil to the focal point in a single lens arrangement. Equations (13) and (14) represent the DFT pair for the mathematical two dimensional (2D) model (Gonzalez, 2002)

$$\Im\{f(x,y)\} = F(u,v) = \frac{1}{MN}\sum_{x=1}^{M}\sum_{y=1}^{N} f(x,y)\exp\left[-i2\pi\left(\frac{ux}{M} + \frac{vy}{N}\right)\right], \tag{13}$$

Sobel		Prewitt		Gradient		Laplacian
$\left\|\frac{\partial f}{\partial x}\right\| =$	$\left\|\frac{\partial f}{\partial y}\right\| =$	$\left\|\frac{\partial f}{\partial x}\right\| =$	$\left\|\frac{\partial f}{\partial y}\right\| =$	$\left\|\frac{\partial f}{\partial x}\right\| =$	$\left\|\frac{\partial f}{\partial y}\right\| =$	
$\begin{pmatrix} 1 & 0 & -1 \\ 2 & 0 & -2 \\ 1 & 0 & -1 \end{pmatrix}$	$\begin{pmatrix} 1 & 2 & 1 \\ 0 & 0 & 0 \\ -1 & -2 & -1 \end{pmatrix}$	$\begin{pmatrix} 1 & 0 & -1 \\ 1 & 0 & -1 \\ 1 & 0 & -1 \end{pmatrix}$	$\begin{pmatrix} 1 & 1 & 1 \\ 0 & 0 & 0 \\ -1 & -1 & -1 \end{pmatrix}$	$\begin{pmatrix} 1 & 1 & -1 \\ 1 & -2 & -1 \\ 1 & 1 & -1 \end{pmatrix}$	$\begin{pmatrix} 1 & 1 & 1 \\ 1 & -2 & 1 \\ -1 & -1 & -1 \end{pmatrix}$	$\begin{pmatrix} 0 & 1 & 0 \\ 1 & -4 & 1 \\ 0 & 1 & 0 \end{pmatrix}$

Table 2. Some 3x3 convolution masks g for high-pass differential filters (Bow, 2002).

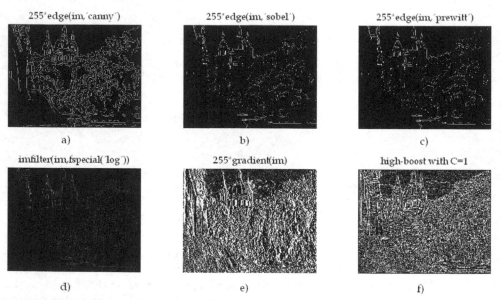

a) b) c)

d) e) f)

Fig. 7. High-pass 3x3 filters examples applied to figure 1a. Matlab parameters and functions used: a) 'canny', b) 'sobel', c) 'prewitt', d) laplacian with 'log', e) *gradient* and f) high-boost filter.

and

$$\Im^{-1}\{F(u,v)\} = f(x,y) = \sum_{u=1}^{M}\sum_{v=1}^{N} F(u,v)\exp\left[i2\pi\left(\frac{ux}{M} + \frac{vy}{N}\right)\right], \tag{14}$$

where (u,v), MxN and $\mathfrak{I}^{-1}$ are the Fourier space coordinates, the image size, the inverse Fourier transform operator, respectively. Matlab has *fft2* and *ifft2* special functions for equations (13) and (14), respectively, where FFT is the acronyms of Fast Fourier Transform. Other functions of Fourier transforms are *fft*, *ifft* for one dimension, and *fftshift* for the shifting of the zero-frequency component to spectra center. An important characteristic obtained from the Fourier transform is that it gives the frequencies content of the image. Due to this property, frequency filter design is a very straight forward task. Low frequencies are located into the matrix around the central coordinates, while frequencies gradually increase as are spread out from its center in a radial form. This characteristic is ideal for frequency filtering (low-pass, high-pass, band-pass, and band-stop). The frequency filtering process consists in the multiplication between image Fourier transform with a binary circular mask. Figure 8 shows the filtered Fourier spectra and the resulting filtered images for a high-pass, low-pass, band-pass and band-stop.

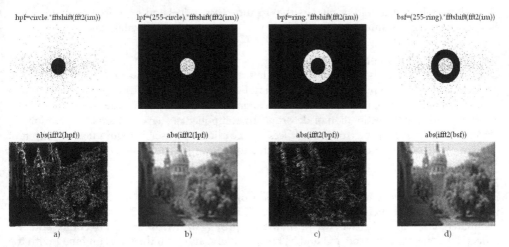

Fig. 8. Fourier filtering applied to figure 1a. a) high-pass, b) low-pass, c) band-pass and d) band-stop. Where, circle and ring are masks of 30 and 60 pixels radii.

2.4.2 Radon transform
Radon transform applied in pattern recognition or digital image processing may be considered as the image's gsl projection over a given angle with respect to x axis. The mathematical model of the Radon transform is (Bracewell, 1995)

$$\mathfrak{R}\{f(x,y)\} = \int\limits_{-\infty}^{\infty} \int\limits_{-\infty}^{\infty} f(x,y)\delta(R - x\cos\theta - y\sin\theta)\,dxdt, \tag{15}$$

where $\mathfrak{R}$, δ, R and θ are the Radon transform operator, the Dirac delta function, the distance from the origin to the profile line and the angle of direction of the same line, respectively. Each of these parameters can be observed in figure 9, Q is the origin of the profile line to be obtained (thick blue bold line). Equation (15) is implemented in Matlab with the special function *radon*.

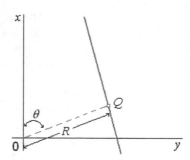

Fig. 9. Radon transform parameters.+

3. Optical metrology fundamentals

Optical metrology is a field of physics that include theoretical and experimental methods to estimate physical parameters using the light wavelength as fundamental scale.

3.1 Optical interferometry

Optical interferometry is based in the light interference phenomenon to determine different physical variables. A typical application is in nondestructive optical testing that requires high accuracy. The interferometer is the optical system used by this technique, which allows by interfering fringes the estimation of deformation components, shapes, strains or vibrations in objects with polished or rough surfaces. According to users' requirements, different configurations of interferometers can be selected to measure displacements components.

3.1.1 Interference

Figure 10 shows the schematic of a common optical arrangement used in interferometry well known as Michelson interferometer. The beam splitter (BS) splits the incident collimated laser light in two wavefronts that propagate in different directions and are reflected by the plane mirrors M1 and M2 respectively, and then they are combined with the same BS to form an interference pattern that can be observed directly on the screen.

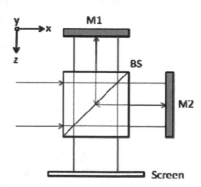

Fig. 10. Michelson interferometer.

The superposition of the two wavefrons at a position (x,y) is expressed by the complex sum:

$$U(x,y) = a_1(x,y)\exp[i\phi_1(x,y)] + a_2(x,y)\exp[i\phi_2(x,y)], \qquad (16)$$

where $a_1(x,y)$ and $a_2(x,y)$ are the amplitudes and its respective phases $\phi_1(x,y)$ y $\phi_2(x,y)$. The intensity at a point in the interference pattern is determined with the product of perturbation U multiplied by its complex conjugated U^*, this is

$$I(x,y) = U(x,y) \cdot U^*(x,y), \qquad (17)$$

then, the resulting intensity is given by

$$I(x,y) = I_1(x,y) + I_2(x,y) + 2\sqrt{I_1(x,y)I_2(x,y)}\cos[\phi(x,y)], \qquad (18)$$

where $I_1(x,y)=a_1^2(x,y)$ and $I_2(x,y)=a_1^2(x,y)$ are the intensities for each wavefront and $\phi(x,y)$ is the phase difference between them, since these propagate along to different paths before the interference.

Due to cosine of equation (18), $I(x,y)$ reaches its maxima when $\phi(x,y)$ corresponds to even multiples of π (constructive interference) and its minima for odd multiples of π (destructive interference) (Gasvik, 2002). In general, optical interferometry is applied to estimate this phase difference, which can arise due to geometrical variations or deformations in a testing object. In figure 11 are shown two synthetic interference patterns when is replaced a mirror: a) with tilt in y and defocus and b) with defocus and coma in the interferometer of figure 10. The phase difference involving the geometrical variations of the mirrors is given by $\phi(x,y)=4\pi\Delta z/\lambda$, where λ is the wavelength of the illumination source and Δz is the shape phase difference introduced by the mirrors.

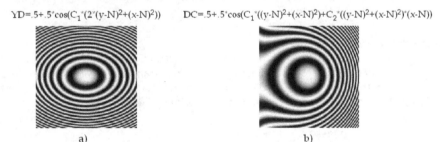

$\mathrm{YD}=.5+.5^*\cos(C_1^*(2^*(y\text{-}N)^2+(x\text{-}N)^2))$ $\mathrm{DC}=.5+.5^*\cos(C_1^*((y\text{-}N)^2+(x\text{-}N)^2)+C_2^*((y\text{-}N)^2+(x\text{-}N)^2)^*(x\text{-}N))$

a)   b)

Fig. 11. Fringe patterns of mirrors with: a) tilt in y and defocus, YD; and b) defocus and coma, DC. These wavefronts were generated using nested for loops. For these cases N=128 pixels; C_1=0.01 and C_2= 0.00001 are the numerical parameter of each aberration.

Another way to generate fringe patterns is by replacing a mirror of the interferometer for a testing object with an optically rough surface that experiments a deformation. In this case, the interference fringe pattern is not observed directly on the screen as in the previous described case. The superposition of a wavefront reflected by a rough surface (object beam) with a regular wavefront (reference beam) as the reflected by a plane mirror in the Michelson interferometer causes that I_1, I_2 and ϕ of equation (18) vary fast and randomly, normally obtaining a speckle pattern. In speckle pattern interferometry the fringe patterns are obtained by the correlation of two speckle patterns recorded using a CCD camera placed at the screen position of the interferometer for the object before and after a deformation $\Delta\phi(x,y)$. Assuming $I_i(x,y)$, $I_f(x,y)$ are the intensities of the speckle patterns for the initial no-deformed state and the final deformed state respectively, the fringe patter can be calculated by (Lehmann, 2001)

$$\left| I_f(x,y) - I_i(x,y) \right|, \tag{19}$$

and the phase difference involving the deformation of the object is given by $\Delta\phi(x,y) = 4\pi z'/\lambda$, where z' is the displacement of the object in z direction (Waldner, 2000).

3.1.2 Phase shifting

In order to determine the phase $\phi(x,y)$ from fringe patterns, is applied a procedure well-known as phase shifting. For this procedure can be registered several images introducing a phase difference which experimentally is achieved with a piezoelectric (PZ) that modifies the optical path length of one of the beams. A widely used algorithm to calculate the phase employs four consecutive images shifted by $\pi/2$ (Huntley, 2001)

$$\phi(x,y) = \tan^{-1}\left[\frac{I_d(x,y) - I_b(x,y)}{I_a(x,y) - I_c(x,y)}\right], \tag{20}$$

where $I_a(x,y)$, $I_b(x,y)$, $I_c(x,y)$ and $I_d(x,y)$ are the intensities of the shifted images. Due to the inverse tangent, in this pattern arise an effect of wrapping in a 2π module; moreover can be affected by noise of high frequency in the case of speckle interferograms. If the interest of the user is to explore the reduction of speckle noise and phase unwrapping techniques can consults references (Sirohi, 1993) and (Ghiglia, 1998).

In figure 12 are shown the wrapped phases calculated with equation (20) using the fringe patterns presented in the section.

3.2 Image diffraction

The mathematical representation for a collimated wavefront passing through a convergent optical system until the focal point is given by the Fourier transform, as is observed in figure 13. By setting a diffraction grating in the entrance pupil of a convergent lens, a Fraunhofer diffraction pattern is obtained in the focal point (Goodman, 2005), given by

$$U_o(u,v) = \frac{A \cdot \exp\left[j\frac{\pi}{f\lambda}\left(u^2 + v^2\right)\right]}{j\lambda f} \int\limits_{-\infty}^{\infty} \int r(x,y) \cdot \exp\left[-j\frac{2\pi}{f\lambda}(xu + yv)\right] dx dy, \tag{21}$$

wpYD=255*(atan2(YD_d-YD_b,YD_a-YD_c)+π)/(2π)   wpDC=255*(atan2(DC_d-DC_b,DC_a-DC_c)+π)/(2π)

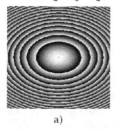

a)

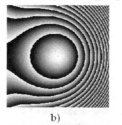

b)

Fig. 12. Calculated wrapped phases for: a) tilt in y and defocus, wpYD; and b) defocus and coma, wpDC.

where $U_o(u, v)$, $r(x, y)$, A and λ are the complex amplitude distribution of the field in the back focal plane of the lens, the grating function, the amplitude of the monochromatic plane wave and the illumination wavelength, respectively. The result of equation (21) varies depending on the function of the grating. For our purposes, those functions are binary and sinusoidal.

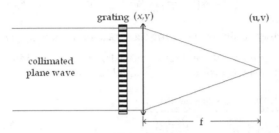

Fig. 13. Diagram for performing the Fourier transform of a grating with a positive lens.

3.2.1 Binary grating

A binary grating can be mathematically represented by a Fourier series expansion of a step function (*fstep*) bounded in the $[0,T]$ interval, see figure 14a. The function is defined by:

$$f_{step}(x,y) = \begin{cases} a, & 0 < y < \frac{T}{2} \\ 0, & \frac{T}{2} \le y \le T \end{cases}, \tag{22}$$

and its Fourier series expansion is given by (Tolstov, 1962)

$$r_{bin}(x,y) = \frac{a}{(2\pi)^2} \sum_{m,n=-\infty}^{\infty} \frac{[(-1)^n - 1]}{mn} \exp[i\omega_0(mx + ny)], \tag{23}$$

where T and a are the grating period and the amplitude, respectively. Then the intensity profile at the focal plane is calculated from equations (17) and (21), with $r(x,y)$ as vertical binary grating of equation (23), giving (Mora-González et al., 2009)

$$I_{bin}(u,v) = h_0^2 \sum_{k=-\infty}^{\infty} \left(\frac{\sin\left(k\frac{\pi}{2}\right)}{k\frac{\pi}{2}} \right)^2 \cdot \delta\left[Ku, K\left(v - \frac{k\omega_0}{K}\right) \right], \tag{24}$$

here $h_0 = \frac{2Aa\pi^2}{f\lambda}$ is the zero diffraction order amplitude, $K = \frac{2\pi}{f\lambda}$ is the scale factor at the focal plane and $\omega_0 = \frac{2\pi}{T}$ is the angular frequency. The binary grating intensity profile presents an infinite number of diffraction orders (harmonics) modulated by a sinc function (see figure 14b).

3.2.2 Sinusoidal grating

In order to observe the sinusoidal grating profile, it must be above x axis because negative gsl cannot be observed. The equation proposed for the vertical sinusoidal grating is given by (see figure 14c)

$$r_{\sin}(x,y) = a\left[\tfrac{1}{2} + \tfrac{1}{2}\sin(\omega_0 y)\right]. \tag{25}$$

The intensity profile at the focal plane from equation (21) with $r(x,y)$ as vertical sinusoidal grating of equation (25), giving (Mora-González et al., 2009)

$$I_{\sin}(u,v) = h_1^2 \delta\left[Ku, K\left(v + \tfrac{\omega_0}{K}\right)\right] + h_0^2 \delta[Ku, Kv] + h_1^2 \delta\left[Ku, K\left(v - \tfrac{\omega_0}{K}\right)\right], \tag{26}$$

where $h_1 = \frac{Aa\pi^2}{f\lambda}$ is the ±1 sinusoidal diffraction orders amplitude. The sinusoidal grating intensity profile only presents three diffraction orders (see figure 14d), those harmonics are characteristic of the Fourier transform of sinusoidal functions.

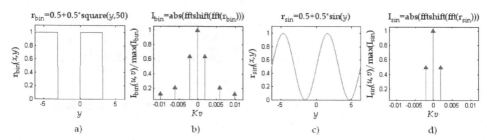

a)   b)   c)   d)

Fig. 14. Functions of a) binary and c) sinusoidal gratings. Fourier spectra of b) binary and d) sinusoidal gratings.

4. Aplications

As shown in previous sections, Digital Image Processing is a useful tool to obtain improved results in Optical Metrology. Applications details are presented in following subsections.

4.1 Fringe analysis

Fringe analysis refers to the process of finding the phase associated to physical variables that are being estimated. A typical case consists in the interpretation of the fringe patterns that can be achieved with phase shifting techniques, when the object under study remains static while three or more frames are acquired when the experiment conditions are free of environmental perturbations. Another case is when the environmental conditions are not met, and then the analysis of a single interferogram is more convenient. In both cases a wrapped phase is obtained before the related continuous phase is assessed.

Phase unwrapping is a numerical technique for retrieving a continuous phase from the calculated phase by using the arctangent (*atan2*) of the sine and cosine functions of the phase. In its simplest form, phase unwrapping consists in the addition or subtraction of a 2π multiple when a discontinuity bigger than π is found between adjacent pixels (Robinson, 1993). This approach however is very sensitive to noise, and is said to be path dependent. It means that any error may propagate along the path followed to phase unwrapping. In this study we will review the least square method (Ghiglia, 1998). Basically, it consists in the integration of the phase gradient by solving a linear equation system employing a numerical technique. Lets assume $\phi^x(x,y)$ and $\phi^y(x,y)$ as the phase differences in the horizontal and vertical directions, respectively. These phases are calculated from the wrapped phase $\phi^w(x,y)$ as follows:

$$\phi^x(x,y) = \tan^{-1}\left\{\frac{\sin\left[\phi^w(x,y) - \phi^w(x-1,y)\right]}{\cos\left[\phi^w(x,y) - \phi^w(x-1,y)\right]}\right\} p(x,y)p(x-1,y), \tag{27}$$

and

$$\phi^y(x,y) = \tan^{-1}\left\{\frac{\sin\left[\phi^w(x,y) - \phi^w(x,y-1)\right]}{\cos\left[\phi^w(x,y) - \phi^w(x,y-1)\right]}\right\} p(x,y)p(x,y-1), \tag{28}$$

In the above equations $p(x,y)$ is a pupil function equal to one inside of an interferogram field and zero otherwise. A discretized Laplacian equation is then obtained from the phase differences:

$$\begin{aligned}
L(x,y) &= \phi^x(x+1,y) - \phi^x(x,y) + \phi^y(x,y+1) - \phi^y(x,y) \\
&= -4\phi(x,y) + \phi(x+1,y) + \phi(x-1,y) + \phi(x,y+1) + \phi(x,y-1)
\end{aligned}. \tag{29}$$

This equation represents a linear equations system that can be solved with iterative algorithms. In particular, is employed an overrelaxation method (SOR) due to it may be easily programmed. The following equation is then iterated until the solution converges:

$$\begin{aligned}
\phi^{k+1}(x,y) = &\, \phi^k(x,y) + \\
&+ \frac{\left[d\phi^k(x,y) - \phi(x+1,y) - \phi(x-1,y) - \phi(x,y+1) - \phi(x,y-1) + L(x,y)\right]r}{d},
\end{aligned} \tag{30}$$

where, $d=p(x+1,y)+p(x-1,y)+p(x,y+1)+p(x,y-1)$, and r is a parameter of the SOR method that must be set between the [1,2] range. Figure 15 shows the wrapped phase ϕ^w obtained from the sine and cosine of the phase and the unwrapped phase ϕ. A simple iterative algorithm that unwraps the phase from the discretized Laplacian is given as:

```
Algoritm 1.  % Unwraps phase.
while (q<max)%q is the number of iterations (500 for this case)
 q=q+1;
 for i=1:n
  for j=1:m
   if p(i,j)==1
    t=p(i+1,j)+p(i-1,j)+p(i,j+1)+p(i,j-1);
    g(i,j)=g(i,j)-((t*g(i,j)-g(i+1,j)-g(i-1,j)-g(i,j+1)-g(i,j-1)+L(i,j))*1.95/t);%iterated equation
   else
    g(i,j)=0;
end,end,end,end
```

A single interferogram with open fringes may also be analyzed for phase recovering (Creath & Wyant, 1992). Experimentally an open fringe interferogram can be achieved if a tilt term is added to the phase, usually by tilting the reference beam in an interferometer. Equation (18) can be modified in order to include a tilt term in the x direction, this is as follows:

wrapped phase $\phi w(x,y)$ unwrapped phase $\phi(x,y)$

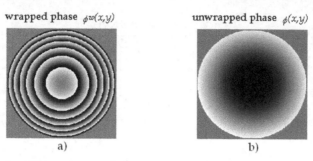

a)   b)

Fig. 15. a) wrapped and b) unwrapped phase.

$$I(x,y) = a(x,y) + b(x,y)\cos\left[\phi(x,y) + 2\pi tx\right] \tag{31}$$

where $a(x,y)=I_1(x,y)+I_2(x,y)$ is known as the background intensity and $b(x,y)=2[I_1(x,y)I_2(x,y)]^{\frac{1}{2}}$ is the modulation or visibility term. The Fourier transform of the expression below can be written as:

$$\tilde{I}(u,v) = \tilde{a}(u,v) + C(u+t,v) + C*(u-t,v). \tag{32}$$

Then the Fourier spectra of an open fringe interferogram contains three terms, $\tilde{a}(u,v)$ is a narrow peak at the center of the Fourier spectra and $C(u+t,v)$ and $C*(u-t,v)$ are shifted complex conjugate intensities symmetrically located respect to the origin of the Fourier

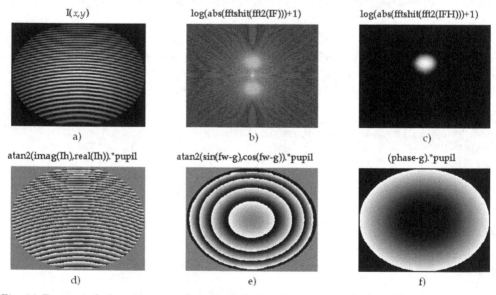

Fig. 16. Process of phase recovery from a single interferogram with closed fringes, as shown in algorithm 2. a) Interferogram, b) Fourier spectrum, c) filtered Fourier spectrum, d) wrapped phase with tilt, e) wrapped phase without tilt, and f) unwrapped continuous phase.

domain (Takeda, 1982). The Fourier procedure to recover the phase consist in isolating either $C(u,v)$ or $C^*(u,v)$. Then the inverse transform is taken in order to retrieve the wrapped phase from the imaginary and real parts of the filtered spectra. The last step, as done with phase shifting procedures, is to apply a phase unwrapping procedure to recover the continuous phase. The complete process of phase recovery from an open fringe interferogram is observed in figure 16.

```
Algoritm 2.  % Phase recovery from a single interferogram
for i=1:256
  for j=1:256
    if sqrt((i-128)^2+(j-128)^2)<126 %creates a function pupil
      pupil(i,j)=1;
    else
      pupil(i,j)=0;
    end
    x=(i-128)/128;
    y=(j-128)/128;
    phase(i,j)=2*pi*(4*(x^2+y^2)+16*x);
    g(i,j)=2*pi*16*x;
    back(i,j)=128*exp(-1*(x^2+y^2));
    mod(i,j)=127*exp(-1*(x^2+y^2));
    I(i,j)=(back(i,j)+mod(i,j)*cos(phase(i,j)))*pupil(i,j); % Interferogram with closed fringes
    H(i,j)=exp(-180*((x-0.25)^2+y^2));%Band-Pass filter
    G(i,j)=1-exp(-1000*(x^2+y^2));%High pass filter
end,end
IF=fftshift(fft2(I));%Fourier transform of the interferogram
IFH=IF.*H.*G; %Filtered Fourier transform
Ih=ifft2(fftshift(IFH)); %Inverse Filtered Fourier transform
fw=atan2(imag(Ih),real(Ih)).*pupil;%Wrapped phase with tilt
fw1=atan2(sin(fw-g),cos(fw-g)).*pupil; %Wrapped phase without tilt
phase1=(phase-g).*pupil; %Unwrapped phase
```

4.2 Wavefront deformation analysis

Optical metrology applied for the determination of different physical variables has greatly contributed with the constant advance of technology at a point that it is becoming a powerful measurement alternative for the solution of problems in engineering and sciences.

4.2.1 Deformation analysis using speckle interferometry

In this section, is presented a deformation analysis for the estimation of out-of-plane displacement components in a simulated model of a cantilever made of aluminum with a load applied at its free end. The example corresponds to a typical problem in structural mechanics where the Young´s modulus can be determined from the displacement of the loaded bar made of an isotropic material. The suggested arrangement for the testing in electronic speckle pattern interferometry (ESPI) is shown in figure 17. The laser light beam is divided by the beam splitter BS1. One beam is reflected by a mirror attached to a piezoelectric PZ (PC controlled), and then is expanded to uniformly illuminate at a small angle respect to the normal of the object surface, and the other beam is coupled into an optical fiber to obtain the reference illumination. The light reflected by the object and the reference beam introduced with BS2 interfere on the CCD.

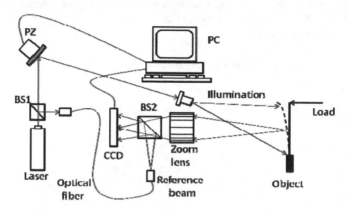

Fig. 17. Electronic speckle pattern interferometer.

The object was simulated by considering the following dimensions: 15 cm length and 3 cm height with a thickness of 0.5 cm. Using the two intensities $I_i(x,y)$, $I_f(x,y)$ of the speckle patterns generated by ESPI arrangement seen in the CCD image plane before and after applying a force of 0.1 N, the correlation fringes using equation (19) is shown in figure 18a and in figure 18b is shown the wrapped phase calculated by equation (20). In figure 18c is shown the filtered and unwrapped phase using a conventional spatial average filter of 3 x 3 pixels and an iterative least-squares algorithm.

fringe speckle pattern   wrapped phase   unwrapped phase

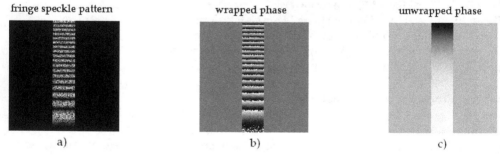

a)   b)   c)

Fig. 18. Deformation analysis of a cantilever with ESPI. a) interference fringe pattern; b) wrapped phase and c) unwrapped phase.

4.3 Wavefront detection
Optical testing using diffraction gratings as wavefront modulators is another alternative to detect wavefront aberrations.

4.3.1 Grating diffraction
Diffraction gratings are optical devices commonly used on physics. There are several gratings types, but as shown in 3.2 section, sinusoidal gratings only diffracts three harmonic

modes, due to this property, sinusoidal gratings have been developed by different techniques. According to the method reported by (Mora-González et al., 2009), is possible to generate these gratings by laser printing on acetates. In figure 19, are shown different increment sizes (Δy) of three sine profiles and the corresponding spectra of equations (25) and (26), respectively. It must be pointed that for larger Δy values, the resolution diminishes and more diffraction orders emerge.

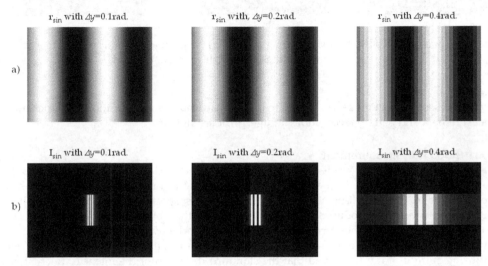

Fig. 19. Sinusoidal gratings generated in Matlab. With a) grating $r_{sin}=255*[.5+.5*sin(y)]$ and b) Fourier spectra $I_{sin}=fftshift(fft2(r_{sin}))$.

4.3.2 Ronchi test

The Ronchi test is one of the most non invasive optical tests used in optical workshops, due to the simplicity for observing aberrations over the optical surface. The test only needs to propagate a convergent aberrated wavefront through a diffraction grating to obtain a modulated fringe pattern (ronchigram) (Mora-González et al., 2001, 2003, 2011). In figure 20 is shown the typical diagram of the Ronchi test using a collimated illumination system.

In figure 21 are shown the ronchigram before and after circular low-pass filtering and their corresponding wrapped phase calculated with equation (20).

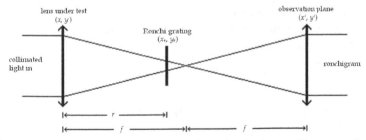

Fig. 20. Collimated light Ronchi test diagram. Where f is the focus of lenses and r is the distance between lens under test and Ronchi grating.

ra(x,y)   raf=abs(ifft2(mask.*fftshift(fft2(ra))))   wp=255°(atan2(rdf-rbf,raf-rcf)+pi)/(2°pi)

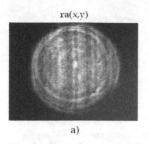 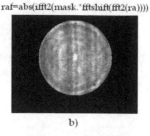 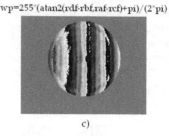

a)   b)   c)

Fig. 21. Ronchi test results. a) ronchigram a: ra(x,y); b) frequency filtered ronchigram a and applied pupil: raf(x,y); and c) wrapped phase of ronchigrams a, b, c and d: wp(x,y).

4.4 Bio-metrology
In the present subsection several functions of Matlab and their applications as blood flow measurement and pattern recognition in fingerprint are shown.

4.4.1 Blood flow measurement
Laser speckle effect is an interference phenomena that is produced when an optical rough surface is illuminated by a laser source that can be observed directly or imaged by using an optical system. The resulting intensity well known as speckle pattern is the result of multiple interferences produced by the roughness of the object under test. The speckle pattern consists in a distribution of brilliant points and dark points.

By assuming ideal conditions like high coherent light source, unique frequency and perfect diffusing surface. It can be proved that the standard deviation of the intensity fluctuations from a speckle pattern is equal to the same that the average of the intensity. Speckle pattern contrast is defined by the relationship between standard deviation (σ) and the averaged intensity (I) (Goodman, 2005):

$$speckle contrast = \frac{\sigma}{\langle I \rangle}. \tag{33}$$

If the illuminated surface is static, the contrast observed in the speckle pattern is maximum, however, if the surface is moving, the speckle patterns changes completely. This phenomenon is known as "decorrelation" and can be observed when light is dispersed by a great number of moving dispersers, i. e. moving particles into a fluid. The decorrelation is used for fluid velocity quantification considering that a speckle pattern photography taken at a finite time is blurred (contrast losing) in flowing areas. Contrast changes depend on fluid velocity and photography exposure time (T). By assuming a Lorentzian velocity distribution, speckle contrast ($\sigma/<I>$) is defined as correlation and exposure time function (τ_c/T).

$$\frac{\sigma}{\langle I \rangle} = \left\{ \frac{\tau_c}{2T} \left[1 - \exp\left(-\frac{2T}{\tau_c} \right) \right] \right\}^{\frac{1}{2}}. \tag{34}$$

Correlation time τ_c is inversely proportional to local velocity of the dispersing particles. The following code calculates a contrast image from a speckle image. Local blood flow velocity can be found from image contrast information and equation (34). Figure 22 shown speckle images before and after processing.

Algoritm 3. % Calculation of speckle contrast.
Im2 = imread('speckle_img.bmp'); % load the bmp image file into the memory.
Im2 = im2double(Im2);
windowSize = 5; %define the window size for the filter.
avgFilter = fspecial('average',windowSize); % generate an averaging filter.
stdSpeckle = stdfilt(I,ones(windowSize)); %caculates the local standar deviation of image.
avgSpeckle = imfilter(I,avgFilter,'symmetric'); %calculates the average of each pixel
ctrSpeckle = stdSpeckle./avgSpeckle; %caculates the speckle contrast image

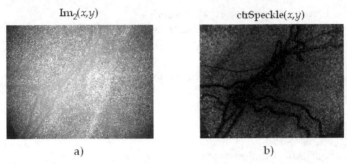

$Im_2(x,y)$ ctrSpeckle(x,y)

a)   b)

Fig. 22. Blood flow measurement results. a) speckle image of a rat cortex. b) speckle image of contrast after processing with the code of algoritm 3.

4.4.2 Fingerprint measurement

Several applications in pattern recognition are also utilized in optical metrology, finger print parameters measurements is an example. The present subsection shows a new form for fingerprint core determination based in the Radon transform of a fingerprint image, applied in x and y axes directions. The core is located by the interception of the extremes (local minimum and maximum) of the Radon transforms (Mora-González et al., 2010).

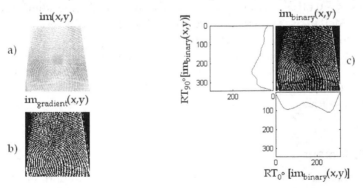

Fig. 23. Images for fingerprint core point detection. a) original fingerprint im(x,y), b) gradient of original fingerprint im_gradient(x,y), and c) binarized gradient im_binary(x,y) and its 0° - 90° Radon transforms.

The process for core finding is very simple. First, a high-pass filter with a gradient type convolution mask is applied to a fingerprint image in order to enhance the contrast. Next the image is skeletonized, and the Radon Transform (RT) is applied in the x and y directions to obtain RT_{90} and RT_0 profiles, respectively. Finally, the noise produced from ridges and rows in the fingerprint is minimized by a least-squares algorithm. The whole process is illustrated in figure 23 by using the following algorithm:

```
Algoritm 4.  % Fingerprint analysis.
[im,map]=imread(FileName); %read fingerprint
im=double(im); %change image format
[Nx,Ny]=size(im); %image size
im_gradient=gradient(im); %gradient spatial filter
level = graythresh(im_gradient); %finding the threshold of gradient
for x=1:Nx
  for y=1:Ny
    if (im_gradient(x,y)>15*level) %fingerprint skeletonization
      im_binary(x,y)=1;
    else
      im_binary(x,y)=0;
end,end,end
[RT,xp] = radon(bg,[0 90]); %Radon transform
leastsq_0=polyfit(xp,RT(:,1),21); %21° polynomial adjustment for 0° Radon transform
leastsq_90=polyfit(xp,RT(:,2),21); %21° polynomial adjustment for 90° Radon transform
y_leastsq0=polyval(leastsq_0,xp); %least square approximation of 0° Radon transform
y_leastsq90=polyval(leastsq_90,xp); %least square approximation of 90° Radon transform
```

5. Conclusion

Mathematical fundamentals for Digital Image Processing and their implementation by means of algorithms and Matlab commands were established. It has been demonstrated according to some Optical Metrology applications, the Matlab algorithms efficiency. This confirms that Matlab is a computational powerful tool. However, optical metrology applications are not only limited to the discussed examples in the present chapter. Applications of all the proposed algorithms can be extended without any problem from deformation analysis by another interferometric techniques (Speckle photography, Moiré, etc.) or optical tests (Hartmann, Foucault, etc.), until analysis and pattern recognition in medicine (X-Ray images, tomography, etc.), among other branches of science and engineering.

6. Acknowledgment

The authors wish to express their gratitude for financial support of this project to *Departamento de Ciencias Exactas y Tecnología*, of *Centro Universitario de los Lagos, Universidad de Guadalajara*. The image of figure 22 courtesy of Julio Cesar Ramirez San-Juan, Ph.D (*Instituto Nacional de Astrofísica Óptica y Electrónica*).

7. References

Bow, S.T. (2002). *Pattern Recognition and Image Preprocesing* (2nd Ed.), Marcel Dekker, Inc., ISBN 0-8247-0659-5, New York, USA.

Bracewell, R.N. (1995). *Two-Dimensional Imaging*, Prentice Hall, ISBN 0-13-062621-X, New Jersey, USA.

Canny, J. (1986). A Computational Approach to Edge Detection, *IEEE Trans. on Pattern Analysis and Machine Intelligence*, Vol.PAMI-8, No.6, (November 1986), pp. 679-698, ISSN 0162-8828.

Creath, K.; Schmit, J. and Wyant, J.C. (2007), Optical Metrology of Diffuse Surfaces, In: *Optical Shop Testing, 3th ed.*, Malacara, D., pp. 756-807, John Wiley & Sons, Inc., ISBN 978-0-471-48404-2, Hoboken, New Jersey, USA.

Gasvik, K.J. (2002). *Optical Metrology*, John Wiley & Sons, Ltd., ISBN 0-470-84300-4, Chichester, West Sussex, England.

Ghiglia, D.C., Pritt, M.D. (1998), *Two-Dimensional Phase Unwrapping: Theory Algorithms and Software*, Wiley-Interscience, ISBN 0-471-24935-1, New York, USA.

Gonzalez, R.C. & Woods, R.E. (2002). *Digital Image Procesing* (2nd Ed.), Prentice Hall, ISBN 0-201-18075-8, New Jersey, USA.

Goodman, J.W. (2005). *Introduction to Fourier Optics* (3rd Ed.), Roberts and Company Publishers, ISBN 0-9747077-2-4, Englewood, USA.

Huntley, J. M. (2001), Automated analysis of speckle interferograms, In: *Digital Speckle Patter Interferometry and Related Techniques*, Rastogi, P. K., pp. 59-140, John Wiley & Sons, Ltd., ISBN 0-471-49052-0, Chichester, West Sussex, England.

Lehmann, M. (2001). Speckle Statistics in the Context of Digital Speckle Interferometry, In: *Digital Speckle Patter Interferometry and Related Techniques*, Rastogi, P. K., pp. 1-58, John Wiley & Sons, Ltd., ISBN 0-471-49052-0, Chichester, West Sussex, England.

Mora González, M. & Alcalá Ochoa, N. (2001). The Ronchi test with an LCD grating, *Opt. Comm.*, Vol.191, No.4-6, (May 2001), pp. 203-207, ISSN 0030-4018.

Mora-González, M. & Alcalá Ochoa, N. (2003). Sinusoidal liquid crystal display grating in the Ronchi test, *Opt. Eng.*, Vol.42, No.6, (June 2003), pp. 1725-1729, ISSN 0091-3286.

Mora-González, M.; Casillas-Rodríguez, F.J.; Muñoz-Maciel, J.; Martínez-Romo, J.C.; Luna-Rosas, F.J.; de Luna-Ortega, C.A.; Gómez-Rosas, G. & Peña-Lecona, F.G. (2008). Reducción de ruido digital en señales ECG utilizando filtraje por convolución, *Investigación y Ciencia*, Vol.16, No.040, (September 2008), pp. 26-32, ISSN 1665-4412.

Mora-González, M.; Pérez Ladrón de Guevara, H.; Muñoz-Maciel, J.; Chiu-Zarate, R.; Casillas, F.J.; Gómez-Rosas, G.; Peña-Lecona, F.G. & Vázquez-Flores, Z.M. (2009). Discretization of quasi-sinusoidal diffraction gratings printed on acetates, *Proceedings of SPIE 7th Symposium Optics in Industry*, Vol.7499, 74990C, ISBN 978-0-8194-8067-5, Guadalajara, México, September 2009.

Mora-González, M.; Martínez-Romo, J.C.; Muñoz-Maciel, J.; Sánchez-Díaz, G.; Salinas-Luna, J.; Piza-Dávila, H.I.; Luna-Rosas, F.J. & de Luna-Ortega, C.A. (2010). Radon Transform Algorithm for Fingerprint Core Point Detection. *Lecture Notes in Computer Science*, Vol.6256, No.1, (September 2010), pp. 134-143, ISSN 0302-9743.

Mora-González, M.; Casillas, F.J.; Muñoz-Maciel, J.; Chiu-Zarate, R. & Peña-Lecona, F.G. (2011). The Ronchi test using a liquid crystal display as a phase grating, *Proceedings of SPIE Optical Measurement Systems for Industrial Inspection VII*, Vol.8082 part two, 80823G, ISBN 978-0-8194-8678-3, Münich, Germany, May 2011.

Oppenheim, A.V.; Willsky, A.S. & Nawab, S.H. (1997). *Signasl and Systems, 2nd ed.*, Prentice Hall, Inc., ISBN 0-13-814757-4, New Jersey, USA.

Pratt, W.K. (2001). *Digital Image Processing* (3th Ed.), John Wiley & Sons, Inc., ISBN 0-471-22132-5, New York, USA.

Robinson, D.W. (1993). Phase unwrapping methods, In: *Interferogram Analysis*, Robinson, D.W. and Reid, G.T., pp. 195-229, IOP Publishing, ISBN 0-750-30197-X, Bristol, England.

Sirohi R. S. (1993), *Speckle Metrology*, Marcel Dekker, Inc., ISBN 0-8247-8932-6, New York, USA.

Takeda, M.; Ina, H. & Kobayashi, S. (1982). Fourier-transform method of fringe-pattern analysis for computer-based topography and interferometry, *J. Opt. Soc. Am.*, Vol.72, No.1, (January 1982), pp. 156-160, ISSN 0030-3941.

Tolstov, G.P. (1962). *Fourier Series*, Dover Publications, Inc., ISBN 0-486-63317-9, New York, USA.

Waldner, S. P. (2000). *Quantitative Strain Analysis with Image Shearing Speckle Pattern Interferometry (Shearography)*, Doctoral Thesis, Swiss Federal Institute of Technology, Zurich, Swiss.

10

Selected Methods of Image Analysis in Optical Coherence Tomography

Robert Koprowski and Zygmunt Wróbel
University of Silesia, Faculty of Computer Science and Materials Science
Institute of Computer Science, Department of Biomedical Computer Systems
Poland

1. Introduction

OCT is a new technique of picturing that uses uninvasional and contactless optical method based on interferometry of partially compact light for receiving sections images of human eyes in vivo. It allows picturing structural changes caused by eyes diseases, mapping thickness of retina and analyses shield of optical nerve and coats of nerve fibers. OCT has been developed since 1995 when it was initiated by measurement of intraocular distance by A.F. Frechera (Fercher el at., 1995) in years 2002-2004 the quick growth of quality and speed of eye picturing acquisition was observed but particularly in 2003 linear picturing and 2004 fast picturing with high resolution –Fig. 1. (Leitgeb el at., 2004; Ozcan el at., 2007; Bauma B. E. & Tearney, 2002).

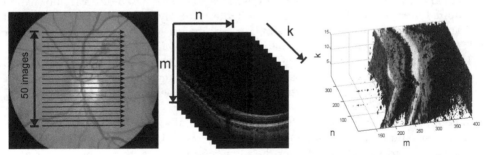

Fig. 1. The comparison of normal optic nerve head images with differential optical coherence tomography (OCT) technologies M×N×K=740×800×50

In work have been won input images L_{GRAY} in number near 1000 from optical tomograph SOCT Copernicus in the following parameters: wave length of light source: 840nm, width of spectrum: 50nm, pivotal resolution width (longitudinal): 6μm, traverse resolution: 12-18 μm of tomograph window: 2mm, speed of measurement: 25 000 scans in k pivot per second, maximum width of scanning: 10mm, maximum number of punctual scans in k pivot falling to n pivot: 10 500, become write down in gray levels about resolution M×N×K=740×800×50 where for each pixel falls to 8 bits.

The next part of considerations will be concerned with methods of analysis and processing of images automatically appointing layers borders visible on fig. 2 like: RPE – Retinal

Pigment Epithelium, OPL – Outer plexiform layer, IS/OS – Boundary between the inner and outer segments of the photoreceptors.

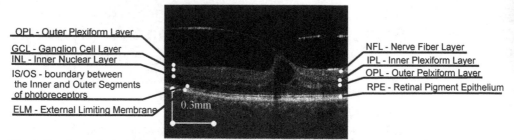

Fig. 2. Section scheme of individual layers along with marked characteristic gauged areas – image taken from SOCT Copernicus.

These considerations will be concerned with analysis of images sequences that have been already archived. Therefore, the possibilities of interference with the OCT device's apparatus will not be considered for increasing range of brightness level. Data from images sequence will not be taken into account, either - each image is analyzed independently. The source of acquiring given images assigned for analyses described by algorithms is free, i.e. any OCT device which allows to receive 2D image about minimum resolution 300×400 pixels.

The need of thickness analysis of individual layers RPE, IS/OS, NFL or OPL results from necessity of quantitative assessment but not qualitative, e.g. disease progression or efficiency of therapy, e.g. diabetes or Birdshot Chorioretinopathy.

Four methods of individual visible layers analyses will be discussed on Fig. 2 namely:

- Method of modified active contour – ACM. This method is based on basic information acquired from image like for example: the lightest RPE layer which will be identified in first period and on its base the remaining layers analysis will be carried out as OPL or IS/OS method of modified active contour for implemented line.

- The wandering small part method in discovering Canny edge - CCA. This method relies on preliminary edge detection using Canny detector and next continuity of lines correction on ends and conducting their connection with remaining ones (Canny, 1986; Koprowski & Wróbel, 2008).

- Random method of contour analysis – RAC. Points that start marking the edges are chosen at random during the preliminary image period, next the correction of their numbers is carried out in order for the remaining numbers, that come up to certain expectations, to become the first points of the lines appointed with the wandering small part method (Koprowski & Wróbel, 2009).

- Method based on hierarchic approach - HAC . There is preliminary identification of main layers like OPL or RPE on the smallest resolution and then the remaining layers are identified like IS/OS and the layers reconnaissance accuracy is gradually improved OPL and RPE (Koprowski & Wróbel, 2009).

2. Present state of knowledge - results acquired with known algorithms

Among results acquired with known algorithms there is in this chapter the description of the results:

- Acquired by other authors
- Acquired by authors of this work which have not brought satisfactory results in this application.

2.1 Results acquired for algorithms processed by authors not bringing desired results for OCT images

Among these results there have been methods which have not given satisfactory results as:

1. Method using Hough transform (Gonzalez & Woods, 1992). This method in this case did not give satisfactory results because the wanted layers on OCT image can change thickness and in general case can not be continuous. Additionally, the radius of curvature describing border of layers can be changed in wide ranges (Koprowski & Wróbel, 2009). It happens for example in shield of optical nerve (Costa el at., 2006) where individual OPL layers , RPE or IS/OS they are much worse visible (Klinder el at., 2009). Certain improvement of this method would be area analysis in which individual areas (with given width) would be brought closer by the lines. However, in this case emerges their mutual connections problem and problem of computational complexity.

2. Method of active contour in its typical version also does not produce desired results (Liang el at., 2006). At automatic selection of starting points using for example, method of Canny contour discovering or Gabor's filters (Gonzalez & Woods, 1992) only borders between the layers with the greatest contrast are discovered – RPE. In other cases, for the others layers, the method does not produce the expected results unless it is applied interactively with the user. Because the considerations in this work are applied only to fully automatic methods, the above method cannot be taken into account because of the mentioned interaction with the user. The method after the modifications introduced by the authors will be presented later in the algorithm ACM and CCA.

3. Method of texture analysis. In this case individual OPL layers, RPE or IS/OS are similar in case of texture which almost by definition disqualifies the described method. Despite this fact, the methods of texture analysis can be successfully used for emitting the wanted object from background (vitreous body). For example, for other type of images the methods have been successfully used in segmentation (Farsiu el at., 2008).

4. Also, methods of extended objects analyses (Koprowski el at., 2005) do not find application here because of the possibility of great size change in both the very object and its thickness and also the possibility of the object's division into two or more parts.

Methods suggested below in the work and processed by the authors (Koprowski el at., 2005, 2008, 2009) are a modification of the already mentioned known methods of analyses and processing of images and they are also new algorithms protected by copyright.

2.2 Results acquired by other authors

According to the best of author's knowledge there are no known algorithms analyses of eyes retina taking into account discovering the mentioned borders OPL, RPE or IS/OS including shield of optical nerve. Approaches suggested and introduced in (Chinn el at., 1997) or (Drexler el at., 2003) work only for typical cases in which the degree of pathology is insignificantly small. Applications used and enclosed for OCT device for example Copernicus also do not work successfully. In case of greater pathology, layers identified automatically are not continuous or they are not identified in a correct manner. The erroneus action that occurs often is incorrect connection of the identified layers and erroneous identifying of optical nerve shield. Additionally, the realized applications added to such a device like Copernicus or Stratus they are protected by copyright and rigorous form of algorithm is not rendered accessible outside. It results in the inability to estimate quantitatively the results and their accuracy in comparison with the author approaches suggested in this work.

Despite it, there is a whole big group of methods working correctly for simple cases where in OCT images there are well identified (with sufficient contrast) individual layers. They are the methods processed in LabVieW or in C++ (for example Bauma B. E. & Tearney, 2002) the processed results were also published in user manual Copernicus (Optopol) or in one of the chapters (Barry, 205). In this last position of literature (Farsiu el at., 2008) one of the few applications that analize individually further discussed OPL or RPE layers completely automatically is presented. It seems that OCT image analysis of eye is similar to the analysis of skin, or even coat material of a tennis ball (Thrane, 2001) however, the specificity of approach lies in variability in thickness of layers, individual variability of individual cases. In such cases of thickness changes of individual RPE, IS/OS, NFL or OPL layers, their mutual positions can be so big that typical algorithms work incorrectly. Obviously, there is coordinately a whole remaining group of methods interacting with user in which the user indicates representative or marks of segmentation area, giving off of layer and the implemented algorithm using, for example, the method of area expansion segmentates the marked area (Klinder el at., 2009), or fractal analisys. Algorithms for which correct results were acquired even for images of big radius of pathology distortion that work fully automatically are presented in next chapters in the form of block schemes. Detailed description of individual steps of discussed algorithms and their property like for example sensitivity to parameters change is discussed in given publications (Koprowski el at., 2005, 2008, 2009).

On this basis, taking into account also medical premises and taken attempts introduced below, four algorithms of analyses and processing of images of eye retina layers OCT were suggested.

3. The description of the suggested and compared algorithms

The algorithms presented below are both, known from the literature and modified by the authors and also new ones. Individual layers are marked in Cartesian coordinate match like RPE-y_{RPE}, IS/OS – $y_{IS/OS}$ layer. To avoid the conflict in designation, in chosen cases overhead index indicating algorithm type (ACM, CCA, RAC or HAC) – for example y_{RPE} $^{(CCA)}$ was added.

3.1 Preliminary processing of image

Preliminary processing of image is common for all discussed methods ACM (Koprowski & Wróbel, 2009), CCA -(Koprowski & Wróbel, 2008), RAC (Koprowski el at., 2005) or HAC (Koprowski & Wróbel, 2009). Preliminary algorithms of processing of images include filtration with median filter of square mask sized about 21×21 for elimination of hum and slight artefacts introduced by measuring match in the course of acquisition of image. Selection of size of mask has been carried arbitrarily on base of image resolution M×N=740×800 and width of interests layers(OPL, RPE or IS/OS). Obviously, it must be mentioned here that there are many others methods belonging to filtration in preliminary processing of image like for example adaptation filters, spatially adaptive wavelet filter (Adler et al., 2004; Gnanadurai & Sadasivam, 2005) or fuzzy-based wavelet.

The second element of processing of preliminary image was normalization from minimum-maximum partition of image pixels brightness for full partition from 0 for 1. This procedure is aimed at the expansion of pixel brightness range for image on which the quality of visible object is degraded for different reasons.

So transformed images L_{MED} (after filtration of median filter and normalization) were subjected to analysis with available algorithms and algorithms suggested by authors (ACM, CCA, RAC, HAC).

3.2 Description of ACM algorithm

The ACM method - active modified contour, it is based on basic information acquired from image like for example the plainest RPE layer which will be identified in the first period and on its base the analysis of the remaining layers like OPL or IS/OS will be carried out (Akiba et al., 2003; Choma el at., 2003). The picture 3 presents structure of unit algorithm (block scheme) in which chosen blocks (layer analysis OPL, IS/OS, ELM) can work independently.

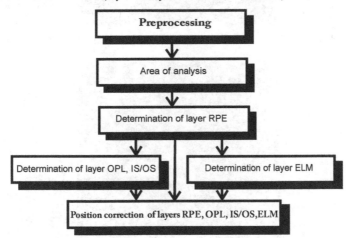

Fig. 3. Block scheme of algorithm

The block scheme introduced in picture 3 divides the work of the whole ACM algorithm into four phases::

- Preliminary processing – filtration with median filter and normalization were described in the former subchapter.
- Appointing of RPE layer site and next using modified active contour method assigning remaining OPL or IS/OS layers.
- Appointment of external border of ELM retina site.
- Correction of the received layers in relation to the   area of analysis - taking into account quality of areas of introduced objects.

After preliminary process of image processing (filtration and normalization receiving L_{MED}) L_{GRAY} image analysis was started by analyzing the place of maximum for next columns of images matrixes. If we mark lines and columns of the image matrixes by m and n new $L_{BIN}{}^{(ACM)}$ image includes value "1" in places where pixels are brighter in given column by

90% for this column maximum taking a stand brightness. In the remaining places there is value "0". On this base calculating of the center sites of longest section for each image column $L_{BIN}^{(ACM)}$ receiving course y_R was carried out (Fig. 2).

Fig. 4. The sum of $L_{BIN}^{(ACM)}$ image in 50% weight and 50% L_{MED} and drawn y_R course (y_{RS}),

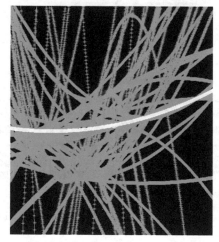

Fig. 5. Functions of 3th row y_{RS} (k_1,k_2) for any possible couples of concentrations

Course of y_R function is further subjected to the operation of concentrations analyses by k-means method acquiring $y_{RS}^{(k)}$ for each k-concentration. Next the operation of approxymation through polynomial of 3 row ($y_{RS}^{(k1,k2)}$) of each couple $y_{RS}^{(k1)}$ and $y_{RS}^{(k2)}$ for $k_1 \neq k_2$ is performed. All polynomial functions $y_{RS}^{(k1,k2)}$ received for all possible pairs of concentration (k_1, k_2) are shown in Fig. 2-3. For each function y_R a number of points is appointed contained in partition ±15 pixels. Next the pair (k_1,k_2) is appointed for which number of point contained in partition ±15 pixels is maximum at chosen $y_{RS}^{(k1^*,k2^*)}$ in simplification further called y_{RPE} function. Result is shown in Fig. 2-3 by white line (course of $y_{RPE}^{(ACM)}$). ELM and IS/OS borders were appointed on the basis of course $y_{RPE}^{(ACM)}$.

Algorithms in both cases were very approximated for each other and they concerned in biggest fragment method of modified active contour (exact differences between suggested method and classic method of active contour is shown in Gonzalez & Woods 1992). According to the introduced visual scheme in Fig. 5 values of medians in areas over and below of analysis pixel in blocks about sizes $p_{yu} \times (p_{xl} + p_{xp} + 1)$ for method of active contour are appointed.

Next the value of their remainder is calculated and written down in matrix ΔS in following form:

$$\Delta S = \begin{array}{c} \cdots \\ 4 \\ 3 \\ 2 \\ 1 \\ 0 \\ -1 \\ -2 \\ -3 \\ -4 \\ \cdots \end{array} \left\{ \begin{array}{cccccc} & & \cdots & & \\ \Delta_{S,4,1} & \Delta_{S,4,2} & \Delta_{S,4,3} & \Delta_{S,4,4} & \\ \Delta_{S,3,1} & \Delta_{S,3,2} & \Delta_{S,3,3} & \Delta_{S,3,4} & \\ \Delta_{S,2,1} & \Delta_{S,2,2} & \Delta_{S,2,3} & \Delta_{S,2,4} & \\ \Delta_{S,1,1} & \Delta_{S,1,2} & \Delta_{S,1,3} & \Delta_{S,1,4} & \\ \Delta_{S,0,1} & \Delta_{S,0,2} & \Delta_{S,0,3} & \Delta_{S,0,4} & \cdots \\ \Delta_{S,-1,1} & \Delta_{S,-1,2} & \Delta_{S,-1,3} & \Delta_{S,-1,4} & \\ \Delta_{S,-2,1} & \Delta_{S,-2,2} & \Delta_{S,-2,3} & \Delta_{S,-2,4} & \\ \Delta_{S,-3,1} & \Delta_{S,-3,2} & \Delta_{S,-3,3} & \Delta_{S,-3,4} & \\ \Delta_{S,-4,1} & \Delta_{S,-4,2} & \Delta_{S,-4,3} & \Delta_{S,-4,4} & \\ & & \cdots & & \end{array} \right. \qquad (1)$$

Where $\Delta S = med(Lu) - med(Ld)$ for Lu and Ld that are areas of the size properly $p_{yu} \times (p_{xl} + p_{xp} + 1)$ and $p_{yd} \times (p_{xl} + p_{xp} + 1)$ and

p_{yu} -   value of Lu line,
p_{yd} -   value of Ld line,
p_u -   partition of relocation pixel and areas Lu i Ld for top,
p_d -   partition of relocation pixel and areas Lu i Ld to bottom,
p_{xl} -   number of column on the left of the analyzed pixel,
p_{xp} -   number of column on the right of the analyzed pixel,
p_{ly} -   distance in pivot oy respect $y_{RPE}{}^{(ACM)}$
p_{xud} -   distance between neighbor pixels in pivot oy,
med –   medians.

After creating ΔS matrix about size $(p_u + p_d + 1) \times N$ sorting is performed for next columns begining from biggest values of remainders between Lu and Ld areas. Next the analysis of individual values for the following columns so that the pxud remainder does not surpass the assumed level is performed. For 1000 pieces of test images this value was established at the level of 2. The remaining parameters like pyu and pyd influence the sensitivity of the method and p_u and p_d are the range of searching possible pixels sites. By increasing p_{yu} and pyd values, time of calculations is increased. Searching for the new values of sites points of $y_{IS/OS}{}^{(ACM)}$ layer is started from course $y_{RPE}{}^{(ACM)}$. Points of initial $y_{IS/OS}{}^{(ACM)}$ layer emerge from slip by ply in attitude of $y_{RPE}{}^{(ACM)}$ course.

New sites are appointed in partition from $y_{IS/OS}{}^{(ACM)} - p_{yu}$ to $y_{IS/OS}{}^{(ACM)} + p_{yd}$.

The received $y_{IS/OS}{}^{(ACM)}$, $y_{RPE}{}^{(ACM)}$, $y_{ELM}{}^{(ACM)}$ course (layers) must additionally grant the following conditions from premises subsequent of eye structure (these conditions will be served in Cartesian coordinate match) (Hausler & Lindner, 1998):

- $y_{RPE}^{(ACM)} < y_{IS/OS}^{(ACM)} < y_{ELM}^{(ACM)}$ for each x,
- $y_{ELM}^{(ACM)} - y_{RPE}^{(ACM)} \approx 0.1$ mm –being the initial value starting work of active contour method (Ko el at., 2005),
- $y_{ELM}^{(ACM)} - y_{IS/OS}^{(ACM)} \approx$ od 0 do 1 mm for different x (Yun el at., 2004).

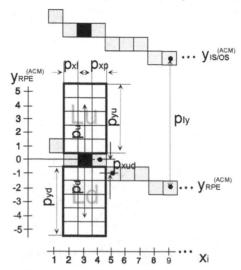

Fig. 6. Scheme of visual values scaling difference of brightness method

Appling this restriction, correct results for automatic achieved RPE, IS/OS or ELM layer finding has been achieved (Fig. 7).

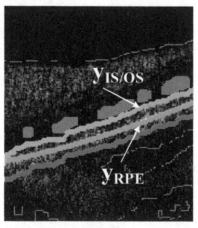

Fig. 7. Accommodation of function course $y_{IS/OS}^{(ACM)}$ and $y_{RPE}^{(ACM)}$.

3.3 Description of CCA algorithm

Method of small part wandering about in discovering Canny edge – CCA relies on preliminary detection of edge using Canny detector and next corrections of lines continuity on ends and performing the connection with the remaining ones– Fig. 8.

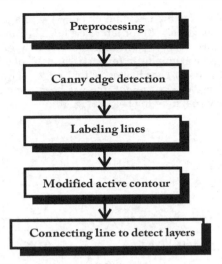

Fig. 8. Block scheme of CCA algorithm

The first period of the used CCA method is discovering edge with assistance of Canny method (Canny, 1986) on L_{MED} image. For so emerged binary $L_{BIN}^{(CCA)}$ the operation of labeling was conducted where each concentration (about value "1") owns label et=1,2,...,Et-1,Et. Next, for each label et labeling is conducted giving each concentration (line) label. Received image $L_{IND}^{(CCA)}$ is shown in pseudocolors on Fig. 7.

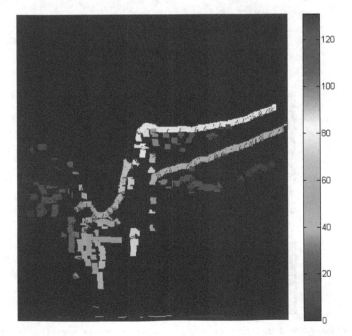

Fig. 9. $L_{IND}^{(CCA)}$ Image in pseudocolors (label Et=131)

Fig. 9 shows values of labels for the next line of $L_{IND}^{(CCA)}$ image. Each continuous line of edge visible on $L_{IND}^{(CCA)}$ image (Fig. 9) for labels $e_t=1,2,...,E_t-1,E_t$ has been transformed for form $k=1,2,3,...,K-1,K$ points $(x_{et,k}$ $y_{et,k})$ in Cartesian match of coordinates. Method of modified active contour has been employed for each "stretch" of edge in both directions. For this purpose for two first pairs of coordinates of first edge $(x_{1,1},y_{1,1})$ and $(x_{1,2},y_{1,2})$ and two last ones $(x_{1,K-1},y_{1,K-1})$ and $(x_{1,K},y_{1,K})$ a straight line has been appointed going through these points, that is according to visual drawing below (Fig. 10):

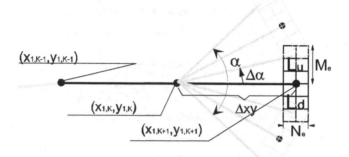

Fig. 10. Graphic interpretation of modified active contour method for appointment of next point beginning from points positions $(x_{1,K-1},y_{1,K-1})$ and $(x_{1,K},y_{1,K})$ for establishing new point (pixel) $(x_{1,K+1},y_{1,K+1})$. For simplification angle of depression of final points of edges was established at $\beta=0°$.

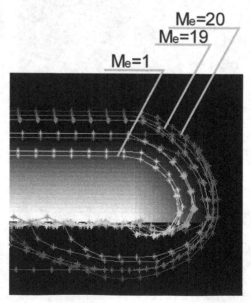

Fig. 11. Artificial image and fragment of modified active contour operation for $\alpha=40$, $\Delta\alpha=1$, $\Delta xy=N_e=4$, M_e changed in range $(1,20)$

Fig. 11 presents the ideas of method of active contour where beginning from points position $(x_{1,K-1}, y_{1,K-1})$ and $(x_{1,K}, y_{1,K})$ straight line going through them is established with an angle of depression β_1 and in distance Δxy appointing of the position of new point $(x_{1,K+1}, y_{1,K+1})$ for different potential positions (in angle partition $\beta_1(1) \pm \alpha$ through $\Delta\alpha$). The choice of proper position of contour point acquired through adding next points for existing edge is acquired on base of analyses of average values from areas Lu and Ld about size $M_e \times N_e$ (Fig. 3-8). α angle for which the best adjustment for the analyzed point $(x_{1,K+1}, y_{1,K+1})$ exists is the one for which the remainder in average values between areas Lu and Ld is the biggest.

As it happens, the suggested method of modified active contour has very curious properties. The parameters of this algorithm are as follows:

α -   Angle in which range the best adjusting for the given criterion is searched,

$\Delta\alpha$ -   Accuracy with which we search for the best adjusting,

Δxy -   the distance between the present and the next searched point of active contour $(x_{1,K+1}, y_{1,K+1})$, $(x_{1,K+2}, y_{1,K+2})$ and so on,

Me -   Height of analyzed Lu and Ld area

Ne -   Width of analyzed Lu and Ld area

On the base of the above-mentioned findings and realized measurements (Koprowski & Wróbel, 2009) values of parameters of active contour on α=45, $\Delta\alpha$=1, Δxy=1, Me=11, Ne=11 were established. Iterations for individual et edges of active contour method have been interrupted, then if one of the following situations happened:

The possible number of iterations has been surpassed - established arbitrary for 1000,

For this point the condition of remainder in average values between areas Lu and Ld has not been granted

At least two points own the same coordinates - it precludes to looping of algorithm.

For parameters established this way, the results have been acquired that are presented below Fig. 10, Fig. 11).

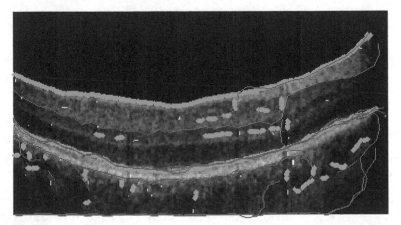

Fig. 12. Operation of modified active contour on real image for α=40, $\Delta\alpha$=1, Δxy=Ne=11, Me =10. The green line marks the contour acquired with Canny method, the red line marks next points of active contour method.

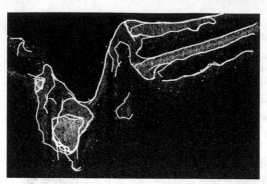

Fig. 13. Operation of modified active contour after the described correction on real image for $\alpha=40$, $\Delta\alpha=1$, $\Delta xy=Ne=11$, Me $=11$

As shown on drawings above (Fig. 10, Fig. 11) the suggested method discovers correctly individual layers on OCT image of an eye.

3.4 Random method of contour analysis – RAC

Points starting the operation of the algorithm – RAC are chosen at random in the preliminary period (Koprowski & Wróbel, 2009). Next, the correction of their number is performed, so that the remaining ones, granting proper conditions become the first points for the appointed RPE, IS/OS, NFL or OPL layers. This line become stretched further by method of modified active contour introduced in description of CCA algorithm (Fig. 14).

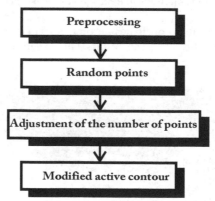

Fig. 14. Block scheme of RAC algorithm

It has already been mentioned that preliminary position of starting points was chosen at random. random values from monotonous partition were acquired (0,1) for each of new points of image matrixes - Lo (about resolution of L_{MED} image there is.: M×N). For Lo image pixels created this way (random) binarization with threshold pr is carried out . Each new pixel with value "1" will be further starting point $o^*_{i,j}$ (where index "i" means next starting point however, "j" means next points created on its base). This way, by selecting value of threshold pr in range (0.1) we influence the number of starting points. In the next period, the position of starting points is modified in the assigned H area of the sizes $M_H \times N_H$. The modification relies on correction of point position $o^*_{i,1}$ with coordinates $(x^*_{i,1}, y^*_{i,1})$ to new coordinates $(x_{i,1}, y_{i,1})$ where possibly relocation is in range $x_{i,1} = x^*_{i,1} \pm (N_H)/2$ and $y_{i,1} = y^*_{i,1} \pm (M_H)/2$. Change of coordinates follows in area $\pm(M_H)/2$ and $\pm(N_H)/2$ in which the biggest value is achieved in remainder between pixels in eight- neighbor match. Next the correction of repeating points is performed- this which have the same coordinates are deleted.

For assigning layers on OCT image the component of contour were later indicated in meaning of his fragments subjected later to modification and processing in the following manner. For each $o^*_{i,1}$ point chosen at random with coordinates $(x^*_{i,1}, y^*_{i,1})$ iteration process is performed relying on searching of next $o_{i,2}, o_{i,3}, o_{i,4}, o_{i,5}$ points and so on, according to dependence described in CCA algorithm (Fig. 8).

In the described case of iteration appointment contour component becomes essential introduction of limitation range (next parameters) which includes:

- j_{MAX} - maximum number of iterations - limitation whose purpose is to eliminate algorithm looping if every time, points $o_{i,j}$ will be appointed with different locations and contour will have for example spiral form.

- Stopping the iteration process if it will be discovered that $x_{i,j} = x_{i,j+1}$ and $y_{i,j} = y_{i,j+1}$. This situation happens most often if Lu and Ld areas are of a similar size as area H or are bigger (about sizes $M_H \times N_H$). As for the random choosing and correcting starting points, here might also appear the situation that after the correction there will be $x_{i,j} = x_{i,j+1}$ and $y_{i,j} = y_{i,j+1}$

- Stopping the iteration process if $y_{i,j} > M_M$ or $x_{i,j} > N_M$ or in cases where the indicated $o_{i,j}$ point will be outside the picture.

- Stopping the iteration process if still better matching point in respect does not grant condition admissible $\Delta\alpha$ (allowable curvature contour).

At this stage, components of the outline for the given parameters are obtained. These parameters include:

Size of h_x and h_y mask is strictly related to resolution of image and size of identified area accepted for $M_M \times N_M = 864 \times 1024$ on $M_H \times N_H = 23 \times 23$

p_r –   threshold responsible for the number of starting points - changed practically in range 0-0.1,

j_{MAX} -   maximum admissible number of iterations - established arbitrarily at 100,

$\Delta\alpha$ -   partition of angle established in partition 10-70°,

$M_H \times N_H$ -size of correction area, square area, converted in range $M_H \times N_H = 5 \times 5$ to $M_H \times N_H = 25 \times 25$

$\Delta\alpha$ –   admissible maximum change of angle between the folowing points of contour established in partition 10-70°.

The analyzing the acquired values it must be noticed that stopping the iteration process happens only when $x_{i,j} = x_{i,j+1}$ and $y_{i,j} = y_{i,j+1}$ (as it was said earlier). Or then only if points $o_{i,j}$ and $o_{i,j+1}$ have the same position. This condition does not concern oi,j points which have the same coordinates but for different "i", that is the ones that emerged in definite point of iterations from different initial points. Easing of this condition leads to generation overlap on the elements of contour which must be analyzed.

As it has been presented above, the performed iteration process can cause overlapping of $o_{i,j}$ points with the same coordinates $(x_{i,j}, y_{i,j})$ emerged from different initial oi,1points. This property is used for ultimate appointment of contour layers on OCT image.

In a general case, it can happen that despite relatively small values of the accepted p_r threshold, the randomly chosen $o_{i,1}$ starting point is placed beyond the edge of object. Then, the next iterations can join it with the remaining part. In such a case the deletion process of outstanding branch is performed – alike for lopping off of branch in frameworking (Gonzalez & Woods, 1992).

Exemplary results showed on Fig. 15 are acquired for real OCT image for p_r=0.02, $\Delta\alpha$=80°, $M_H \times N_H$=35×35.

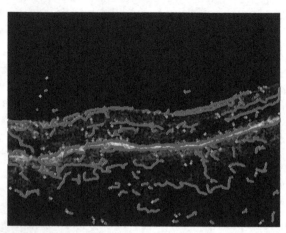

Fig. 15. Exemplary results acquired for real image OCT for p_r=0.02, $\Delta\alpha$=80°, $M_H \times N_H$=35×35.

Fig. 1 - correctly indicated contour components are visible and other fragments of contour which from the point of view of limitation are not deleted. However, on the other hand number of available parameters and its form allow enough liberty in their selection in order to get desired results. In majority of cases, obtaining the intentional form of contour is possible for one established $M_H \times N_H$ value. However, it can turn out that the use of hierarchic approach is required for which $M_H \times N_H$ size will be decreased, thanks to which greater accuracy of the suggested method will be acquired and it will introduce weight (hierarchies) of importance of individual contours.

3.5 Method based on hierarchic approach – HAC

The method based on hierarchic approach – HAC (Koprowski & Wróbel, 2009).The main NFL or RPE layers are initially identified on image of the smallest resolutions and next remaining layers are identified like for example IS/OS and accuracy reconnaissance of NFL and RPE layers (Fig. 3-2) is gradually increased.

From foundation, described algorithm should give satisfactory results mainly from part of criterion operation speed. The described methods (algorithms) are characterized by big accuracy of account, however, they are not sufficiently fast (it is hard to get analysis speed of single 2D image in time not surpassing 10ms or 50 ms on processor PII 1.33 GHz). Thus, decrease of L_{MED} image resolution was suggested about near 50% for such value of pixels number in rows and columns (with $M \times N$=740×800) which is power of value "2" there is $M \times N$=256×512 (L_{MED2}) applying further decomposition for L_{D16} image (where symbol "D" – means decomposition and symbol "16" means block size for which it has been received). Any exit (output) image pixel after decomposition has value equal median from area (block) of 16×16 size entrance (input) image according to Fig. 17.

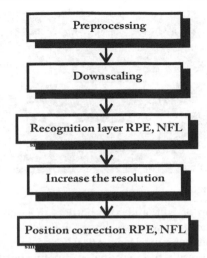

Fig. 16. Block scheme of HAC algorithm

$A_{1,1}$	$A_{1,2}$	$A_{1,3}$	
$A_{2,1}$	$A_{2,2}$	$A_{2,3}$	
$A_{3,1}$	$A_{3,2}$	$A_{3,3}$	

Fig. 17. Location of blocks na obrazie L_{MED2}

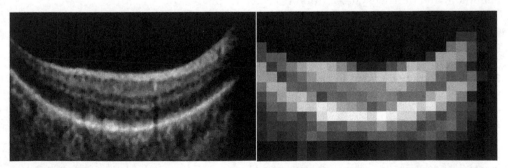

Fig. 18. Image before and after decomposition – L_{MED2} i L_{D16}

Exemplary L_{D16} result and input L_{MED2} image are shown on Fig. 18. L_{D16} Image will be subjected to the operation of appointment of pixel positions with maximum value for each column. Applying this thresholding method by maximum value in rows, in 99% of cases only one maximum value in column is received.

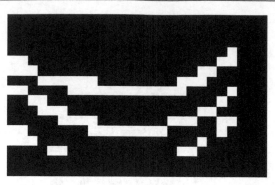

Fig. 19. Exemplary L_{DB16} image

In order to appoint position of NFL and RPE borders precisely, the use one more L_{DB16} image was essential. This image is a binary image with white pixels placed in places for which remainder between neighbor pixels in vertical tis greater than assigned pr threshold – accepted in range (0, 0.2). In result, the cooridnates of points border locations $y_{NFL}^{(HAC)}$ and $y_{RPE}^{(HAC)}$ are received as locations of values "1" in L_{DB16} image for which $y_{NFL}^{(HAC)}(x) \leq y_{RPE}^{(HAC)}(x)$. This relative simple approach gives unbelieveably satisfactory results. This method for selection of pr threshold on level 0.01 gives satisfactory results in nearly 70% of images in not compound cases (that is, the ones which are not images with visible pathology or shield of optical nerve). Unfortunately, for the remaining 30% of cases, selection of p_r threshold in accepted borders does not decrease the emerging errors (Fig. 19).

The correction of erroneous reconnaissance of $y_{NFL}^{(HAC)}$ and $y_{RPE}^{(HAC)}$ layers is important because for this approach these errors will be copied (In presented further hierarchic approach) for next exact approximations. After correction taking into consideration number of white pixels for individual L_{DM16} image columns, and mutual situating taking into consideration NFL and RPE layers position, presented correction gives for above-mentioned images class efficiency at the level of 99% of cases. Despite the accepted limitations, this method brings erroneous results for initial columns of image (with hierarchic approach definition) unfortunately, these errors are copied further.

The cause of erroneous reconnaissance of layers locations is the difficulty in distinguishing proper layers in case of discovering three "line", three points in given column in which position is changed in admissible range for individual x.

3.6 Decrease of decomposition area

Relatively simple period of processing of tomographyc image with particular consideration of speed of operation is escalation of accuracy and the same decrease of $A_{m,n}$ area's size (Fig. 17) – block on L_{MED} image. It was assumed that $A_{m,n}$ areas will be decreased in sequence to 1×1 size by a half in each iteration. Decrease of $A_{m,n}$ area is equivalent with next period execution of NFL and RPE line position approximation.

Increase of accuracy (precision) position of NFL and RPE lines indicated in former iteration is tied with two periods:

- Coordinate condensing (x,y) in meaning of indirect appointment (in center of point (x,y) put exactly) using method of linear interpolation.
- Change of position of the condensed points so that they bring closer the wanted borders in a better way.

If first part is intuitive and it leads to resampling process, the second requires exact explanations.The second period relies on adjusting individual point to wanted layer. Because in ox axis the image is from definition already decomposed and pixel brightness in the analyzed image is similar to median value of the primary image, properly in window A (Fig.17) modification of RPE and NFL point position follows in vertical axis only. Analysis of individual RPE and NFL points is independent in meaning of addiction from the position of point in line.

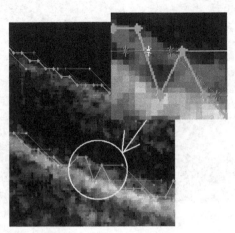

Fig. 20. Results of the processes of adjusting for two iterations. White color marks input RPE points and red and green color mark next approximations.

Each RPE point remaining from the previous iteration and new arising from the interpolation, are in various stages of the algorithm matched to RPE layer with ever greater precision. Change of the position of $y_{RPE}^{(HAC)}$ point (x) is in the range $\pm p_u$ where range of variation is not dependent on the scale of considerations (size of A area) and follows closely the distance between the NFL and RPE. For blocks A of size 16×16 to 1×1 p_u is constant and is 2. This value was adopted on the basis of the typical average for examined hundreds of L_{GRAY} images the distance between the NFL and RPE of about 32 pixels which means that the decomposition into A blocks of size 16×16 are two pixels so $p_u=2$. In this regard, ± 2 is looking for maximum L_{DM} image and it adopts a new position of RPE NFL point. This way the process of RPE or NFL is more similar to the actual conduct of the analyzed layer. Results obtained from the fit shown in Fig. 3-6. The white color shows the input RPE values as input data for this stage of the algorithm and the decomposition on A blocks of size 16 x 16 (L_{DM16} and L_{D16} images), red matching results for A blocks of size 8 x 8 (L_{DM8} and L_{D8} images) and green match results for A blocks of size 4 x 4 (L_{DM4} and L_{D4} images). As shown in Fig. 3-6 further decomposition and the next smaller and smaller A areas and hence higher resolution, image is obtained with greater accuracy at the expense of time (Indeed, increasing the number of analyzed $y_{RPE}^{(HAC)}(x)$, $y_{NFL}^{(HAC)}(x)$ points and their neighborhoods $\pm p_u$).

This method for A size 16×16 has large enough properties of the Global Approach to the brightness of pixels that there is no need to introduce at this stage the additional treatment to distinguish between closely spaced layers (that were not previously visible because of image resolutions). By contrast, with the A areas of sizes 4 x 4 other layers are already visible, which should be further analyzed correctly. Increasing accuracy makes IS/OS layer visible which is located near the RPE layer (Fig. 20). Thus, in a circled area there is high fluctuation of position in oy axis of RPE layer. Therefore, a next algorithm step was developed taking into account the partition on RPE and IS/OS layers for appropriate high-resolution. As shown in Fig. 21. presented method copes perfectly with detection of NFL, RPE and IS/OS layers marked appropriately by colors red, blue and green.

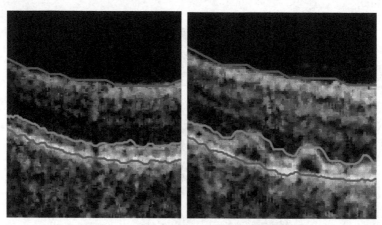

Fig. 21. Fragments of L_{MED} images with drawn NFL course– red, RPE – blue and IS/OS – green

4. Summary

Presented methods ACM, CCA, RAC or HAC give correct results at detection (identifying) RPE, IS/OS, NFL or OPL layers on tomographyc image of eye. Differences in suggested methods are visible only at their comparison of efficiencie for analysis of some hundreds mentioned tomographyc images. Comparing the mentioned methods we must bear in mind accuracy of reconnaissance of layer, reactions of algorithms on pathologies, shields of optical nerves and speed of operation in this case for computer (P4 CPU 3GHz, 2GB RAM).

The following table Tab 1 shows composite comparison of the suggested algorithms and Tab. 2. comparison of result acquired with assistance of the discussed algorithm taking into consideration typical and critical fragments of operations of individual algorithms.

Algorithm/Feature	ACM	CCA	RAC	HAC
Total error in the diagnosis of layers	5%	4%	7%	2%
The rate of detection layer RPE - MATLAB	15 s	5s	10s	1s
The rate of detection layer RPE - C++	0.85 s	0.27s	1.2s	50ms

Table 1. Composite comparison of the suggested algorithms

Random. Described method gives correct results at appointment of contour (separation of layers) equal on OCT images and for other images for which classic methods of appointment of contour they not bring results or results do not supply continuous contour. Big influence of hum on the acquired results is one of the algorithm's defects. It results from fact that number of pixels with big value that is the disturbance increases the possibility of choosing at random the starting point in this place and in consequence element contour. Time of account is the second defect which is greater if the number of chosen points is greater /or cause for which next $o_{i,j+1}$ points search has been detained.

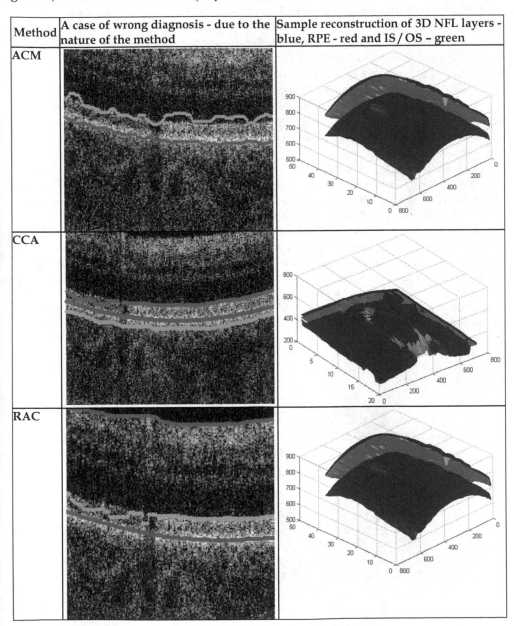

Method	A case of wrong diagnosis - due to the nature of the method	Sample reconstruction of 3D NFL layers - blue, RPE - red and IS / OS - green
ACM		
CCA		
RAC		

Table 2. Comparison of the results obtained by the described algorithms

Hierarhic. Presented algorithm discovers NFL, RPE and IS/OS layers in time for 50ms on computer with processor 2.5GHz Intel Core 2 Quad. Performed measurement of time was measured as value of average analysis 700 images dividing individual images on A blocks (Fig. 3-3) about sizes 16×16, 8×8, 4×4, 2×2. It is possible to decrease this time by modifying number of approximation blocks and simultaneously boosting identification error of position of layer - results shown in a table below.

Summary of the various stages of analysis time algorithm presented in the table above clearly indicates that the first phase of the longest pre – stage processing image where the dominant importance (in terms of execution time) has a filtration of median filter and the final stage of determining the exact location of the RPE and IS/OS layers. The exact breakdown of RPE and IS / OS, in fact involves an analysis of and the correction of the position of credits primarily RPE and IS / OS in all columns for the most accurate image zoom (due to the small distance between the RPE and IS / OS is not possible to carry out this division in the previous approximations). The reduction in computation time can therefore occur only by increasing the layer thickness of measurement error. And so, for example, for analysis in the first approximation for a size 32×32 and then 16×16 thick errors arising in the first stage and reproduced in subsequent. For the approximations for A of size 16×16 and then 8×8, 4×4, 2×2 and 1×1 the highest accuracy is achieved but the calculation time increases approximately twice.

A key element that crowns the results obtained from the proposed algorithm is a 3D reconstruction based on the sequence of $L_M^{(i)}$ images. The sequence of images and more precisely the location sequence of $NFL^{(i)}(n)$, $RPE^{(i)}(n)$ and $IS/OS^{(i)}(n)$ layers based 3D reconstruction tompgraphyc image. For example a sequence of 50 images and the resolution of one $L_M(i)$ image on level $M×N=256×512$ is obtained through the 3D image composed of three layers of the NFL, RPE and IS/OS of size 50×512. The results shown in (Koprowski & Wróbel, 2008),for example the reconstruction of the original image (without the treatment described above) based on the pixel brightness - reconstruction performed using the algorithm described above based on the $NFL_{(i)}(n)$, $RPE^{(i)}(n)$ and $IS/OS^{(i)}(n)$ information.

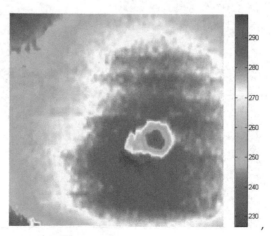

Fig. 22. Spatial location layers RPE

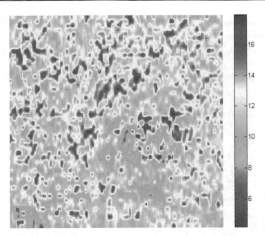

Fig. 23. Layer thickness IS/OS-RPE

It is clearly apparent from the layers of the ability to automatically determine locations of thickest positions or the thinnest between any points.

5. References

Adler D. C., Ko T. H., & Fujimoto J. G., "Speckle reduction in optical coherence tomography images by use of a spatially adaptive wavelet filter," Opt. Lett. 29, 2878–2880 (2004).

Akiba, M., Chan, K. P. & Tanno, N., Full-field optical coherence tomography by twodimensional heterodyne detection with a pair of CCD cameras. Optics Letters, 2003. 28(10): p. 816-18.

Barry C.: Optical Ccoherence tomography for retinal imaging dissertation, De promotor: Prof. Dr. T.G. van Leeuwen, De copromotor: Prof. Dr. J.F. de Boer 2005

Bauma B. E. & Tearney G. J.: Handbook of Opticall Coherence Thomography, MarcelDekker 2002

Canny J.: A Computational Approach to Edge Detection, IEEE Transactions on Pattern Analysis and Machine Intelligence, Vol. 8, No. 6, Nov. 1986.

Chinn, S. R. & Swanson, E. A. e Fujimoto, J. G., Optical coherence tomography using a frequency-tunable optical source. Optics Letters, 1997. 22(5): p. 340-342.

Choma MA, Sarunic MV, Yang C & Izatt JA. Sensitivity advantage of swept source and Fourier domain optical coherence tomography. Opt Express 2003 11:2183–9.

Costa, R. A., Skaf, M., et al., Retinal assessment using optical coherence tomography. Progress in Retinal and Eye Research, 2006. 25(3): p. 325-353.

Drexler W, Sattmann H, Hermann B, et al. Enhanced visualization of macular pathology with the use of ultrahigh-resolution optical coherence tomography. Arch Ophthalmol 2003;121:695–706. [PubMed: 12742848]

Farsiu S, Chiu SJ, Izatt JA. & Toth CA. Fast detection and segmentation of drusen in retinal optical coherence tomography images. Proceedings of Photonics West, San Jose, CA, February 2008; 68440D1-12 and Proc. SPIE, Vol. 6844, 68440D (2008);

Fercher AF, Hitzenberger CK, Kamp G. & Elzaiat SY. Measurement of intraocular distances by backscattering spectral interferometry. Opt Commun 1995;117:43–8.

Gnanadurai D. & Sadasivam V., "Undecimated wavelet based speckle reduction for SAR images," Pattern Recognition Letters, 26, 793-800 (2005).

Gonzalez R. & Woods R.: Digital Image Processing, Addison-Wesley Publishing Company, 1992, Chap. 4.

Hausler G. & Lindner MW. Coherence radar and spectral radar-new tools for dermatological diagnosis. J Biomed Opt 1998;3:21–31.

Klinder T., Ostermann J., Ehm M., Franz A., Kneser R. & Lorenz C., Automated model-based vertebra detection, identification, and segmentation, Medical Image Analysis 13 (2009) 471–482

Ko, T. H., Fujimoto, J. G., et al., Comparison of ultrahigh- and standard-resolution optical coherence tomography for imaging macular pathology. Ophthalmology, 2005. 112(11): p. 1922-1935.

Koprowski R., Izdebska-Straszak G., Wróbel Z. & Adamek B. The cell structures segmentation with using of decision trees. Pattern Recognition and Image Analysis, Vol. 15, No. 3, 2005,

Koprowski R. & Wróbel Z.: Hierarchic Approach in the Analysis of Tomographic Eye ImageAdvances in Soft Computing, Springer Berlin / Heidelberg Volume 57, 2009, p 463-470

Koprowski R. & Wróbel Z.: Identyfication of layers in a tomographic image of an eye based on the Canny edge detection, Conference on Information Technologies in Biomedicine, 2008

Koprowski R. & Wróbel Z.: Layers Recognition in Tomographic Eye Image Based on Random Contour Analysis Advances in Soft Computing, Springer Berlin / Heidelberg Volume 57, 2009, p 471-478

Koprowski R., Wróbel Z.: Determining correspondence in stereovision images of patients with faulty posture Congress on Image and Signal Processing, 2008

Leitgeb, R. A., Drexler, W., et al., Ultrahigh resolution Fourier domain optical coherence tomography. Optics Express, 2004. 12(10): p. 2156-2165.

Liang J, McInerney T. & Terzopoulos D.:United Snakes, Medical Image Analysis, Volume 10, Issue 2, April 2006, Pages 215-233

Ozcan A., Bilenca A., Desjardins A. E., B. E. Bouma B. E., & Tearney G. J., "Speckle reduction in optical coherence tomography images using digital filtering," J. Opt. Soc. Am. A. 24, 1901-1910 (2007).

Thrane L.: Optical Coherence Tomography: Modeling and Applications, Risø National Laboratory, Roskilde, Denmark, May 2001

Permissions

The contributors of this book come from diverse backgrounds, making this book a truly international effort. This book will bring forth new frontiers with its revolutionizing research information and detailed analysis of the nascent developments around the world.

We would like to thank Dr. ir. Clara M. Ionescu, for lending her expertise to make the book truly unique. She has played a crucial role in the development of this book. Without her invaluable contribution this book wouldn't have been possible. She has made vital efforts to compile up to date information on the varied aspects of this subject to make this book a valuable addition to the collection of many professionals and students.

This book was conceptualized with the vision of imparting up-to-date information and advanced data in this field. To ensure the same, a matchless editorial board was set up. Every individual on the board went through rigorous rounds of assessment to prove their worth. After which they invested a large part of their time researching and compiling the most relevant data for our readers. Conferences and sessions were held from time to time between the editorial board and the contributing authors to present the data in the most comprehensible form. The editorial team has worked tirelessly to provide valuable and valid information to help people across the globe.

Every chapter published in this book has been scrutinized by our experts. Their significance has been extensively debated. The topics covered herein carry significant findings which will fuel the growth of the discipline. They may even be implemented as practical applications or may be referred to as a beginning point for another development. Chapters in this book were first published by InTech; hereby published with permission under the Creative Commons Attribution License or equivalent.

The editorial board has been involved in producing this book since its inception. They have spent rigorous hours researching and exploring the diverse topics which have resulted in the successful publishing of this book. They have passed on their knowledge of decades through this book. To expedite this challenging task, the publisher supported the team at every step. A small team of assistant editors was also appointed to further simplify the editing procedure and attain best results for the readers.

Our editorial team has been hand-picked from every corner of the world. Their multi-ethnicity adds dynamic inputs to the discussions which result in innovative outcomes. These outcomes are then further discussed with the researchers and contributors who give their valuable feedback and opinion regarding the same. The feedback is then collaborated with the researches and they are edited in a comprehensive manner to aid the understanding of the subject.

Apart from the editorial board, the designing team has also invested a significant amount of their time in understanding the subject and creating the most relevant covers. They scrutinized every image to scout for the most suitable representation of the subject and create an appropriate cover for the book.

The publishing team has been involved in this book since its early stages. They were actively engaged in every process, be it collecting the data, connecting with the contributors or procuring relevant information. The team has been an ardent support to the editorial, designing and production team. Their endless efforts to recruit the best for this project, has resulted in the accomplishment of this book. They are a veteran in the field of academics and their pool of knowledge is as vast as their experience in printing. Their expertise and guidance has proved useful at every step. Their uncompromising quality standards have made this book an exceptional effort. Their encouragement from time to time has been an inspiration for everyone.

The publisher and the editorial board hope that this book will prove to be a valuable piece of knowledge for researchers, students, practitioners and scholars across the globe.

List of Contributors

Cristina-Maria Dabu
CRIFST – Romanian Academy, Romania

Qiang Li
Jilin University, P. R. China

Sidonie Costa, Fernando Duarte and José A. Covas
University of Minho, Portugal

K. Senthil Kumar
Division of Avionics, Department of Aerospace Engineering, Madras Institute of Technology, Anna University, India

G. Kavitha
Department of Electronics and Communication Engineering, Madras Institute of Technology, Anna University, India

R. Subramanian
Division of Avionics, Department of Aerospace Engineering, Madras Institute of Technology, Anna University, India

G. Ramesh
National Aerospace Laboratories (NAL) Bangalore, India

Vladimir Gostev
State University of Information and Communication Technologies, Ukraine

F. Gascón
Departamento de Física Aplicada II, ETS Arquitectura (US), Avda. Reina Mercedes 2, 41012 Sevilla, Spain

F. Salazar
Departamento de Física Aplicada, ETSI Minas (UPM), C/Ríos Rosas 21, 28003 Madrid, Spain

Emerson Carlos Pedrino
Federal University of Sao Carlos, Department of Computer Science, Brazil

Valentin Obac Roda
Federal University of Rio Grande do Norte, Department of Electrical Engineering, Brazil

Jose Hiroki Saito
Federal University of Sao Carlos, Department of Computer Science, Brazil
Faculty of Campo Limpo Paulista, Brazil

Maria Lyra, Agapi Ploussi and Antonios Georgantzoglou
Radiation Physics Unit, A' Radiology Department, University of Athens, Greece

Miguel Mora-González, Jesús Muñoz-Maciel, Francisco J. Casillas, Francisco G. Peña-Lecona, Roger Chiu-Zarate and Héctor Pérez Ladrón de Guevara
Universidad de Guadalajara, Centro Universitario de los Lagos, México

Robert Koprowski and Zygmunt Wróbel
University of Silesia, Faculty of Computer Science and Materials Science, Institute of Computer Science, Department of Biomedical Computer Systems, Poland

Printed in the USA
CPSIA information can be obtained
at www.ICGtesting.com
JSHW011434221024
72173JS00004B/803